WOMEN, GLOBALIZATION AND FRAGMENTATION IN THE DEVELOPING WORLD

WOMEN'S STUDIES AT YORK SERIES

General Editors: Haleh Afshar and Mary Maynard

Haleh Afshar
ISLAM AND FEMINISMS: An Iranian Case-Study
WOMEN AND EMPOWERMENT: Illustrations from the Third World (*editor*)
WOMEN IN THE MIDDLE EAST: Perceptions, Realities and Struggles for Liberation (*editor*)

Haleh Afshar and Stephanie Barrientos (*editors*)
WOMEN, GLOBALIZATION AND FRAGMENTATION IN THE DEVELOPING WORLD

Haleh Afshar and Carolyne Dennis (*editors*)
WOMEN AND ADJUSTMENT POLICIES IN THE THIRD WORLD

Judy Giles
WOMEN, IDENTITY AND PRIVATE LIFE IN BRITAIN, 1900–50

Mary Maynard and Joanna de Groot (*editors*)
WOMEN'S STUDIES IN THE 1990s: Doing Things Differently?

Haideh Moghissi
POPULISM AND FEMINISM IN IRAN: Women's Struggle in a Male-Defined Revolutionary Movement

---

Women's Studies at York
Series Standing Order ISBN 0–333–71512–8
(*outside North America only*)

You can receive future titles in this series as they are published by placing a standing order. Please contact your bookseller or, in case of difficulty, write to us at the address below with your name and address, the title of the series and the ISBN quoted above.

Customer Services Department, Macmillan Distribution Ltd
Houndmills, Basingstoke, Hampshire RG21 6XS, England

Women, Globalization and Fragmentation in the Developing World

Edited by

Haleh Afshar
Reader
Department of Politics
University of York

and

Stephanie Barrientos
Senior Lecturer
Department of Economics
University of Hertfordshire

First published in Great Britain 1999 by
MACMILLAN PRESS LTD
Houndmills, Basingstoke, Hampshire RG21 6XS and London
Companies and representatives throughout the world

A catalogue record for this book is available from the British Library.

ISBN 0–333–73927–2 hardcover
ISBN 0–333–73928–0 paperback

 First published in the United States of America 1999 by
ST. MARTIN'S PRESS, INC.,
Scholarly and Reference Division,
175 Fifth Avenue, New York, N.Y. 10010

ISBN 0–312–21659–9

Library of Congress Cataloging-in-Publication Data
Women, globalization and fragmentation in the developing world /
edited by Haleh Afshar, Stephanie Barrientos.
 p. cm.
Includes bibliographical references and index.
ISBN 0–312–21659–9 (cloth)
1. Women in development—Developing countries. 2. Women–
–Developing countries—Economic conditions. 3. Women—Developing
countries—Social conditions. I. Afshar, Haleh, 1944– .
II. Barrientos, Stephanie.
HQ1240.5.D44W657   1998
305.42'09172'4—DC21   98–23858
                                                                                                CIP

Selection, editorial matter and Introduction © Haleh Afshar and Stephanie Barrientos 1999
Text © Macmillan Press Ltd 1999

All rights reserved. No reproduction, copy or transmission of this publication may be made without written permission.

No paragraph of this publication may be reproduced, copied or transmitted save with written permission or in accordance with the provisions of the Copyright, Designs and Patents Act 1988, or under the terms of any licence permitting limited copying issued by the Copyright Licensing Agency, 90 Tottenham Court Road, London W1P 9HE.

Any person who does any unauthorised act in relation to this publication may be liable to criminal prosecution and civil claims for damages.

The authors have asserted their rights to be identified as the authors of this work in accordance with the Copyright, Designs and Patents Act 1988.

This book is printed on paper suitable for recycling and made from fully managed and sustained forest sources.

10 9 8 7 6 5 4 3 2 1
07 06 05 04 03 02 01 00 99 98

Printed and bound in Great Britain by
Antony Rowe Ltd, Chippenham, Wiltshire

Contents

Acknowledgements		vii
Notes on the Contributors		ix
1	Introduction: Women, Globalization and Fragmentation *Haleh Afshar and Stephanie Barrientos*	1
2	Fractioned States and Negotiated Boundaries: Gender and Law in India *Shirin M. Rai*	18
3	Right-wing Mobilization of Women in India: *Hindutva*'s Willing Performers *Jahnavi Phalkey*	38
4	The Impact of Global and the Reconstruction of Local Islamic Ideology, and an Assessment of its Role in Shaping Feminist Politics in post-Revolutionary Iran *Haleh Afshar*	54
5	The Informal Sector and the Conservative Consensus: a Case of Fragmentation in Egypt *Noha El-Mikawy*	77
6	Women-headed Households: Global Orthodoxies and Grassroots Realities *Sylvia Chant*	91
7	Women, Industrialization and the Environment in Indonesia *Ines Smyth*	131
8	Gender and the Global Food Chain: a Comparative Study of Chile and the UK *Stephanie Barrientos and Diane Perrons*	150
9	Women's Work in Changing Labour Markets: the Case of Thailand in the 1980s *Rachel Kurian*	174

10	Health Education for Women as a Liberatory Process? An Example from Tajikistan *Colette Harris*	196
11	Why Rural Technologies Fail to Meet the Needs of Nigerian Women: Evidence from Hausa Women's Groups in Kano State *Sintiki Tarfa*	215

Index   226

Acknowledgements

We would like to thank the Development Studies Association for funding and supporting the Women and Development Study Group, and the Political Studies' Association for funding and supporting the Women's Group. We would also like to thank members of these groups for participating in the meeting held at York in May 1996 where earlier drafts of these papers were discussed. Thanks are similarly due to the University of York's Centre for Women's Studies and its members for hosting the PSA and DSA's women's groups' annual meeting and offering kind hospitality to many of the participants.

We would like to thank the contributors to this volume for generously giving us much of their time; they have come to meetings to present their papers, to discuss the drafts of the chapters and to comment and contribute to one another's work. For us it has been a most enriching experience and we thank them all for so cheerfully putting up with the exacting editorial demands showered on them. We are particularly grateful to the contributors to this volume for heroically meeting the deadline and patiently waiting for the latecomers; and to Sue Barker for her administrative support. The pervasive good humour and supportive and sisterly responses were invaluable.

Last but not least we would like to thank Molly and Ali, Kym and Rici for giving us the time and even giving up their beds, desks and computers to accommodate contributors and enable us to work. We would also like to thank Maurice Dodson and Armando Barrientos for holding the fort and for all their support.

Haleh Afshar and Stephanie Barrientos

Notes on the Contributors

Haleh Afshar teaches Politics and Women's Studies at the University of York and Islamic Law at the Faculté Internationale de Droit Comparé at Strasbourg. She was born and raised in Iran where she worked as a journalist and a civil servant before the revolution. She has served as the Chair of the British Association of Middle Eastern Studies (1995–7) and is the joint convenor of the Development Studies' Association's Women and Development Study Group and has edited several books produced by this group. The most recent include *Women in the Middle East* (Macmillan 1994); and jointly edited with Mary Maynard *The Dynamics of Race and Gender* (Taylor & Francis 1994). Jointly with Mary Maynard she is the series editor for the York Women's Studies Series, published by Macmillan. She is the editor of the most recent book published for this series, *Women and Empowerment* (1998). Afshar remains active in feminist Iranian politics and has recently published a book entitled *Islam and Feminisms* (Macmillan 1998).

Stephanie Barrientos is a Senior Lecturer in Economic Development at the University of Hertfordshire. She completed her PhD on Unequal Exchange in Trade at the University of Kent, and taught for a number of years at City of London Polytechnic. Her research is on gender and development in Latin America, and gender and non-traditional agricultural exports. She has written a number of articles on the subject and is co-writing a book (with Anna Bee, Ann Matear and Isabel Vogel), *Women in Agribusiness, Working Miracles in the Chilean Fruit Export Sector*, to be published by Macmillan.

Sylvia Chant is Reader in Geography at the London School of Economics and has specialist interests in gender and development in Mexico, Costa Rica and the Philippines. She is author of several books and articles including *Women and Survival in Mexican Cities: Perspectives on Gender, Labour Markets and Low-income Households* (Manchester University Press 1991), *Women of a Lesser Cost: Female Labour, Foreign Exchange and Philippine Development* (with Cathy McIlwaine) (Pluto 1995), and *Gender, Urban Development and Housing* (UNDP 1996). Her most recent book is entitled *Women-headed Households: Diversity and Dynamics in the Developing World* (Macmillan 1997). Sylvia Chant has recently become President of the Society of Latin American Studies, UK.

Noha El-Mikawy obtained her BA degree in Cairo and her Masters and PhD degrees from the University of California in Los Angeles. She taught at the American University in Cairo and the Free University of Berlin. She is currently teaching at the University of Erlangen Nurnberg, where she is a research fellow. El-Mikawy is also editor of the international book review section of al-Siyasa al-Dawliya, the only Arabic language journal specializing in international relations, and is a member of the New Civic Forum, a private association in defence of liberalism established in Cairo in 1991.

Colette Harris is currently preparing her PhD dissertation, 'Gender, Socialism, and Islam in Tajikistan', at the Institute of Development Research of the University of Amsterdam. Believing that researchers should return something to the communities they research, Colette implemented a development project in the field of health in Tajikistan in 1997. She has given talks on women in Tajikistan at conferences in Mexico, Turkey, Russia, England and the Netherlands, and has published a number of articles on women. Before concentrating on Tajikistan Colette did research on women in Russia, China, Indonesia, Cuba and Mexico. She is also involved in a project financed by the University of Amsterdam, which will examine the interventions of aid agencies in regard to women's reproductive health in countries in crisis.

Rachel Kurian is a Senior Lecturer in International Labour Economics at the Institute of Social Studies in The Hague. She has done research and written on trade liberalization, labour markets and employment patterns with a special emphasis on women's work. Her recent publications include *Social Development: Past Trends and Future Scenarios* (with Lucia Hanmer, Niek de Jong and Jos Mooij) (Sida 1997); 'Tamil Women on Sri Lankan Plantations' in *Working Women in Third World Plantations* (edited by Shobita Jain and Rhoda Reddock) (Berg forthcoming). Her current work includes a research project on a gender critique of the World Employment Report 1995 (with Ruth Pearson).

Jahnavi Phalkey studied Political Science at the University of Bombay and the School of Oriental and African Studies, University of London. She is now a Research Fellow at the Asiatic Society of Bombay, working on a gendered understanding of the left in Maharashtra, India. She is also working on an oral history project for Sparrow (Sound and Picture Archives for Research on Women). Her primary research interest is in the area of political theory and sexuality.

Notes on the Contributors

Diane Perrons is a lecturer in Geography at the London School of Economics. She is a specialist in gender and employment with particular interests in Europe. She is author of *Arena of Capital* (with Mick Dunford) (Macmillan 1983); *Making Gender Work* (co-author Jenny Shaw) (Open University Press 1995); and she edited a special issue of European Urban and Regional Studies (1998, Vol. 5 No. 1) on Gender Inequality in Europe. She is presently co-ordinating a comparative study of flexible working for the European Union.

Shirin M. Rai is a Senior Lecturer in Politics at the University of Warwick. She also teaches at the Centre for the Study of Women and Gender. She is the co-editor of *Women in the Face of Change* (1992), and of *Women and the State: International Perspectives* (1997). She has written extensively on issues of gender, democratization and development.

Ines Smyth has a PhD in Social Anthropology from University College, London. She has taught at the Institute of Social Studies (in the Hague) and at the Development Studies Institute at the London School of Economics. She has recently joined Oxfam as a Policy Adviser. Her research interests and expertise cover issues of gender theory, industrialization, reproductive rights and population policies. Her most recent publications are an edited volume (with Isa Baud) entitled *Gender and Insecurity in an International Perspective: Women's Responses to Economic Transformations*, (Routledge 1997), and a forthcoming paper (with M. Grijns) for the *Bulletin of Concerned Asian Scholars* on female workers' labour militancy in the Indonesian industrial sector.

Sintiki Tarfa is a lecturer in the Department of Agricultural Economics and Rural Sociology, at the Ahmadu Bello University, Zaria and is currently completing her doctorate in Women and Technology at the University of Reading. She has been actively involved in the Institute of Agricultural Research, Technology for Women Project, Farmer Participation in Irrigation Management, the National Livestock Project on Dairy Technology Development and Transfer to women in Nigeria; and co-authored research and technical reports. She was also involved in the preparatory investigations for the establishment of a Women's Studies and Resource Centre at the Ahmadu Bello University, Zaria. Her main areas of interest are Agriculture and Rural Development.

1 Introduction: Women, Globalization and Fragmentation
Haleh Afshar and Stephanie Barrientos

Changes in the global political economy since the 1980s have had a dramatic effect on the lives of women, who have become increasingly integrated as players in the world's production and consumption processes. Women have been affected by globalization in the most diverse aspects of their lives and in the furthest reaches of the world. The effects have been multiple and contradictory, inclusionary and exclusionary. This book explores gendered implications of globalization at the grass roots in developing countries. It considers the conflicting interactions between the global and local political economies, cultures and faiths. Our main focus is to explore the very specific effects of increased global integration on women in developing countries, and how they have had to negotiate complex and rapid changes in diverse and contrasting circumstances.

GLOBALIZATION

The term 'globalization' has been used to define various aspects of global expansion in the past decade. It has been associated with key areas of change, which have led to a marked transformation of the world order. At a political level the process of deregulation and liberalization has led to an apparent diminution of the state and a general assumption that all states everywhere must become more democratic and secure 'good governance' over their people. At the level of the economy, globalization has been associated with the trend towards increasing economic liberalization. This has been reflected in freer trade and more deregulated labour, goods and financial markets. Combined with this has been an increasing dominance in global capital and financial deepening as capital movements across countries have been facilitated by the removal of regulation and national barriers. Transnational corporations, which have benefited from the removal of national constraints on their activities, now occupy an increasingly dominant position. Within the developing world, the process of economic liberalization has been heralded by the International Monetary Fund (IMF) and World Bank, which have imposed the new economic order on the more vulnerable debt-ridden countries through conditionality in their programmes. At the technological level, globalization has been facilitated by the innovation of mass rapid transportation and global communications networks, leading to the information revolution. The overall result has been the emergence of a global consumer society with a tendency to greater cultural homogenization. The process has had a remarkably wide impact, affecting not only the first and the third worlds but also the former Soviet economies, which have been subjected to the 'shock' of rapid political transformation and economic liberalization.

At its most expansive, the global 'vision' has been presented as a borderless world, in which national economic boundaries are dissolving, and all countries are integrated into a unified global order. The result is an 'interlinked economy' in which there is a free flow of capital, people, goods, services and information, and where national government is displaced by global governance (Ohmae 1990). It has been countered that the move to globalization is not necessarily a new phenomenon, and that national capital, national markets and nation-states continue to play a significant role (Hirst and Thompson 1996). In this view interaction on the world stage is a set of complex relations between nation-states, which between them ultimately determine international, as opposed to global, activity. A more pessimistic view contends that globalization is no more than the integration of the powerless marginal third world into the agenda set by the West (Dibaja 1997: 112) – a process that is not open to rigorous analytical examination since globalization, which is rooted in modernist thinking, is unable to provide a theory which accounts for the failure of the development process in the third world (Dibaja 1997:123).

Although the uneven nature of globalization and its unequal impact on developing countries have been analysed by some writers (for example Amin 1997; Hoogvelt 1997; Sklair 1991; Sklair 1994), it is glossed over in the mainstream debate. The debate on globalization has largely ignored the effects on marginalized groups, ethnic minorities and the experiences of women, as well as the specificities of major creeds and cultures, particularly in developing countries. The almost exclusively male elite who head the transnational companies and the national and international bureaucrats who facilitate the process have profited most, and have enthusiastically welcomed the new global order. They are extremely optimistic about the potentials of its all-embracing hold, which spans national barriers. Yet the expansion of liberalized global markets has been a refracted process. The mainstream proponents of globalization focus on one side of the mirror, ignoring its opposite dimensions. In the refracted mirror of globalization, an analysis of its contradictory opposites is equally important to understanding the whole, especially from the standpoint of gender – the focus of this book.

GENDER AND GLOBALIZATION

The Economic Dimension

The various analyses of globalization reflect the difficulties of coming to terms with its multidimensional nature and containing it within the formal boundaries of theory and grand narratives. From the standpoint of developing countries, one of the main vehicles of globalization has been the implementation of structural adjustment and stabilization policies, implemented largely as a result of IMF and World Bank conditionality. These policies forced many developing countries into an economic and political straitjacket, so integrating them into the global process. The effects of these policies on women have been profound and well analysed (see for example Afshar and Dennis 1992; Bakker 1994; Elson 1992b; Elson 1995; Singer 1991, Sparr 1994). As the consequences of structural adjustment have become institutionalized in the global development process, the coping strategies developed by women in times of crisis have now become embedded in their daily lives. The case studies in this volume explore some of the longer-term consequences of these for women in developing countries.

Structural adjustment has forced the pace of global integration through its emphasis on free trade and free markets, broadly defined as 'neo-liberal' economic policies. It has led to a shift away from a state-led national approach to development, epitomized in many countries by the policy of import-substitution industrialization, to an open economy, free market approach. Traditional trading relations and patterns have been undermined as countries have liberalized their economies and sought to specialize according to their 'comparative advantage' in global free trade. Underlying traditional trading patterns were a specific set of gender relations in production and employment. Whilst there were variations between countries and over time, the predominant pattern was for men to be located in waged employment in the productive sector, with women primarily located in unpaid household and subsistence work in the reproductive sector. The labour market was envisaged in terms of workers who were heads of household and whose survival needs were met by the unpaid domestic labour of women. This assumption of domesticity in turn made women low-waged workers once they offered their labour to the 'productive' sector. As the process of expansion of capitalism and globalization continued, capital proved gender-blind and the cheap, efficient labour of women was found to be preferable to that of men (Elson and Pearson 1981). The further impact of trade liberalization has had a significant effect on women, as export-oriented production has expanded female employment in most sectors in many developing countries (Joekes and Weston 1994; Standing 1989).

Much analysis of the effects of globalization in developing countries has stemmed from the overarching influence of the expansion of transnationals and the new international division of labour (Frobel et al. 1980; Jenkins 1987). Within the literature, there has been a focus on both negative and positive effects, particularly on women (Elson and Pearson 1981; Mitter 1986; Stichter and Parpart 1990; Ward 1990). Most studies of the effects of transnational production have tended to concentrate on the specific effects of industrialization and the increase of industrial employment for certain groups of women in developing countries. In the early stages transnational expansion was often concentrated in 'special economic zones' such as the *maquiladora* in Mexico. Here employment and other regulations were minimal, and many companies employed young unmarried women (Fernandez-Kelly 1994). As economic and trade liberalization expanded beyond the zones and became more generalized across developing countries, so did paid female employment; anecdotal evidence suggests that women of all ages are increasingly being employed in many countries. Transnational production has also increasingly extended into agriculture through the expansion of agribusiness, and women are a significant part of the labour force in much non-traditional agricultural production (Barrientos 1996; Barrientos et al. forthcoming; Macintosh 1989; Sachs 1996). Female employment in global production has thus become more extensive.

Patriarchal structures within the labour force have not disappeared, but have been transformed through the changing demands of global capital. The combination of global integration and fragmentation has been facilitated by economic liberalization. Women's work is often insecure, temporary or part-time, with little protection and few fringe benefits. Female employment has long been concentrated in the 'informal' sector, and gender segregation has cut across both the 'formal' and 'informal' sectors (Scott 1995). The removal of state regulations and changing production practices by large companies and transnational corporations facilitated significant changes in the gender division of labour and increased fragmentation in the processes of production. Deregulation of labour markets, fragmentation of production processes, deindustrialization and new areas of export specialization have all generated an increased demand for low-paid, 'flexible' female labour. Through outsourcing and subcontracting women of all ages are often employed in smaller firms, workshops or at home producing for transnational companies. The consequence has been an erosion of any separation between the 'formal' and 'informal' sectors as linkages between the two have been reinforced and changes have occurred in previous forms of gender segregation across different types of economic activity. Female labour is thus increasingly integrated into global production, but in a fragmented form with contradictory consequences.

The fragmentation of the labour process combined with the feminization of labour markets has imposed new demands on women's time. So the process of exploitation and gender divide is perpetuated, based on the assumption that women's time can extend infinitely (Elson 1992a). But it also institutionalizes the fragmentation of this provision, and thus women's integration perpetuates their marginalization as an essential element within the new global structures. Structural adjustment generated the triple burden for women (Moser 1992), and globalization has reinforced its consequences. As state welfare systems have been disbanded, much provision has shifted onto unpaid female labour, community organization and/or the free market necessitating money income. In the new global labour market based on low-paid, flexible work, poor households cannot depend on a single (traditionally male) breadwinner to survive (Standing 1989). Women have become an integral part of this liberalized labour market, but have simultaneously been marginalized within it as they have had to develop coping strategies for dealing with conflicting demands of fragmented insecure work, domesticity and community participation (Moser 1992).

The contradictory effects of globalization have been both empowering and disempowering for women (Afshar 1998; Rowlands 1997; Ward 1990). Frequently, the immediate employer is a kinsman or a relative, and the patriarchal politics of the family essentially prevent women from embarking on any form of active self-protection. However, the potential for new forms of resistance is emerging as women are drawn further into the global production process (Rowbotham and Mitter 1994; Ward 1990). Cross-country dialogue and alliances between networks of women activists and academics (Hale 1995) enhance a gendered approach to global political economy. Increasing household dependence on female income-earning capacity helps to raise the status of women, giving them the potential for greater independence and empowerment (Afshar 1998; Afshar and Alikhan 1997; Kabeer 1994; Rowlands 1997). However, changes in gender relations within the household often lag behind those in the labour force. There is a strong resistance on the part of men to accept the possible reversal of roles and domestic responsibilities. There is also a trend for men to migrate, nationally and internationally, in search of paid employment thereby creating an increasing number of female-headed households (Chant 1997). The extent to which the globalization of the economy and its employment patterns have empowered women, or would in the long run, is open to discussion. Although there are benefits in gaining access to paid employment, the pay and conditions are often such that in the short run it is not easy to conclude that the majority of working women have necessarily benefited from the process (Afshar and Dennis 1992).

Some discussants of the advance of globalization have highlighted the inability of capitalism to 'develop' equally. But the all-embracing tendencies within the process of globalization means its effects on non-industrial employment and economic activity, as well as those excluded and marginalized by the process altogether, often need greater focus within the analysis. The impact of globalization on women has often been complex and contradictory, both in the context of their 'inclusion' and 'exclusion'. To be understood it needs to be analysed not only at the global but also at the local and household levels. Feminists have been disaggregating the specificities of women's experiences in the context of the global process, but this work has yet to find its way into much of the core debate over globalization.

The Political Dimension

The effects of globalization have been made more complex by the inability of states to defend their national interest and include any kind of explicit gendered politics. The global political economy with international institutions and government and governmental agencies dictate global political and economic terms, simultaneously demanding 'good governance' and the retractions of state-funded welfare programmes. Good governance is advocated as a political panacea and has found a myriad of definitions (Currie 1996: 803; Leftwich 1993): it is intended to curb corruption, increase democratic controls and transparency, while at the same time the state is to shed its apparatus and cut its payroll (World Bank 1992). But the new orthodoxy which dominates the thinking about good governance takes little account of the trade-offs and conflicts between the different aims of the states in developing countries. The blanket assumption is that without any special preconditions stable democracies could be introduced anywhere, at any time, and would 'enhance, not hinder, further development' (Leftwich 1993: 605).

In practice this simplistic assumption has proved inadequate and the result has been patchy over time. Good governance cannot be provided on command. Often the scope for state autonomy and exclusive control of internal politics is reduced (Sideri 1997). Where the policies have been least successful – and sometimes where they have been more successful, as in the case of India – there has been a reaction, and a return towards different forms of 'fundamentalism' and/or direct violent action. The impoverished poorest sections of society, who have been abandoned by the little subsidized health and welfare that the state could afford, and given no power in return, have rejected 'modernity' with all that it entails and have juxtaposed a glorified notion of return to the sources of their faith against the global policies inflicted upon them.

What is left of the services of the state has been devolved to nationally and internationally funded, non-governmental agencies, frequently organized and run by women. Grassroot organizations as well as development projects are much more likely to attract international funds if they are decentralized (Schuurman 1997: 151). As the state loosens its hold, an increasingly layered, multidimensional and overlapping system of governance is being developed locally to provide a level of protection for individuals, frequently against the policies of the national government, which is perceived as merely an agent of the global institutions (Mittelman 1994). Often the activists are women working with and for women, a process which has heightened the political profile and presence of women in the public arena. But many women activists are paying a high price for their struggles. Landed with the triple burdens of paid and unpaid work and political activism (Moser 1992), such women have to stretch the little time that they have even further (Elson 1992a) to fulfil all the moral and economic duties imposed on them by their kin (Afshar 1989). At the same time, the new burdens placed on non-governmental agencies have changed the nature of these organizations from small, egalitarian democratic units into larger organizations with new hierarchies, often without the appropriate career structures and organizational infrastructures. Once more it is the time and the goodwill of women that is usually exploited.

Changing gender patterns of paid productive employment have, of necessity, led to renegotiation within the household. The burden on women has increased, and many women have not been able to continue their traditional role simply by virtue of their absence through paid employment. Gender has gained increasing importance because of the increased role of women as breadwinners. This has impacted on local communities, which have not responded or been able to respond in terms of provision of nurseries, crèches, etc., forcing an increased reliance on kinship and neighbourhood. The reconstruction of a fragile network of extended families also suffers from instability and economic insecurity, and the need to be mobile in search of employment opportunities. Different and shifting opportunities could erode or undermine the support of this network, which does not have the strength of traditional moral obligations to hold the kinship patterns together.

Fragmentation within the neo-liberal market economy has thus been accompanied by a similar political process and a 'hollowing out' of the state. An approach that was formulated in the West to deal with the problems of post-Fordist working processes has been exported across the globe (Schuurman 1997; Singer 1991). The market has extended deeper into the functioning of women's lives. Traditional subsistence production has been undermined, entitlements and capabilities depend more and more on money income, and even the poorest in many developing countries are drawn into a fantasy world of global consumerism (Sklair 1991). Poverty is now often associated with those in insecure, flexible, waged employment: the 'working poor'. But many of the poor are sucked into a consumer-led debt spiral. When poor households are in debt, it is often women who make the bigger sacrifices, searching for work on any terms to keep the debt collector from the door, at the same time reinforcing the triple burden women carry.

THE REACTION

In some countries women's social integration through the process of globalization has led to the potential for new forms of participation and empowerment. In some places, greater participation by women in the political and social process has helped to raise their awareness and level of activism. This is reflected in the growth of women's groups, community organizations run by women and local NGO support for women's initiatives within developing countries (Rowbotham and Mitter 1994). These have often been fragmented, locally specific and frequently concerned with particular demands. They are neither homogeneous nor cohesive, but are nevertheless partly the outcome of women's collective responses to the impact of globalization.

In other cases the process has led to a reaction against modernity and a variety of forms of revivalism. The failure of westernization and modernization to deliver on its promise of universal prosperity has opened the arena for political discourse, where both men and women have come to express grave doubts about the validity as well as the social and economic sustainability of modernization. An important anomaly of the free market has been its corrosive effect on 'moral principles' such as the sanctity of marriage, motherhood and the family. Erosion of the social and economic standing of men and women and greater social instability have in some cases led to a reconsideration. This process has had different reactions in different contexts. In some cases there has been some pressure on the state to give some consideration to the increasing numbers of marginalized people. Sadly, usually the reaction has not been in terms of better provisions for working women, rather it has been a populist rejection of modernity and a 'return' to some form of 'fundamentalism' (Afshar 1998; Kandiyoti forthcoming; Moghissi forthcoming).

As changing gender relations have been a central aspect of the global process, some international organizations now give greater importance to gender. Significant amongst these has been the United Nations, which organized the Conference for Women in Beijing in 1995 (Krause 1996). Some states have also been forced to recognize the importance of gender, and elite women have succeeded in placing their rights and the state's obligations at the heart of political discourse (Afshar 1998; Moghissi 1996). Responding to the political struggles of feminist and women activists, some developing countries have instituted women's ministries or taken gender issues on board, at least formally, though often the practice is different from the rhetoric. As the debates of the nature of globalization exemplify, the role of the state in this process remains a problematic issue. The problems of legitimacy, the extent to which the state has or has not disappeared, and whether it can really deal with social issues, especially relating to gender, remains unresolved. This raises the question of whether the gender dimensions of state policies have really changed or have merely shifted onto a different plane.

This book draws together different case studies which show the complex ways in which the effects of globalization are mediated through to the grassroots, and specifically how this has affected women in different contexts. The contributors to this book are not exploring generalized abstract perspectives, but focus on the more specific aspects, particularly in terms of the impact of global changes on the daily lives of women. This work contributes to a 'delayering' of the analysis by examining the contradictory ways in which globalization has affected women at different levels and in different countries as it has percolated down to the grassroots. It thus explores the multipolarity of globalization from a gender perspective, encompassing some of the more general issues as well as specific case studies.

THE POLITICAL CONTEXTS AND NEGOTIATIONS

The book begins by exploring these issues within the broader political context, before going on to examine the economic myths and realities of globalization. It starts with two chapters on the relationship of women and the state which examine two contrasting strategies by different women in dealing with the post-colonial state in India. These present contrasting experiences of the poorest of women in India seeking different economic and political goals using diverse strategies to articulate their demands. Shirin Rai focuses on street vendors who gain their livelihood on the margins of the global village, trading from the pavement and/or heading households and working in what has been called the informal sector. Rai highlights the complexities of the bargaining processes and the ways that women traders negotiate terms and conditions with the various tiers of politicians and bureaucrats who affect the very survival of their trading activities. These negotiations for space to pursue economic activity are conducted in the context of the fractured terrain of the post-colonial Indian state. Their experience demonstrates the splintered complexity of the Indian state formation, the multiplicity of strategies of struggle needed by women to confront and use the state factions in their own interests, and the unpredictable implications of globalization. Rai argues that class as well as the gender positioning of these women street traders mean that they operate, economically and politically, in the interstices of the system, only occasionally moving on to the ground for legal arrangements.

Jahnavi Phalkey's study of violent protests by slum-dwelling women, which led to the demolition of the Babri Mosque, in Ayodhya, presents a very different form of political engagement in India. Here the mobilization of women in the name of the global phenomenon of religious fundamentalism is conducted using the local concepts of populism and direct action. Women as standard-bearers of the faith, traditions and morality resort to violence to defend the sanctity of these precepts and as such offer their lives for a cause that they view as eternal and essential. These women are defending a position that may well confine them to their homes and domesticity, but their intention is to secure a respected, morally sound base which provides an alternative to the isolated, poorly paid situation offered to them by multiculturalism as well as the feminist movement in India.

The chapter by Afshar on Iran that follows presents the interaction between 'fundamentalism' in theory and practice, and the analysis offered by Middle Eastern elite women living in Iran and in exile of the policies of Islamification. Afshar contends that the impact of the activities of elite Islamist women in Iran (Moghissi 1996) has altered these policies to a point well beyond recognition. Faced with the reality of fundamentalism, elite Islamist women have chosen to look to the world and use its standards to voice demands that would be recognized as feminist in most global discourses.

Noha El-Mikawy analyses the trajectory of fundamentalist views taking root in the informal sector in Egypt. El Mikawy argues that global liberalization measures have helped to reify the liberal belief in the free movement of capital and the liberating effect of the separation of private and public spheres. This liberal ideology encouraged feminists and liberal activists to look for ways to defend the rights of women as mothers, workers and citizens. But it also provoked critics of modernity to defend women against the evils of globalization. In Egypt the analysis points to legitimate doubts about the liberating impact of the distinction between private and public spheres and equal doubt about the liberating effect of informal economic activities. The arguments El-Mikawy presents indicate that reifying motherhood and the family and celebrating the empowering potential of the informal sector take place against a background of an increasingly conservative consensus. Thus liberalization in Egypt has provoked a reaction which effectively undermines consciousness and political competence. El-Mikawy concludes that liberalization has mobilized views, which in Egypt undermine the citizenship of women rather than help bring it about.

THE ECONOMIC SPECIFICITIES: MYTHS AND REALITIES

The second part of this volume focuses on the economic interaction of globalization and the lives of women in specific circumstances. This part begins with two chapters dedicated to exploding some of the myths concerning women and poverty. Sylvia Chant deals with the stereotyping of women-headed households that has frequently, and with little substantiation by place-specific empirical evidence, assumed the status of 'global orthodoxies'. This is particularly the case with the notion, first, that women-headed households are the 'poorest of the poor', and second, that they are responsible for the inter-generational transmission of disadvantage to children. With particular reference to case study material from low-income communities in Mexico and Costa Rica, Chant challenges the relevance of negative portrayals emanating from national and international policy discourses, and points to the importance of bringing more evidence of this nature into the public arena. Chant also considers the impact of popular stereotypes on the lives of households headed by lone women at the grassroots and suggests key research and policy implications.

This is followed by Ines Smyth's critique of the general assumption in the literature that environmental deterioration always has a more severe impact on women than on any other social group. The assumption is that women have a special bond with nature, and that the gender division of tasks, especially in the household, is fixed. Smyth's chapter shows that in the case of Java (Indonesia), environmental deterioration has resulted in a more complex picture than one of unmitigated negative consequences for women. While women in Java continue to carry out the tasks related to the use of natural resources to a greater extent than men, this is not because of their innate bond with nature, but because of the combination of very specific local conditions. Furthermore, gender norms and responsibilities have clearly not been inflexible, and women have made use of the opportunities offered by the rapid industrialization taking place there to increase their personal and economic security.

The opening up of the world's export markets has to some extent provided similar experiences for women in developing and developed countries. An example is provided of women working at different ends of the global food chain. Stephanie Barrientos and Diane Perrons focus on non-traditional exports from developing countries which provide northern supermarkets with a wide range of produce throughout the year, reflecting both technological innovation in the production and distribution of fresh produce and changing consumption and retailing patterns in developed countries. Large numbers of women have been integrated into flexible employment at both ends of the food chain, and this case study examines the comparative effects of flexible female employment in contrasting nodes of the fruit supply chain which links Chile and the UK. They explore the ways in which women mediate the tensions of entry into non-standard forms of flexible work and their 'traditional' role within the household in very different contexts. Globalization is found to have mediated gender relations in similar and contradictory ways in both a developing and developed country. Barrientos and Perrons provide a comparative exploration of the different household strategies which have evolved to cope with the specificities of global integration. They analyse the different forms of the dual burden women bear, and the potential enhancement of their independence and empowerment, within contrasting but interlinked circumstances.

The effect of the 'feminization' of the labour market is further explored by Rachel Kurian with respect to Thailand. She examines the consequences of foreign direct investment in the country in terms of expanding female employment. Thailand's economic success during the 1980s was based on an expanding, export-oriented manufacturing sector. Kurian considers how labour market segmentation was accentuated through the fragmentation of female employment in a 'flexible' labour market. This is clearly demonstrated in the case of temporary migration of women from agriculture to work in export-oriented manufacturing. Kurian explores the dynamics of urban and rural employment in the context of expanding foreign direct investment in order to assess the factors underlying female rural–urban migration. She then considers the effect this has on the women themselves in terms of their contribution to household income and needs. She argues that the multiple roles women play increase the fragmentation of their lives, and that global integration locks women into insecure low-skilled employment and offers them few if any alternatives.

The difficulties of integrating women into national and international programmes within a 'transitional economy' are analysed by Colettte Harris. She focuses on the attempts by NGOs to shore up the deteriorating conditions of women in Tajikistan following the break-up of the Soviet Union. Harris contends that whilst Tajikistan is comparable to many developing countries, post-Soviet development requires a different approach from that of third world countries. The basic infrastructure of Soviet dogma and authoritarianism, together with isolation from other cultures, have made it harder for the people to take the initiative and work out new ideas and approaches outside the Soviet framework; today it still remains very difficult to do so. Harris discusses the problems involved in the establishment of a grassroots women's health centre focusing on reproductive health care and health education, and their relation to the problems of women and development in general in Tajikistan. She explores aspects of working on development with local women's organizations, the Tajik authorities and international organizations, in the context of economic and political transformation.

Sintiki Tarfa's chapter demonstrates that similar difficulties arise when central organizations seek solutions for difficult local problems without taking into account the specificities of the conditions that prevail. Tarfa examines the experience of Hausa women in Nigeria, who as rural producers play a very important role in agricultural production, marketing and in the management of community resources. Tarfa shows how a government programme of technological support, stimulated by international concern for women, failed to meet the needs of women cultivators. This was largely because of the top-down implementation of the programme, in the formulation of which the women cultivators had no say. Tarfa argues that although technologies can be developed in agriculture and related areas which do not have such negative effects on women, in this particular case they failed. Tarfa contests that, as this case study shows, if the underlying issues of female subordination are not addressed, then globalization and development policies are unlikely to result in practical measures that meet gender needs.

The chapters in this volume highlight the intricacies of the interconnections between women's lives and the global process. They clearly demonstrate that from the national and international arena to the poorest women in the far-flung villages of Africa, the global political economy has begun making unexpected impacts. The articulation of the needs of national and international agencies and those of women do not always result in anticipated solutions. The reactions have ranged from integration and greater empowerment to rejection and even violence and a return towards a lost and idealized past reconstructed in terms of a futuristic conservative agenda. However, if the analyses of the authors in this volume are correct, it would be facile to assume that there is any possibility of return. The twenty-first century will present women with difficult choices, but will also pose severe threats to the patriarchal order that has shaped their lives, and so will provide them with new challenges and opportunities.

REFERENCES

Afshar, H. (1989) 'Gender Roles and the "Moral Economy of Kin" among Pakistani Women in West Yorkshire', in *New Community* 15(2), January, pp. 211–25.

Afshar H (ed.) (1998) *Women and Empowerment: The Politics of Development*, Basingstoke: Macmillan.

Afshar H. (1998) *Islam and Feminisms: an Iranian Experience*, Basingstoke: Macmillan.
Afshar, H. and Dennis, C. (eds) (1992) *Women and Adjustment Policies in The Third World*, Basingstoke: Macmillan.
Afshar, H. and Alikhan, Fatemeh (eds) (1977) *Empowering Women for Development*, Hyderabad: Booklinks Corporation.
Amin, S. (1997) *Capitalism in the Age of Globalization*, London: Zed Books.
Bakker, I. (ed.) (1994) *The Strategic Silence, Gender and Economic Policy*, London: Zed Press.
Barrientos, S. (1996) 'Flexible Work and Female Labour: the Global Integration of Chilean Fruit Production', in R. Auty and J. Toye (eds), *Challenging the Orthodoxies*, Basingstoke: Macmillan.
Barrientos, S., Bee A., Matear, A. and Vogel, I. (forthcoming) *Women and Agribusiness – Working Miracles in the Chitean Fruit Export Sector*, Basingstoke: Macmillan.
Chant, S. (1997) *Women Headed Households: Diversity and Dynamics in the Developing World*, Basingstoke: Macmillan.
Currie, B. (1996) 'Governance, Democracy and Economic Adjustment in India', *Third World Quarterly* 17(4), pp. 787–807.
Dibaja, Z. (1997) 'Globalisation: the Last Sky', *The European Journal of Development Research* 9(1), June.
Elson, D. (1992a) 'Male Bias in Structural Adjustment', in H. Afshar and C. Dennis (eds) *Women and Adjustment Politics in the Third World*, Basingstoke: Macmillan.
Elson D. (1992b) 'From Survival Strategies to Transformation Strategies: Women's Needs and Structural Adjustment', in L. Benería and S. Feldman (eds), *Unequal Burden, Economic Crises, Persistent Poverty, and Women's Work*, Boulder: Westview Press.
Elson, D. (ed.) (1995) *Male Bias in the Development Process*, Manchester: Manchester University Press.
Elson, D. and Pearson, R. (1981) 'The Subordination of Women in the International Factory Production', in K. Young, C. Wolkowtiz and R. McCullagh (eds) *Of Marriage and the Market*, London: CSE Books.
Fernandez-Kelly, M.P. (1994) 'Making Sense of Gender in the World Economy: Focus on Latin America', *Organization* 1(2), pp. 249–75.
Frobel, F., Heinrichs, J. and Kreye, O. (1980) *The New International Division of Labour*, Cambridge: Cambridge University Press.
Hale, A. (1995) *World Trade is a Women's Issue*, Women Working Worldwide, Briefing Paper, Manchester.
Hirst, P. and Thompson, G. (1996) *Globalisation in Question*, Cambridge: Polity Press.
Hoogvelt, A. (1997) *Globalisation and the Postcolonial World, The New Political Economy of Development*, Basingstoke: Macmillan.
Jenkins, R. (1987) *Transnational Corporations and Uneven Development, The Internationalization of Capital and the Third World*, London: Methuen.
Joekes, S. and A. Weston (1994) *Women and the New Trade Agenda*, New York: UNIFEM.
Kabeer, N. (1994) *Reversed Realities*, London: Verso.

Kandiyoti, D. (1998) 'Beyond Beijing: Obstacles and Prospects for the Middle East', in M. Afkhami and Loefflar (eds) *Beyond Beijing*, Syracuse, NY: Syracuse University Press.
Krause, J. (1996) 'Gender Inequalities and Feminist Politics in a Global Perspective', in E. Kofman and Youngs, G. (eds) *Globalization Theory and Practice*, London: Pinter.
Leftwich, A. (1993) 'Governance, Democracy and Development in the Third World', *Third World Quarterly*, vol. 15, no. 3.
Macintosh, M. (1989) *Gender, Class and Rural Transition, Agribusiness and the Food Crisis in Senegal*, London: Zed Press.
Miller B, (1981) *The Endangered Sex – Neglect of Female Children in Rural North India*, Ithaca, NY, Cornell University Press.
Mittelman, J.H. (1994) 'The Globalisation Challenge: Surviving at the Margins', *Third World Quarterly* 15(3), September.
Mitter, S. (1986) *Common Fate Common Bond, Women in the Global Economy*, London: Pluto Press.
Moghissi, H. (1996) 'Factionalism and Muslim Feminine Elite in Iran', in Saeed Rahnema and Sohrab Behdad (eds) *Iran after the Revolution*, London: I.B. Tauris.
Moghissi, H. (forthcoming) '*Feminsimeh populismy va "feminismeh Eslami"*', *Kenskash*.
Moser, C. (1992) 'Adjustment from Below: Low Income Women, Time and the Triple Role in Guayaqui, Ecuador', in H. Afshar and C. Dennis (eds), *Women and Adjustment Politics in the Third World*, Basingstoke: Macmillan.
Ohmae, K. (1990) *The Borderless World, Power and Strategy in the Interlinked Economy*, London: Fontana.
Rowbotham, S. and Mitter, S. (1994) *Dignity and Daily Bread, New Forms of Economic Organising among Poor Women in the Third World and the First*, London: Routledge.
Rowlands, J. (1997) *Questioning Empowerment, Working with Women in Honduras*, Oxford: Oxfam.
Sachs, C. (1996) *Gendered Fields, Rural Women, Agriculture and the Environment*, Boulder: Westview Press.
Scott, A.M. (1995) 'Informal Sector or Female Sector? Gender Bias in Urban Labour Market Models', in D. Elson (ed.), *Male Bias in the Development Process*, Manchester: Manchester University Press.
Schuurman, F.J. (1997) 'The Decentralisation Discourse: Post-Fordist Paradigm or Neo-liberal Discourse?', *The European Journal of Development Research* 9(1), June.
Sideri, S. (1997) 'Globalisation and Regional Integration', *The European Journal of Development Research* 9(1), June.
Singer, H.W. (1991) 'Food Aid and Structural Adjustment in sub-Saharan Africa', in R. Prendergast and H.W. Singer (eds) *Development Perspectives for the 1990s*, Basingstoke: Macmillan.
Sklair, L. (1991) *Sociology of the Global System*, Hemel Hempstead: Harvester Wheatsheaf.
Sklair, L. (1994) *Capitalism and Development*, London: Routledge.
Sparr, P. (ed.) (1994) *Mortgaging Women's Lives, Feminist Critiques of Structural Adjustment*, London: Zed Books.

Standing, G. (1989) 'Global Feminisation through Flexible Labour', *World Development* 17(7), 1077–95.
Stichter, S. and Parpart, J. (eds) (1990) *Women, Employment and the Family in the International Division of Labour*, Basingstoke: Macmillan.
Ward, K. (ed.) (1990) *Women Workers and Global Restructuring*, New York: ILR Press, Cornell University.
World Bank (1992) *Governance and Development*, Washington, D.C.

2 Fractioned States and Negotiated Boundaries: Gender and Law in India[1]//
Shirin M. Rai

This chapter poses questions about the relationship of Indian women to post-colonial state formation. In the context of the liberalization policies of the Indian government in the 1990s, I would suggest that strategy change would become ever-more complex. As the global reach of social movements increases through technological and information networks, and as the pressures of international trade and markets begin to impinge significantly on national economies, the relationship between local struggles, social movements and the nation-state will be mediated by forces of globalization. This would, perhaps, be more visible a trend in countries such as India, where liberalization and structural adjustment policies are quite new and deeply contested. In the context of a multi-party democratic political system, weak infrastructural power of the state and the growing pressures on the political system because of increasing social disparities and new social coalitions, the rate and pace of globalization become unpredictable. This unpredictability could then become part of the negotiations that take place between local struggles and state fractions.

In this chapter I examine the experience of 40 Gujrati women in New Delhi who became engaged in a dispute with the metropolitan authorities in 1991–2 about their right to trade from the street pavement on which they had been working for the preceding five years, and focus on several different agents/actors and the space(s) that they occupy within the Indian political context. I argue that the case of the Gujrati women demonstrates both the splintered complexity of a post-colonial state formation, such as India, and the multiplicity of strategies women need to confront and/or use state fractions in their own interests. I argue first, that the class as well as the gender positioning of these women mean that they operate, economically and politically, in the interstices of the system, only occasionally moving on to the ground of legal arrangements. Second, that feminists need to recognize the importance of state structures and the targeting of these through struggle in the lives of women, while being aware of the limitations of strategies directed only at state organizations. I conclude by arguing for an understanding of the Indian state formation informed by issues of the relative autonomy of state fractions from existing social relations and infrastructural capacity on the one hand, and state embeddedness in social relations and the consequences of such embeddedness for women on the other. Such an approach, derived from analysis of a particular struggle, also points to the potential for a strategy that is both 'in and against' the state.

The chapter is organized in two sections. In the first, I describe and analyse the struggle of the Gujrati women in New Delhi, and in the second, analyse the struggle in the context of the role of legal institutions, in particular the Supreme Court of India and its support of the public interest litigation movement in India.

WOMEN IN STRUGGLE

Exoticism and Profit

Perhaps the most well-known handicrafts from India come from the northwestern state of Gujrat and are available in most parts of the world. These products have earned the Indian state millions in much-needed hard currency and have become tourist attractions in the own right. Janpath is one of the premier shopping districts of Delhi, and is renowned for shops selling handicrafts from all parts of India. Janpath Lane runs off this road; it has no street lighting and was scarcely used until about 40 Gujrati women were relocated there by the New Delhi Municipal Corporation (NDMC). 'We have kept the ethnic trade going in Delhi,' said Ratan, one of the women traders on Janpath Lane. 'The foreigners spend so much money here. The government has benefited from our trade, but has given us nothing in return. We want the government to at least let us put up some sort of shelter. Our wares get wet in the rain. But they are not bothered.'

The women come from the *banjara* (gypsy) community of Gujrat. There are more than 1,800,000 *banjaras* in India. They are low caste and not integrated into the Hindu communities in their villages. 'They are so low in caste that they are not even registered as having any caste; they can't even draw water from the village wells,' said Livleen Sharma, herself from the *banjara* community and a social worker who works with the women on Janpath Lane. Traditionally, the *banjaras* travelled from one region of the state to another, grazing their animals, working as blacksmiths and engaging in petty trade to survive. These people have remained marginalized in Indian society and the economy, despite the changing nature of their economic activities over a period of time. They are not considered politically relevant because they do not form a settled community to be wooed by politicians for their votes. The *banjaras*, therefore, cannot easily be characterized in terms of class, caste or even religion. The best description given them is a situational one – they are subaltern (Guha 1982–7).

In the last two decades, there has been a gradual 'exoticization' of such peoples to create an image of and for India as the home of beautiful handicrafts (Said 1979). This exoticization has been a conscious policy and one which reaps rich rewards for the Indian state. Handicrafts earn the Indian government more in exports than any other commodity, and the growth of the sector since 1970 has been remarkable. (Handicrafts as an export category include pearls and jewellery which are the major earners, but more traditional crafts such as embroidery or patchwork form a considerable part of India's export earnings.) 'During 1989–90, handicrafts exported were of the order of Rupees 6285 crores [£1256 million]' (Dutt and Sundaram 1991: 627).

Hawking in the City

Street-trading (or 'hawking' in India) is a tradition among the *banjaras*. What is distinctive is that it is the women who sell goods on the street, while the men act as suppliers, travelling to their villages to collect items for sale. As a result the women are extremely articulate and self-confident. 'These are ambitious women. They come from women-oriented clans that believe in Durga and Kali.[2] They are very aggressive saleswomen which is why they posed a threat to other traders in the area,' said Livleen Sharma.

Most of these women have grown up on the streets of Delhi helping their mothers in the trade. They know the market, the constraints and the areas of opportunity in the city. 'We have been doing this work for the last 20 years', said Ratan, 'and we want to continue this way.' Because of their success they are not poor. They have been able to build a significant clientele among local and foreign buyers. This is not to say that all *banjara* women, or even those working in big cities, are in such a fortunate economic position. Most lead a precarious existence and have no hope of earning anything more than the minimum to support themselves and their families. Within Delhi, Janpath Lane is unique in its concentration of *banjara* women and their crafts, allowing them to sell not only their own goods but the goods of other *banjara* women who have been unable to secure a pitch on the street. The importance of the right to trade from a particular place is therefore very great.

Forty women were involved in the court case that is the subject of this study. Before they were 'relocated' to Janpath Lane they squatted on the pavement outside the Imperial Hotel on Janpath itself. They had traded from there for more than ten years, until the hotel administration put enough pressure on the NDMC to have them evicted. The women are convinced that this was because they were competition for the very expensive boutiques within the hotel. Five years ago the 40 women were given 'notice to quit' from their site outside the hotel and moved to Janpath Lane ('dumped', said one). 'Five years ago there was no lighting here (there still isn't, as you can see) and it was absolutely *sunsan* (deserted) on this road. This is not a main road, but it soon began to prosper once we started trading from here,' said Radha. Very soon the lane had gained a reputation for Gujrati handicrafts that were both 'authentic' and affordable. Foreign tourists were drawn there and trade prospered. The Gujrati women's aggressive but engaging style of selling – many speak enough English, German and French to be able to negotiate with foreign customers – meant more profit for them, but also brought them into conflict with the traders on Janpath itself.

These traders have proper (*pucca*) shops and more capital to invest than their competitors on Janpath Lane. As they began to feel the pinch of losing their customers to the women on Janpath Lane they put pressure on the local NDMC officials to 'do something about this situation'. In 1991 matters came to a head, when the Gujrati women were served notice to quit yet again. The NDMC declared it was going to build a public lavatory on the pavement; and the women decided that they had no option left to them but to fight for their right to trade from the pavement of Janpath Lane.

A Case of Rights

The women decided to approach the Thareja Committee which had been set up in 1989 by the Supreme Court of India to investigate the trading rights claims of large numbers of pavement hawkers. In a landmark case, *Sodan Singh et al.* v. *NDMC et al.* (1989), it was argued that the fundamental rights of the petitioners under Articles 14, 1 9(l)(g) and/or 21 of the Indian Constitution to equal protection (as other traders), freedom to practise any profession or to carry on any occupation, trade or business and protection of life and personal liberty had been violated by the NDMC in not allowing them to trade from the streets within its jurisdiction. The NDMC contended that the 'grant of exclusive right to occupy any part of the road amounts to the negation of the Common Law theory of dedication of a road for public use' (Supreme Court 1989: 10). In its judgment the Supreme Court concluded that 'The petitioners do have the fundamental right to carry on a trade or business of their choice, but not to do so on a particular place' (1989: 18). It rejected the right-to-life plea of the petitioners. A one-person committee headed by Additional District Judge G.P. Thareja was appointed by the Supreme Court to 'examine the claims made by the squatters [pavement traders] in the light of the said scheme and the decision [of the Supreme Court], and identify street pavements in different areas where street hawking could be regulated without being a hindrance to other users' (Supreme Court 1992: 10).

While all these legal and procedural issues were being aired, the *banjara* women continued to trade on Janpath Lane. They were harassed regularly by NDMC officials and the local police, *challaned* (fined), but allowed to continue working. Corruption is part of the network of administration, and petty corruption is endemic. Police routinely take *hafta* (literally 'week' – i.e. a weekly payment/bribe) from traders of all descriptions and in exchange allow them to operate illegally. Though the women of Janpath Lane did not admit to bribing the police, both Livleen Sharma and Judge Thareja said that they did. The Supreme Court in its judgment made reference to the fact that 'corruption at a large scale was rampant and huge amounts of money were being realised illegally by some of the servants of the Municipalities from the poor hawkers' (Supreme Court 1989: 22).

In November 1991 things came to a head when the demands of the NDMC officials became too great for the women to meet. They were in no position to compete with the shopkeepers on Janpath who could afford to pay far larger sums to the officials and police. In November 1991, just before the Hindu festival of Diwali, when trade is generally brisk, the Gujrati women were ordered to cease trading, but they decided not to give up. A rather unusual protest 'strike' followed.

The Strike

'We decided we will not move from here,' Ratan said. 'It is the NDMC who put us there, so why should we move? They never gave us anything in writing, but always ask for written proof from us. We have been paying *challans* of Rs. 200–250 every time they decided to trouble us, two or three times a week, and every time they also take away one or two pieces of work that we sell. That's another Rs. 100–200 gone.' The women knew that if they quit the pavement on Janpath Lane they would never be able to return there. Others, who could afford to pay more, would be granted the right. They also knew that shopkeepers on Janpath would like to expand their shops on to Janpath Lane.

'For four months we didn't move from this pavement,' said Amma, taking up the story. 'We could not trade, but we didn't move. We slept here, cooked here, our men also used to come and stay here with us.' They suffered not only the bitter cold of November nights, but also the increasing impatience of their families. 'For 20 to 25 days we slept here,' said Krishna. 'After that our men started getting irritated with us. They found it difficult to look after children. The children missed us too. So our men took over from us for the night. We used to go back, feed the children, cook for ourselves for the next day, and be back on the pavement at eight in the morning after sending the children off to school.' During the day they kept vigil on the pavement, but as the strike wore on, so did the harassment. They decided to approach politicians and raise the profile of their struggle.

'First we went to the NDMC chief Ramesh Chandra, but he refused to listen to us,' said Ratan. Indeed, even after Judge Thareja decided in favour of the Gujrati women, Ramesh Chandra said, 'I will knock [on] the door of the Supreme Court if they are permitted to legally occupy the pavement' (*The Pioneer* 1992: 2). The women's defiance in the face of NDMC harassment made them particularly vulnerable to the wrath of the local bureaucrats. 'When we got no *sunwai* [hearing] from Chandra, we decided that we must approach the national politicians. We went to prominent Delhi MPs and the Governor General of Delhi and many others whose names we don't remember. We are not educated you see,' Krishna joined in. 'We decided the night before where we would go. We used to gather here at 8 am, hire a *tempo* [small truck], and start off. We never made an appointment; just reached the home or the office of the MP we had decided upon for the day, and waited for them to see us. Some did, others didn't. Some even signed a petition for us,' Krishna recalled. 'Our case was raised in the parliament after we spoke to an MP from Gujrat,' reminded Amma. 'We didn't go to any women MPs', said Ratan 'because we didn't know of any. We weren't very systematic about meeting politicians.' During this period no social or political organization came to these women's aid. The only person who assisted them was Livleen Sharma, an influential person in Delhi, but in her individual capacity. 'Livleen Sharma used to buy fabrics from us. That is how we got to know her. When we started our struggle she got involved... she came to us, we didn't go to her... she came to ask after us,' said Ratan.

The flashpoint came in March 1992 when 'the NDMC... swooped down on them and dug up the entire pavement as part of the anti-encroachment drive. A railing was put up, an NDMC van put on vigil and the women denied permission to sell their handicrafts' (*The Pioneer*, 1992: 2). This was obviously in contravention of the order made by the Thareja Committee in February 1990. A contingent of policewomen were sent to enforce the order. '"Ladies" police came here. They beat us, and locked us up. We were locked up in the police station at 10am and released only at midnight. We came straight back here,' said Krishna.

By this time, however, the story was in the national newspapers. Soon after the NDMC allowed the women to return and they began selling their goods on the pavement again. Other than the high profile that the women had been able to generate for their case, there were also other more cynical reasons why the NDMC had allowed them back. In June there was to be a by-election in Delhi, and the continuing agitation by these women, which was now gaining media support, would not go down well with local people (*The Pioneer* 1992). One phase of the struggle was over, but the legal decision about their position on Janpath Lane itself still had to be taken by the Thareja Committee.

For this, the women had to prove that they had been trading from there since 1985. The Thareja Committee's view was that 'minimum proof as would enable the Committee to weed out bogus claims from genuine ones had to be insisted upon to maintain credibility in regard to the scrutiny' (Supreme Court 1992: 15). In September 1992, 22 women were given *tehbazari* (tenancy) rights, thus regularizing their position. It was only in March 1993 that another 12 women were granted a pitch. Of the 40 women involved, only six were unable to secure *tehbazari* rights because they were unable to provide the required receipts. 'We don't know why we kept these receipts. People told us to. I have receipts since 1976,' said Amma. 'I keep everything that is written; all receipts, all bills, children's school receipts, *challans*, prescriptions. It might come in handy. It took me a long time to get the *challan* receipts sorted, but I got them all in the end.' Not everyone was so aware of the power of the written word when confronting bureaucracies. The six barred from trading on Janpath Lane are among those who did not keep their receipts.

Supporters and Supports

The struggle of the Janpath Lane women was a key one in their lives and for their survival. As their testimony makes clear, they did not seek to establish links outside their own group. Nor, it seems, did groups such as SEWA (Self-Employed Women's Association), which are very active in mobilizing self-employed women across India, offer any help or support. That these women were traders and not engaged in any production of goods, and could be seen as exploiting other women from whom they bought the handicrafts they sold, could be one reason why women's organizations distanced themselves from the Gujrati trader women. As a result, their strategies were *ad hoc*, and their decisions taken by consultation among themselves.

The only outsiders who touched on their struggle in any significant way were Livleen Sharma and Judge Thareja. A sense of moral justice compelled him, the latter said, to favour those who have developed the commercial potential of Janpath Lane rather than the speculators who have risked nothing yet would capitalize on the labour and enterprise of others. The inclusion of both these actors in this narrative is important but for different reasons. Sharma and Thareja represent different and powerful elites in Indian society. Their support for the Janpath Lane women had different sources and forms, but was important to the final outcome. This, of course, does not detract from the struggle itself, but points to the variables that can affect the lives of the less privileged – variables that are not linked to organizations or institutions, and are random though critical. Their inclusion in the story underscores the systemic fragility of the Indian politico-legal system, where random interventions by exceptional individuals rather than an effective machinery to implement state policies become critical to the outcome of the struggle (a point I develop further in the next section).

The story of the struggle of the Janpath trader women is an instructive one in understanding the relations between women and state institutions in India. In the next section I examine the role that the Supreme Court played in this case, how it positioned itself *vis-à-vis* the other fractions of the state, and whether its philosophy of 'soft legalism' allows it to be more responsive to certain struggles.

NEGOTIATING BOUNDARIES

What becomes evident when we read the narratives of the Gujrati women is that they are not reactive or passive, but always conscious of the massive power of the state as exercised in their lives by the petty officials of the NDMC. That power is backed by laws, by the enforcers of laws and by violence. The Indian state for them is a crucial network of power relations which translates into different levels of organization, and they can ill afford to ignore the boundaries that it draws around them. Transgression of these boundaries is a different question, however. Transgression involves knowing the boundaries that are to be pushed. The knowledge of these boundaries comes in different ways to people of different classes, races and cultures. Boundaries may only become visible in the process of transgressing them; whether the transgressors saw their actions as transgression or not forms a critical part of the story. Transgression of boundaries also involves multi-faceted counter-strategies. Acquiescence and opposition, anger and conciliation, idealism and pragmatism – all are interwoven into a complex pattern of interaction with the state institutions and procedures. In the story of the Janpath Lane women we see all these strategies at work.

One of the most significant contributions of poststructuralist arguments to the theorizing of the state is the insistence that there is no unity that we can point to as 'the state'. What we customarily call 'the state' can be regarded only as a network of power relations which exist in cooperation yet also in tension. The study of the functioning of the various agencies in operation in the case discussed illustrates the validity of the poststructuralist approach to the state. Precisely because of this fluidity and dispersal of power we cannot regard the 'touch' of the state as universally suspect and structuring of women's lives. We cannot simply argue – as many radical feminists have done, for example – that an appeal to the state for protection 'involves seeking protection against men from masculinist institutions' (Brown 1992: 9; see also Kapur and Cossman 1993). This is because one implication of poststructuralist arguments about the dispersal of power is the acknowledgement of the varied forms that power takes and the uses to which it is and can be put. If we add to this acknowledgement our understanding of the complexity of civil society, then taking simply an 'against the state' position becomes positively dangerous. Civil society is as deeply masculinist as is the infrastructure of state relations. Women cannot look to one to oppose the other. Both spaces – of informal and formalized networks of power – are imbued with masculinist discourses (Pateman 1989); neither is uncoerced, however different the forms and mechanisms of coercion. A further layer of complexity is added when the global economic forces impinge on national economies and legal and political systems. International discourses of human rights, for example, or growing integration of national economies into the world market system, create an environment in which the nation-state becomes both the transmitter of global economic messages (as opposed to the defender of local economy) and an ambivalent player on the political stage – both more and less in control of various state fractions, as well as its own infrastructural power.

Political Rhetoric and Legitimacy

Through this study we can witness the unfolding character of the Indian state. The different roles played by the Supreme Court and the NDMC, the police and the Thareja Committee in this case indicate the various organizational forms and discourses of the state. The historical importance of the rhetoric of 'socialism' and welfare state in India (embodied, for example, in its constitution in the Preamble, the Directive Principles of State Policy and the First Five-Year Plan) allows the Supreme Court to take positions in cases such as this one that it might otherwise not have taken.

In his study of the Indian state, Sen (1982: 160) argues that one feature of the Indian state that indicated its relative autonomy from social classes was its ability to promote and develop a cultural environment hostile to private capital and conducive to state capital. However, his analysis falls short of acknowledging the relative autonomy of the political. The rhetoric of socialism is cast as a legitimizing instrument in the hands of the state. Its potential to be used by oppositional groups as a means of holding the state organizations accountable, and of delegitimizing state fractions when there is a lack of such accountability, is not analysed. The belief that 'social justice must inform a welfare state' is seriously regarded by many senior legal professionals in India, as is the characterization of the Indian state as a welfare state, despite the lack of resources that severely constrains its welfare functions. That this concern challenges state power is revealed in repeated attempts by the Indian state executive to bring the Supreme Court to heel by seeking to curtail its influence in appointing judges to its bench, as well as the scope of its power to review executive decisions (*India Today*, 28 July 1997).

Taking the relative autonomy of the political seriously would also invite an examination of the democratic processes and functioning in the country for the last 50 years. To dismiss this feature of the Indian political system as a 'charade', as Alavi (1972: 63) did and many others subscribing to the post-colonial state analysis still do, is to fail to see how important this very uneven, pitted and sometimes dangerous political terrain is for mobilization of opposition by various groups, including women. That an important parliamentary by-election in Delhi was approaching when the women traders went on strike was important. Public interest in state functioning was raised at the time and enabled the women to make their campaign more visible than they otherwise might have. In the context of a non-democratic state formation, the struggle might not have had access to the media and local politicians at all. Specificities of the political system are thus important to the nature and scope of women's struggles.

Public Interest Litigation

In asking the Thareja Committee to take into account the economic and social position of the petitioners, the Court moved beyond a purely 'legal' position. This legal interpretation takes into account the socioeconomic position of the litigants on the one hand, and the role of a welfare state on the other, and is called Public Interest Litigation (PIL) in the Indian legal discourse (see also Anthony 1993). Since the 1980s, the Supreme Court has often taken a social interventionist position in its judgments. The Court has increasingly taken as its stand that 'in a developing society judicial activism is essential for participative justice ... Justices are the constitutional invigilators and reformers [who] bring the rule of law closer to the rule of life' (P.N. Singh 1981–2, cited in Cooper 1993: 6). A judgment in a civil liberties case in 1978 established a precedent of interpreting the fundamental rights of Indian citizens in a more flexible way. A leading exponent of PIL, Justice Bhagwati, urged that the Constitution 'must be interpreted creatively and imaginatively with a view to advancing the constitutional values and spelling but and strengthening the basic human rights of the large masses of people in the country' (Cooper 1993: 8). PIL also indicates a certain autonomy for various state fractions from 'peak interest groups' in Indian society. The women on Janpath Lane benefited enormously from this approach to the Constitution and the rights of Indian citizens. The gendered nature of PIL, however, cannot be disregarded. It has been argued that where women are concerned, 'with some notable exceptions, the judicial approach to the equality guarantees of the Constitution [of India] is informed by a problematic approach to both equality and gender difference' (Kapur and Cossman 1993: 1). This can be explained by what Johnson, and before him Karl Polanyi, called the embeddedness of the state.

The state capacity literature regards 'embeddedness' as a characteristic of 'strong' states: its ability to harness 'peak interest groups' in society to the purposes of economic development. It does not, however, reflect on the consequences of this embeddedness on marginal, less powerful or weak social groups. If state fractions are embedded in interest groups, they are also vulnerable to infiltration by these groups and by the discourses of dominant interests in society (see below; and Kandiyoti 1991). Further, this embeddedness is not a neat fit – the levels of embeddedness may vary for differing state fractions functioning in varied social and political contexts. I would argue that, though gendered in its interpretation of the laws of the country, the PIL approach makes a difference to women's lives in particular cases and sets precedents for future judgments.

Infrastructural Power and Political Capacity

While PIL focuses on legal interpretation and decisions, it tells us little about the capacity of the state to implement these decisions. Michael Mann draws a distinction between the 'despotic and infrastructural power' of the state. The former denotes the power of state elites with little 'institutionalized negotiation with civil society groups', while 'infrastructural power' presumes the ability of the state to 'penetrate and centrally coordinate the activities of civil society through its own infrastructure' (Mann 1984: 190 and 188). While we cannot speak of either term as undisturbed by the characteristics of the other, his distinction is useful to emphasize that there exists no direct, linear co-relation between 'state autonomy' and 'state capacity' (Onis 1991: 123). The first will not automatically lead to the other. The public interest concerns of the Indian Supreme Court, themselves not unproblematic for women's struggles, also face considerable constraints from the lack of political and economic resources which go into building a stable infrastructural power. This undermines its capacity to ensure the implementation of its decisions, thereby posing a threat to its legitimacy.

In the case of the Gujrati women both the welfare state rhetoric of the judicial authorities and the coercive and arbitrary power of the local police and administration were evident, pointing to the tensions within and between state fractions. The ability of state organizations to enforce their laws and regulations in this case (as in others) was crucial. As evident in the discussion of state capacity, when the 'infrastructural power' of the state organizations is weak, the implementation of directives can become hostage to random factors. In the Janpath Lane case, the implementation of Supreme Court directives could be read as contingent on the personal attributes of enforcers rather than in the capacity of state institutions to ensure the implementation of legal judgments.

The Indian state organizations are also largely unchecked at the local level in the scale of violence which they inflict on the people. The women's movement in India, for example, is rooted in women's opposition to police brutality (Spivak 1987) in the 1970s. Rape, murder and beatings in police custody continue to be common features of state operations, especially in rural areas. At the time, depending upon their race, class and caste, most third world women have fewer resources to withstand the violations of state authorities. Lack of education, economic vulnerability, weak infrastructural social support and lack of availability of information leave women in these countries more dependent on their own resources, which in themselves are meagre. These also determine to a large extent the options open to women, and that they think they have, in their dealings with state organizations.

Further, 'weak' state capacity does not allow the state organizations to regulate themselves effectively internally, which adversely affects not only the implementation of policies, but the relationship between citizens and state fractions. I have already mentioned the high level of corruption among the Delhi metropolitan bureaucracy. Like that of many other 'weak' states, the Indian administrative bureaucracy is generally too 'flabby' to be effective and too huge to be controlled. As a result, corruption becomes an independent variable in the functioning of the Indian state organizations, further subverting the implementation of policy. This can be partly explained by institutional factors, such as the size of the bureaucracy or the effectiveness of controls put in place by the political executive, and partly by the particularity of the state organizations' 'embeddedness' in civil society (Lie 1991: 220).

While linked to the question of resources and state capacity, corruption as a feature of state functioning in India is often taken for granted or overlooked as an independent factor in the state/citizen relationship and as a mobilizing feature for oppositional groups. Women, of course, are affected in different ways from men; the 'favours' asked for are not just financial, but may also be sexual. That the Janpath Lane women could not afford to pay the NDMC officials the bribes being offered to them by the shopkeepers of Janpath adversely affected their bargaining position. Corruption within the state bureaucracies has increased owing to the opening up of the Indian economy to the global market systems and the attempts of multinationals to function within the bureaucratic boundaries of the Indian state. We can see here the relative autonomy of various state fractions and discover how these might emphasize different aspects of political rhetoric and administrative functioning, which at times create severe tensions within a system and potentially could be taken as an advantage by those struggling against aspects of state policy.

Looking to the state enforcement agencies to implement the decision of the Supreme Court could not therefore be the only way open to the women. The tension between the metropolitan authorities and the police on the one hand, and the Thareja Committee and the Supreme Court on the other, on the substantive issues at stake in this case was evident. Protest had to be organized in tandem with petitioning the courts and, as their strike gained support, mobilized outside the institutions and corridors of state power. This they did.

Visibility as Strategy

First, the women made themselves visible in the public political arena by refusing to vacate the pavement from which they traded. Thus they forced the coercive arm of the state – the police – to become visible too, so exposing it to public scrutiny. When the women were *lathi-* (baton)-charged and arrested, the media took up the story. The support of the socially prominent Livleen Sharma, itself in part the result of increasing public interest in the women's plight, also strengthened their case outside the courtroom. It now became impossible for the state legislative intitution to ignore what was happening. That the Member of Parliament from Gujrat raised a question in parliament on their behalf is indicative of this, as is the fact that some of the randomly approached influential Delhi MPs signed their petition supporting their case to the NDMC.

The functioning of a party political system, however, can be a double-edged sword. On the one hand, groups can at particular times mobilize the support of one party against the other, creating for themselves strategic spaces that they might not otherwise have had, and, on the other, the need for mobilizing votes to legitimize governance means that the parties and state institutions become complicit in not challenging the socioeconomic relations counter to their own rhetoric. Caste, religion and gender relations are particularly sensitive socioeconomic issues, as are those related to property and the redistribution of wealth. The state organizations' embeddedness in civil society also reinforces this complicity.

Civil society is not an uncomplicated 'space of uncoerced human association and ... of relational networks – formed for the sake of family, faith, interest and ideology – that fill this space' (Walzer 1992: 89). Civil society is a deeply fraught space, harbouring hidden and explicit dangers in the garb of national, religious and ethnic identities as fashioned by male-directed movements of various kinds (Rai 1994). In this context, the 'embeddedness' of the state fractions in civil society cannot be regarded in the positive light that many developmental economists do (see, for example, Charlton and Donald 1992: 7). For women, the reinforcing of bureaucratic capacity by social norms can be a terrifying combination, threatening any attempt to change their lived reality. In this context, however, the fractured nature of the state becomes important.

What we begin to piece together from this study, as far as the debate about women and 'the state' is concerned, is a highly complex picture. The Indian post-colonial state formation can be seen to be composed of different fractions acting as oppressors and also resources/supporters in these women's struggles to protect their livelihoods. In conclusion, I argue that the relationship between theory and practice has to be 'foregrounded' if it is to address the question of the political role that women can and need to play in the arena of state citizen interaction.

IN AND AGAINST THE STATE? CONCLUDING THOUGHTS

One of the most startling differences between women in European liberal welfare states and those in India and most of the third world is the extent to which they are directly 'touched' by the regulatory power of state organizations. They are unable to provide the kind of safety network that the European liberal state does with its welfare provision, which depends greatly on social monitoring. Neither upper-class nor lower-class Indian women fall within the ambit of state functioning. In health, education, child care and employment upper-class women have traditionally depended on the private sector and so too do the poorest women – the first group because of access to private, non-state resources, the second, because the state can provide them with very little support. The erosion of even the minimal welfare provision under the conditionalities imposed through liberalization and structural adjustment policies has further emphasized this feature of state/citizen relationship. Further, illiteracy and exclusionary social practices exacerbate this isolation from the processes of state organizations. Political expediency overrules the rhetoric of social justice quite easily; there is a lack of political will to interfere in traditional family relations. Further, the weakness of the infrastructural power of state organizations means that laws are ignored in many parts of the country. So even though Indian women have constitutional rights of inheritance, divorce and maintenance, for example, the enforcement of these rights is at best patchy.

For most women in India state institutions figure marginally in their lives. They loom large only when women transgress the boundaries set by these institutions in various areas of public and private life over which they have jurisdiction. Therefore, for the majority of women the question is not whether to approach state organizations, *it is that they are approached by state organizations*, in many instances in a brutal and violent way. In that context, can one argue that 'to be "protected" by the very power whose violation one fears perpetuates the specific modality of dependence and powerlessness marking much of women's experience across widely diverse cultures and epochs' (Brown 1992: 9). As Patricia Williams writes: 'For the historically disempowered, the conferring of rights is symbolic of all the denied aspects of their humanity: rights imply a respect that places one in the referential range of self and others, that elevates one's status from human body to social being' (Williams 1991: 153). The question surely is not one of simply 'seeking protection', but of fighting state violence. The forms that this struggle can take may vary from country to country, state formation to state formation. But to focus simply on the regulating, structuring, constraining power of state institutions, and to overlook the struggles that challenge and reconfigure state power, is to sell short the daily lives of millions of women.

Finally, I would argue that the question of 'in and against "the state"' has to be looked at afresh. Ehrenreich and Piven (1983) make the case for increasing women's involvement with state institutions by pointing to the radical potential of such a project for women both as individuals and as a growing collective. The London/Edinburgh Weekend Return Group, in their influential book *In and Against the State* make a different point: 'The State, then is not "our" state. It is "their" state, an alien, oppressive state' (1980: 53). However, they remind us that 'we have made positive gains [under this hostile state] not by "winning power" in any formal sense but by taking a degree of control, counter-posing our forms of organisations to theirs' (1980: 147). I further argue, not in opposition but from a different standpoint, that if we do not regard the state as a unity, we cannot look upon struggle as a unified strategy either.

My concern in this chapter is to point to the lack of intentionality of a unified state structure and to point to the spaces that are available and can are created for and through struggle for retrieving, reconstructing and regaining control over the meanings and signifiers in women's lives. They do this in different ways, taking into account their own experience, needs and situations, and they approach the various forms of state differently – in opposition, in cooperation, through subversion not simply of rules but of articulated intentions of state forms, and through negotiations. And they do all this actively, if not always with a coherence and intentionality of their own: 'It is because subjects do not, strictly speaking, know what they are doing that what they do has more meaning than they know' (Bourdieu, in Risseeuw 1991: 154). It is on this struggle – in all its myriad forms – that we must focus to understand the relationship that women construct with the state in which they live.

ACKNOWLEDGEMENTS

I would like to acknowledge the support of the Nuffield Foundation which facilitated my research in Delhi by a grant. I also gratefully acknowledge the tremendous support of the women on Janpath Lane during my research. They opened themselves to me with courage and generosity, without which this research would have been impossible. I also thank Livleen Sharma and Mr Thareja for sharing information and opinions with me. I would like to thank Jeremy Roche, Ann Stewart, Peter Burnham and Sol Picciotto for their comments.

NOTES

1. A version of this chapter was published in *Social Legal Studies*, Vol. 4, 1995, under the title: 'Women Negotiating Boundaries: Gender, Law and the Indian State'. I'm grateful to Sage Publications for permission to reproduce the data here.
2. Durga and Kali are two representations, benevolent and angry respectively, of the goddess Parvati, the consort of Shiva the God of Death in Hindu mythology, and signify *Shakti* or female energy in different forms.

REFERENCES AND BIBLIOGRAPHY

Alavi, Hamza (1972) 'The State in Post-Colonial Societies: Pakistan and Bangladesh', *New Left Review* (July–August) 74: 63.
Allen, J. (1990) 'Does Feminism Need a Theory of the State?', pp. 21–38 in Sophie Watson (ed.) *Playing the State*, London: Verso.
Alvarez, Sonia E. (1990) *Engendering Democracy in Brazil: Women's Movements in Transition Politics*, Princeton, NJ: Princeton University Press.

Amin, Samir (1974) *Accumulation on a World Scale: a Critique of the Theory of Underdevelopment*, New York: Monthly Review Press.
Amin, Samir (1977) *Imperialism and Unequal Development*, Hassocks: Harvester Press.
Anthony, M.J. (1993) *Social Action through Courts: Landmark Judgements in Public Interest Litigation*, New Delhi: Indian Social Institute.
Bamat, T. (1977) 'Relative State Autonomy and Capitalism in Brazil and Peru', in *Insurgent Sociologist* (Spring).
Barrett, Michèlle and Anne Phillips (eds) (1992) *Destabilizing Theory: Contemporary Feminist Debates*, Cambridge: Polity Press.
Brown, Wendy (1992) 'Finding the Man in the State', *Feminist Studies* 18(1): 7–34.
Charlton, Roger and David Donald (1992) 'Bringing the Economy Back in: Reconsidering the Autonomy of the Developmental State', paper presented at the Annual Conference of the Political Science Association, 7–9 April, Belfast.
Cooper, Jeremy (1993) 'Poverty and Constitutional Justice: The Indian Experience', *Mercer Law Review*, 44: 1–25.
Davis, Kathy, M. Leijenaar and J. Oldersma (eds) (1991) *The Gender of Power*, London: Sage.
Davis, Miranda (ed.) (1987) *Third World, Second Sex*, London: Zed Books.
Dutt, R. and K.P.M. Sundaram (1991) *Indian Economy*, New Delhi: S. Chand.
Ehrenreich, B. and F.F. Piven (1983) 'Women and the Welfare State' in Irving Howe (ed.) *Alternatives: Proposals for America from the Democratic Left*, New York: Pantheon.
Eisenstein, Zillah R. (ed.) (1979) *Capitalist Patriarchy and the Case for Socialist Feminism*, New York, Monthly Review Press.
Elson, Diane (1992) 'Gender Analysis and Development Economics', paper presented at ESRC Development Economics Study Group, Annual Conference, March.
Frank, A.G. (1971) *Capitalism and Underdevelopment in Latin America*, Harmondsworth: Penguin Books.
Frank, A.G. (1978) *Dependent Accumulation and Underdevelopment*, London: Macmillan.
Franzway, S., D. Court and R.W. Connell (1989) *Staking a Claim: Feminism, Bureaucracy and the State*, Cambridge: Polity Press.
Guha, Ranjit (1982–7) *Subaltern Studies: Writings on South Asian History and Society*, Delhi: Oxford University Press.
Howe, Irving (ed.) (1983) *Alternatives: Proposals for America from the Democratic Left*, New York: Pantheon.
Johnson, Chalmers (1982) *MITI and the Japanese Miracle: the Growth of Industrial Policy 1925–1975*, Stanford: Stanford University Press.
Joseph, Saud (1993) 'Gender and Civil Society', *Middle East Report* 183 (July–August).
Kandiyoti, Deniz (1991) *Women, Islam and the State*, Basingstoke: Macmillan.
Kapur, Ratna and Brenda Cossman (1993) 'On Women, Equality and the Constitution: Through the Looking Glass of Feminism', Special Issue on 'Feminism and Law', *National Law School Journal* No. 1, pp. 1–61.

Lie, John (1991) 'Embedding Polanyi's Market Society', *Sociological Perspectives* 34(2): 219–35.
London–Edinburgh Weekend Return Group (1980) *In and Against the State*, London: Pluto Press.
Longrigg, Clare (1991) 'Blood Money', *Amnesty* (February/March): 1617.
Mann, Michael (1984) 'The Autonomous Power of the State', *Archives Européennes de Sociologie* 25(2): 185–212.
Mehdid, Malika (1993) 'Feminist Debate on Women and the State in the Middle East', paper presented at the Conference of Socialist Feminists, July 1992, London.
Melotti, Umberto (1977) *Marx and the Third World*, London: Macmillan.
Mernissi, Fatima (1991) *Women and Islam*, Oxford: Basil Blackwell.
Mohanty, Manoranjan (1990) 'Duality of the State Process in India', in Manoranjan Mohanty (ed.) *Capitalist Development: Critical Essays*, Bombay: Popular Prakashan.
Mouffe, Chantal (ed.) (1992) *Dimensions of Radical Democracy: Pluralism, Citizenship, Community*, London: Verso.
Nadkarni, V.C. (1993) 'Crime and Punishment', *Sunday Times of India: Review*, Delhi, 21 November: 1.
Onis, Ziya (1991) 'The Logic of the Developmental State', *Comparative Politics* 24(1): 109–26.
Pateman, Carol (1989) 'Feminism and Democracy', pp. 210–55 in *The Disorder of Women*, Cambridge: Polity Press.
Pathak, Zakia (1992) 'Shahbano', pp. 257–79 in J. Butler and J. Scott (eds) *Feminists Theorize the Political*, New York and London: Routledge.
The Pioneer (1992) 'Janpath Hawker Women Win Legal Battle', 2 October.
Pringle, Rosemary and Sophie Watson (1992) 'Women's Interests and the Post Structuralist State', pp. 53–73 in Michèlle Barrett and Anne Phillips (eds) *Destabilizing Theory*, Cambridge: Polity Press.
Rai, Shirin M. (1994) 'Gender and Democratisation or What Does Democracy Mean for Women in the Third World?', *Democratisation* 1(2): 2809–28.
Risseeuw, Carla (1991) 'Bourdieu, Power and Resistance: Gender Transformation in Sri Lanka', pp. 15–79 in Kathy Davis, Monique Leijenaar and Jantine Oldersma (eds) *The Gender of Power*, London: Sage.
Rosa, Kumudhini (1987), 'Organising Women Workers in the Free Trade Zone, Sri Lanka', pp. 159–4 in Miranda Davis (ed.) *Third World, Second Sex*, London: Zed Books.
Said, Edward (1979) *Orientalism*, New York: Vintage.
Sen, Anupam (1982) *The State, Industrialisation, and Class Formation in India*, London: Routledge and Kegan Paul.
Spivak, Gayatri C. (1987) 'Draupadi', in *In Other Worlds: Essays in Cultural Politics*, London: Methuen.
Supreme Court of India (1989) *Judgement on Sodan Singh et al.* v. *New Delhi Municipal Committee et al.*
Supreme Court of India (1992) *Sodan Singh et al.* v. *New Delhi Municipal Committee et al.*, D. No. 1250/88/Sec.X.
Walzer, Michael (1992) 'The Civil Society Argument', pp. 89–1807 in Chantal Mouffe (ed.) *Dimensions of Radical Democracy*, London: Verso.
Watson, Sophie (ed.) (1990) *Playing the State*, London: Verso.

Weedon, Chris (1993) 'Feminism and Postmodernism', paper presented at the Women's Studies Network (UK) Conference, July.
Williams, Patricia J. (1991) *The Alchemy of Race and Rights*, Cambridge, MA: Harvard University Press.
Wilson, Elizabeth, (1977) *Women and the Welfare State*, London: Tavistock.

3 Right-wing Mobilization of Women in India: *Hindutva*'s Willing Performers

Jahnavi Phalkey

The Indian economy has undergone a significant transformation in the 1990s. This has happened in the form of what the Indian government calls 'liberalization'. The process is broadly seen as an opening up of the Indian market to foreign investment. The logic of this rolling back of relative state control of the production process is largely based in the rhetoric that surrounds what is called 'globalization'. The debate is taking place in the media, academia and political parties and the most frequently voiced argument is that India should not be 'left behind in the rapidly shrinking global village'. The debate also occupies an important place in the study of politics of the developing world, to the extent that liberalization, or the opening up of developing economies to international investment, is seen as a key symptom of development itself, while the viability of domestic industry in the presence of international competition, particularly from establishments in the developed world, is ignored. The argument is rejected on the grounds that such an approach would handicap the viability and growth of domestic industries. This rhetoric is difficult to argue against given its apparent intention of favouring the production process in the developing world, even though it ignores the need for continuing infrastructural support which is most essential to the development, and in many cases the very survival, of domestic industry.

Industrialization is one of the major components of modernization in developing countries such as India. Transformation in the production process and wider economy has been largely government-led, thereby making it a major part of the experience not only of independence, governing and development, but also of modernity. Modernity came to India as a part of the colonial regime, though it evolved in the logic of 'native' institutions as well. Thus, not only the political system but also the direction that the economy has followed were products of this logic. However, over time, it became increasingly clear that the continued adoption of the western political idiom was not helping to explain change or accept responsibility for the malfunctioning of modern institutions, and the state was unable to cope with those social changes that came about as the result of the new system of allocation, utilization and distribution of resources, economic and otherwise. This contributed to the growing dissatisfaction with the political system and governance.[1] In this chapter it is not possible to consider in detail the dissatisfaction that was generated, but one of its effects – the rise of populism in politics – will be discussed.

John Gledhill (1994: 94) described populism as 'based on middle-class leadership which builds a mass base by promising working people jobs and social benefits, using a discourse which tends to be patriotic and anti-imperialist'. Gledhill quotes Bryan Roberts on populism in Latin America;

> [Populist] regimes solve the problems confronting capital at a particular stage of its development. This stage occurs at a time when industrial interests are becoming predominant in the economy, but when their power is not sufficiently consolidated to enable them either to incorporate other groups through economic benefits or coerce them through control of state apparatus. (Roberts 1978: 68–69)

Roberts and Gledhill both cite Latin America in their elaboration of the process and characteristics of populist politics, but these hold true for the Indian polity to some extent. There are, however, certain conditions that are specific to India. These are largely seen in the ways and the rhetoric in which populist politics has manifested itself in India. The discussion involves numerous variants of the Indian political system, but in this chapter we shall restrict ourselves to Hindu nationalist politics.

Roberts talks of an economy in which the interests of capital have gained prominence, but their power to influence the political process is not sufficient. The Indian economy is at a stage where the interests of capital are strongly articulated, but it is *not* characterized by a weak industrial bourgeoisie. The role of the bourgeoise in the political process is substantial but not overwhelming, and this ensures that the state, though a major player, is not the only agent of economic restructuring. India has followed a mixed economy pattern, wherein the state allows investment of private capital in some areas. This means that there has always been a space for non-state investment, which now has the potential to evolve independently with changing circumstances. Another important feature of the Indian polity is its fragmented civil society. Local communities are divided and grouped by loyalties of caste [2] and clan, which follow certain hierarchical patterns. The state does not penetrate or administer the interior or rural areas very effectively. Thus, political representation also shows signs of these hierarchical patterns. The process of representation in effect becomes a mediation of 'gaps' in the local and larger political process, i.e. between social and political organization, for the polity to function. The determinants of mediation and the process of mediation ground power in everyday life. Populist politics contributes to this process.

Hindu nationalist politics[3] can be said to contribute to the mediation of these gaps in its methods of representation. These are illustrative of populism, as Gledhill explains. The leadership is largely middle-class and appeals to the dissatisfied masses by promising jobs and social benefits which they expect but do not receive from the state: a condition that typically arises as a result of the dysfunctional institutions of modernity.[4] Their discourse is overwhelmingly patriotic, however, they set their own terms of the 'national' and therefore of patriotism as well.[5] The nation is defined as a 'Hindu nation', and a patriot is essentially one who identifies with *hindutva*. The culmination of Hindu nationalist political aspirations in the twentieth century was the almost theatrical demolition of the Babri mosque, in Ayodhya in the state of Uttar Pradesh on 6 December 1992. Communal violence followed throughout India. This was not a spontaneous act of violence, as tension around the issue of the mosque had been simmering since even before independence, and more recently since 1989. The mosque is said to have been built by the Moghul emperor Babar, after the destruction of a Hindu temple, on the site that Hindu nationalists claim is the birthplace of Ram, an incarnation of the Godhead. Various contesting histories have been proposed about the mosque ever since the conflict surfaced. *Hindutva* forces wanted to reclaim the site to redress the wrongs of history and establish a continuum of Hindu history. What was interesting about the violence, to my mind, was the visible and substantial participation of women marking their presence in *hindutva* politics. It is not that women were participating in nationalist politics for the first time. Women had participated in the struggle for independence. The focus of this chapter, then, is to examine women's participation in the violence of *hindutva* politics, looking in particular for possible explanations within women's experience of modernity.

WOMEN'S PARTICIPATION IN *HINDUTVA* POLITICS

Women's groups and other voluntary organizations have produced numerous reports describing women's participation in communal violence following the demolition of the Babri mosque. A number of academics also tried to make sense of the phenomenon.[6] This chapter will not look in detail at the locations and number of the events in which women participated. Rather, descriptions and the nature of these events are discussed. What follows, to facilitate further discussion, is a very brief list of some of the incidents. Women generally participated in their capacity as members of the 'women's wings' of the various parties comprising the *hindutva* brotherhood. The Rashtriya Swayamsevika Samiti of the RSS, the Durga Vahini of the VHP, Mahila Morcha of the BJP and the women's wing of the Shiv Sena. Women's role in communal violence was through direct participation, by going out on the streets and hurling stones, throwing crude home-made bombs, and dragging people out of their homes. Then there was indirect participation: helping the rioters by piling up stones, and glass bottles and making crude Molotov cocktails. Women also showed their complicity in the violence by not protesting. They also instigated violence themselves locally, and through public defiance of the Hindu male community such as Sadhvi Rithambara, Uma Bharati and others who made public speeches calling on the valour of Hindu men to protect the honour of the Hindu community. A number of incidents have been requestioned and contested, and the process continues.

Flavia Agnes (1994) reports that in Bombay, Hindu women cheered while Muslim women were raped. Again in Bombay, women lay down in the road in the path of army vehicles when a Shiv Sena MLA was arrested for carrying arms during the riots (Setalvad, 1993: 234). Shiv Sena women blocked the progress of fire engines to prevent them reaching Muslim districts after the men had destroyed and set fire to shops and homes. Women led mobs and dragged Muslim women and children out into the streets, cheered on the gang rapes and joined Hindu men in stoning and setting them on fire (Kishwar, 1993: 23). Two Muslim women were killed in police fire in Pratiksha Nagar, Bombay, yet some Hindu women watching from their balconies insisted that the women died of 'natural causes', and in any event 'Muslims deserved to die'. Hindu women employees of a state-owned corporation in Bombay threatened to strike until the government demolished a nearby Muslim slum (Bhaktal, 1993: 12–13). Twenty thousand women participated in demonstrations in Ayodhya (Basu, 1993: 79). These women are members of the paramilitary groups the VHP is training, as in Ayodhya, and come from both upper- and middle-class backgrounds (Mazumdar, 1995: 15). RSS women are given a thorough grounding in ideology as well as rigorous physical and military training. They are coached to give public speeches and chair meetings. There are intellectual sessions on the history of the Hindu nation, and prayer meetings, etc. (Sarkar, 1993).

The participation of women in *hindutva* politics involves a re-enactment of traditional gendered social roles in the public sphere. Nirupama Gour, the secretary of the Mahila Morcha of the BJP, recalls the preparation for the elaborate ritual to send Kar Sevaks to Ayodhya like warriors sent to the battlefield by women in the past. Food, flower garlands, the *tilak*, etc., were prepared. The women were also responsible in Ayodhya for shielding men from the police crackdown. They would encircle the men in order to prevent the police from wielding *lathis* (batons). However, the women did not scale the mosque during the demolition as it would be undignified for Hindu women to be seen climbing a mosque in their saris (Mala Rustogi to Amrita Basu in an interview in Lucknow, 28 December 1992). Women were involved earlier in door-to-door campaigns, unlike men who generally addressed public meetings. Thus, they came in contact with housewives and the women of the households.

The speeches made by Sadhvi Rithambara and Uma Bharati are interesting. They exemplify a peculiar process of the emasculation of Hindu men. They talk of the sexually aggressive and rapacious masculinity of Muslim men, which is a threat to Hindu women. This they see as the reason for the growing Muslim population, something that threatens the very existence of the (Hindu) nation. Therefore, the logical conclusion is that Hindu men should 'control' and kill Muslim men in order to preserve their masculinity and national pride. It is interesting to note that when Uma Bharati and Sadhvi Rithambara evoke male sexuality in their public speeches, it becomes quite acceptable within patriarchal conventions, which is not the norm. But they can do so only by the simultaneous erasure of their own sexuality, in renunciation and celibacy in this case. The sexuality of the women is also controlled by the men, whose sexuality they seek to address.

Women have served as agents of the *hindutva* forces in politicizing religion, and they themselves have become a vital political force and electoral pool as well. The image of a Hindu woman victimized by Muslim male sexuality, has paradoxically 'empowered' her and legitimized her resort to violence. The Hindu man, on the other hand, is feminised vis-à-vis the sexually aggressive Muslim man, again to legitimize his violence when the goal is a 'just' Hindu nation.

UNDERSTANDING WOMEN IN *HINDUTVA*

It is very tempting to judge this political phenomenon by attempting a rationalist critique of the political agency women alone seem to derive from this participation, but to do so shows an unwillingness to look precisely at that process which is subverting the idiom of modernity, political agency and politics, to suit its own purposes of gaining political power. But again, is it sufficient to say that, or is this a process with its own logic which does not find sympathy in the given political paradigms? It is unfair to construct a discourse around women participants of the Hindu right which reduces their acts to false consciousness. Bourdieu, while elaborating on the concept of habitus, goes on to say that collective mobilization 'cannot succeed without a minimum of concordance between the habitus of the mobilising agent and the dispositions of those whose aspirations and world views they express' (Bourdieu, 1977: 91). This goes some way to explain the reproduction of social and political configurations, and hence the congruence of the dispositions of the Hindu right leaders and the women participants. This does not explain, however, how these dispositions came about; that is, how Hindu nationalist thinking attracted a loyalty for itself in the habitus of the mobilized. There can be no easy answer to this nor a final one, but in this chapter I shall attempt an understanding of this process from the available information. There seem to be sufficient reasons for women to participate in violence, even if their participation cannot be justified. But this analysis does not rule out other possibilities which may be more important and fundamental in explaining their participation.

It is necessary to look at the nature of the politics of the groups involved. The BJP is seen to have a 'modern agenda', and does not openly commit itself to the domestication of women. This makes it difficult for women of the Hindu right to see their politics as restricting their freedom. This contributes to the immense support the Hindu right enjoys from the educated middle-class Hindu population. Nor does the *hindutva* 'brotherhood' seem to be talking an illegitimate language. They largely follow the language of the establishment, and this affords a certain legitimacy to their own work. Thus, the project has a gloss that does not identify it as dissent, as left politics does. This lends a sense of strength and 'security' to those who identify with right politics. Hindu women's purity was already an issue for the Indian state during the partition following independence. The state assumed the role of protector for Hindu women from Muslim men. The state then adopted the same language and rhetoric as present-day Hindu fundamentalists – perceiving and portraying Islamic Pakistan and its Muslim men as sexually aggressive, barbaric, violent and irrational as opposed to (Hindu) India, which is rational, secular and modern. The state's honour was clearly defined in terms of the honour of the majority community and *hindutva* claims to represent the nation of this majority community 50 years after these terms started taking roots in popular political thinking (Butalia and Sarkar 1995).

When religious fundamentalism wields political power, it grossly impinges on the daily lives of its citizens. This involves regulation of both the 'public' and 'private' spheres of social life. In such circumstances, women's public lives are under the direct surveillance of those in power. Women's bodies often become the site of political struggle. A strong reason for the 'veiling' of Muslim women in Islamic countries such as Iran comes from the fact that unveiling is seen as the influence of the West on 'their' women, and therefore control of them. So, to establish and assert their control over their 'own' women, Muslim men insist on Muslim women being veiled. This argument informs the basis for distinguishing between 'communalism' and 'fundamentalism' for Amrita Basu in her work on Hindu women's activism. She observes that since the *hindutva* forces do not apparently and actively seek to re-order women's roles in social life or subjugate them, *hindutva* (Sarkar et al., 1993: 1) cannot be categorized as 'fundamentalism', but rather is 'communalism'. This is no space here for a debate on the etymology of the respective terms. However, as far as the claim that *hindutva* does not actively re-order women's roles goes, it is problematic. Amrita Basu herself speaks of Hindu women's activism having support from households and therefore in a sense it renews their commitment to their domestic roles. The symbolic female figure whom they exalt remains the patriarchal ideal: the eversacrificing and chaste Sita. There is no articulated call for the re-domestication of women and they have a role to play in political activism, but that is not a sufficient reason not to categorize the violence that they initiated against a 'particular community' as fundamentalism. That the violence was initiated to protect the interests of the Hindu community is not convincing in the circumstances, where a mosque built some 100 years ago becomes a symbol of insecurity to the extent that it has to be reconquered, destroyed and replaced. The absence of an active need to articulate a re-ordering of women's role is very much in line with their other policies.

The desire not to disturb the status quo is very strong among all the political forces in India. The widespread dissatisfaction in the population is delicately balanced and it is in the best of the interests of any politics not to disturb too many of these precarious equations at one time. The idea of a Hindu nation actively disturbs the Hindu–Muslim equation, so it is best that other forces remain undisturbed. This also explains the construction of an 'imagined' monolithic Hindu community, which glosses over caste conflicts. Suddenly spaces arise within the *hindu(tva)* fold – the Dalits, neo-Buddhists (new converts, generally belonging to lower castes), Buddhists, Jains, etc. The notions of purity and pollution, which used to be strong among the upper castes, are now ignored and this constructed unity is forged into nationhood. *Hindutva* otherwise has no problem identifying with the globalization process, although there are certain sections within the fold that object to the 'corrupting presence of western culture'.[7] Materially, they are willing to participate in the spoils of capital. They have more in common with capitalist modernity than with the traditions of Hinduism. They have identified women as a potential political force, a vote pool, which also ensures their far-reaching mobilization (to the family as a political unit), more so as women also are useful to *hindutva* as political actors. They form effective shields against police violence. There is no denying the difference political agency makes to the lives of women, but all the same giving *hindutva* the credit for not seeking to re-order women's roles needs to be thought through. For the entire apparatus of *hindutva* activism is blatantly chauvinist in its approach.

Women who participate in 'public' activity, particularly in those areas that are seen to be relatively male-dominated, are criticized for neglecting and abandoning their 'duties as mothers and wives, as nurturers and breeders' within patriarchal conventions. However, women participating in the Hindu right find that they have the approval of 'patriarchy'. These women's activism, by diverting time and other resources from household work and nurturing, is now seen as a sacrifice and not neglect. Their political space becomes an extension of the domestic space, as is evident in the kind of activities they engage in. It reinforces an individualism of the family and re-establishes a domesticated definition of the family as well.

Thirdly, the importance of this activism by itself to the women involved is that of procuring agency. By participating in the violence, the women gain access to political and social agency, which the women's movement sought to work towards but could not decisively deliver, for obvious reasons.[8] This agency becomes a liberating experience and a definite rupture from the traditional and limited role of domesticated wives. The identification of these women as a political force, gives substance to the experience of modernity, which is overwhelmingly present in the rhetoric of post-colonial politics.

Bourdieu's theory of political representation 'assumes that social action is structured by the pursuit of "interests" by human agents, although the content of those interests is always determined culturally....'

Following the logic in Bourdieu's theory, one can see the absorption of women into the *hindutva* political force as a systematic control of their individual agency. The *hindutva* brigade, by recognizing women as a political force, also ensures the women's voluntary identification with the 'cultural' norms that they (*hindutva*) propagate and thus pre-empts the possibility of the translation of these women's experience of modernity and political dissatisfaction into any other allegiance. It is to their advantage that the women identify their own role as coinciding with that of *hindutva* ideology. This serves very well the aim of keeping women within patriarchal bounds, and that too by subversion of the idiom of modernity.

The effectiveness of a political group depends to a large extent on the strategies it employs for mobilization. The *hindutva parivar* propaganda has the confidence of a perceived superior and glorious past, where the existence of equality between the sexes is emphasized. The subjugation of Hindu women (which they do not deny) came with the invasions by Muslims, whose sexual aggression made seclusion and protection of Hindu women a necessary evil. Thus, Hindu men are absolved of any role in the suppression of Hindu women, which takes, rhetorically, the commitment of *hindutva* to freedom and equality of women beyond suspicion. This is history constructed with a definite purpose. Uma Chakravarti discusses the absence of the *dasi* (slave woman) in Vedic history, which *hindutva* draws upon (Chakravarti, 1988). This perception of the Vedic past has no place for ordinary people, servant women and everyday life. It discusses the glory of learned women of higher castes only. It is a telling paradox that the history of those they seek to mobilize is erased from their own memory, not by force, but by memorizing a given perception which has a manufactured consistency and is comfortable. The methods that *hindutva* forces utilize to propagate ideas like these are also theatrical. Although strategies differ according to region and the political party in question, the ideas they seek to spread are similar. The BJP had their *rath yatra*, a chariot journey through India. The 'chariot' was actually a Toyota decorated to look like an ancient carriage of the Hindu gods.[9] The Shiv Udyog Sena was a co-host for the Michael Jackson show in Mumbai, etc. The strategies have one element in common: they seek to make the ordinary citizen believe that she (or he) is the centre of political activity; their job, their physical security, their past, their 'nation', religion, god – all become important in political discourse. How they invoke this centrality, as we have seen, can sometimes even be contradictory to the goal. What is important is that it is evoked at all.

THE SIGNIFICANCE OF WOMEN AS A *HINDUTVA* FORCE

Women *activists* of hindutva stand on the threshold of patriarchy. When discussing the relationship between modernity and identity politics, Sudipto Kaviraj explains that modernity renders new ways of belonging accessible, at the same time as it makes real the possibility of having earlier identities in a different way. *Hindutva* politics gives a different meaning to being a 'Hindu' or a 'Muslim' in India (Kaviraj, 1995) In the case of women activists of *hindutva*, the rhetoric seeks to establish the possibility of a 'new' identity for them as part of the political force. However, that it is a new way of being a (patriarchal) 'woman' is a more convincing proposition. Their participation outside the 'home' renders them visible in the public sphere, but as we have seen, serves only to reinforce their position within the home. *Hindutva* women, as political actors, are still subordinate to *hindutva* men. But, as a political agent, the position of a Hindu woman is 'above' that of a Muslim man and also of a Muslim woman in *hindutva* politics. This contributes to problematizing earlier feminist assumptions of women as victims of patriarchal violence and beliefs. These women are constantly moving between the various positions that arise out of their political activism. What is of concern is whether the movement is an internalized choice or simply an external 'manipulation'. Do women activists of *hindutva* have their own political agenda, which may not coincide with their women and men co-activists?

Women's participation brings about a change in their own lives as well as in the texture of political process in India. If women's agency in *hindutva* is a result of manipulative politics, it still has the potential for change. Manipulative politics rests on delicate equilibria and when these are disturbed, for example by the caste system, the possibility of subversion is always present. The visibility of women's agency does not contribute towards an explanation of the process by which this came about. The *hindutva* platform itself is not uniform on women's issues, and there are different stands within the brotherhood. For example, one rarely finds the BJP or the RSS making misogynist remarks in public as the Shiv Sena do.[10] Yet, the question remains, how is one to react to this as a feminist? Feminist politics actively intervenes to enable women to demand access to agency and in this case women are agents, although in a limited sense. It is dangerous not to take a stand *vis-à-vis* this politics. The stand, however, has to be informed by an understanding of the larger political process, which includes patriarchal politics as well.

The success of *hindutva* politics shows the weakness of any organized secular critique of the state. The left has not become an effective alternative nor are there any other critiques of the state that have materialized as a strong political force, whether feminist or any other movement.[11] This leaves a vacuum in the political process which *hindutva* followers can exploit. A large part of the effectiveness of *hindutva* mobilization rests on their incisive critique of the governing process so far, and the 'crisis of governability' that characterizes Indian politics today. They have managed to expose the impotence of socialist rhetoric which has been used and abused in the 50 years of Indian independence. They have also managed to prove that the popular is all about laying claim to and demonstrating power. Opportunism alone cannot explain of the success of *hindutva* politics or disorganized secular forces. The entire process is situated in what Adorno calls the 'psychodynamics of modernity'. This is not to put the responsibility of delineation onto psychologism, but to emphasize the complexity of political configurations. It highlights questions of human intention, agency and autonomy of the individual which are the primary concerns for explanation of human behaviour.

The developing world has a complex relationship with modernity. There are two kinds of reactions, very broadly, that modernity evokes in these countries: it is either accepted as an inevitable part of colonial history, or rejected at a more rhetorical level, in arguments around neo-imperialism, which include primarily discussions on cultural imperialism. The debate the authenticity of modernity takes is forceful in the developing world. The history of modernity in India is a little younger than it is in England. The logic of the growth of modernity, however, differs in the two contexts. The origins of Indian modernity come from colonial experience, while that of England extends in colonizing. The events were also shaped by different factors: India was denied industrial experience for a long time, while it was one of the primary experiences in England. The social fabric of both the countries was different. What, then, prevents India from claiming this modernity as its own in spite of its long history? Why does the process become inauthentic in spite of its 'native' experience? It is precisely this process that India needs to reclaim as its own and understand the logic of its own modernity. A continuing reliance on the West for explanations of change is a journey further from lived experience and serves only to alienate.

When a nation's experience of modernity is in question, it is all too apparent that women's specific experience of modernity will not be an important political issue, whether in India, in the developing world, or even in the developed world. Modernity is linked to globalization and international relations, which also exhibit a lack of concern for gender issues. When industrialization is seen as an important characteristic of modernization, it is never an issue that Filipino women work long hours for poor pay in appalling conditions. It is never asked (with the exception of some radical writers) why only women are chosen to work in the factories set up in the developing countries by multinational companies. Urbanization again characterizes modernization, but it is never asked why Nepalese women are sold to the brothels of major Indian cities. Issues such as these, of gender, are never on the agenda of international politics.

The debate and the process of 'globalization' are rapidly changing political configurations in the world. There is an increasing desire in the developing countries to belong to the 'world' as defined by the interests and media of the developed world. Somewhere in this process of mass-producing world citizens the value of the authentic has simultaneously suddenly sharpened, and various social and political forces are defining the 'authentic' in their own context, like *hindutva* does for India by identifying the 'Hindu' as authentic. The process by which the authentic is arrived at is not an issue, although it is characteristically negotiated from within modernity. The situation is no longer about globalization only, but is accompanied by fragmentation, which may not be necessarily an anti-globalization politics. It could be a politics, like *hindutva*, that sets the terms of acceptance of the 'global', in rhetoric only.

The participation of Hindu women in politics based on religion separates them violently from the experiences of patriarchy and modernity as shared by women of the other religions in India. Their insensitivity to the vulnerability of a minority community fragments not only the Indian nation but denies the rich possibility of any global experience. *Hindutva* politics also subjects Hindu men to regimentation, both physically and psychologically.[12] But, as Marilyn Strathern has argued, 'it is not just a question of relations between the sexes. It is a part of the system of producing differences' (Strathern, 1988: 65). These differences are not a cultural continuity, but are reconstituted and constructed at different points of time, between men and women, Hindus and Muslims, the East and the West and other such corresponding binaries. Thus, even though communal politics is predominantly male-directed, it is not based exclusively on the agency of masculine sexuality. This is made clear by events such as women's participation, evocation of male aggression by women activists, the 'victim' status of Muslim men, the absence of active space for older men, etc. Hindutva is a part of the historical materiality in the lives of its women followers. If feminism seeks to constitute this materiality differently, then, as Rajeswari SunderRajan (1992: 129) points out it calls for 'an alertness to the political process that naturalises and coercively structures self-representation'. It has never been easy to do justice to the complexity of political processes and also take a political stand that calls for active intervention. All feminist politics is affected by this dilemma and I hope that my commitment to social science is asserted as I stand by SunderRajan, as alert as possible and willing to intervene politically when the need arises.

NOTES

1. The conditions that I seek to explain above deserve more space than is possible within the limits that are set by the focus of this chapter. The process is undoubtedly more complex and needs expert elaboration.
2. Social divisions based on caste are strong grounds for identity politics. However, these boundaries should not be taken as rigid or non-negotiable. Sudipto Kaviraj calls them 'fuzzy boundaries' in his discussions on caste politics. Although upward mobility is difficult in this four tier caste system with another rung of outcasts, horizontal mobility is perceivable. This moving between castes is determined by local and temporal factors, and also depends on the mobility of the individual in the literal sense. These divisions are effectively used by political leadership to create or demolish political forces and pool of voters.
3. To present a sketchy history of Hindu nationalist politics, its rise can be traced back to the late nineteenth century. The British introduced western education in India, which had two broad effects: it created a group of people who were trained in 'reason' and Enlightenment idiom. They started questioning the basis of Hindu beliefs and rituals. In reaction to this and the proselytizing activities of the missionaries, there was a second group who began to emphasize the validity and sometimes the superiority of Hindu ways of being. The Rashtriya Swayamsevak Sangh (RSS) was established in 1925. It is the ideological inspiration for most of Hindu nationalist politics. It is not a political party but claims to be a cultural organisation that works for the rejuvenation of Hindu society and *dharma*. The Hindu Mahasabha, which was a contemporary of the RSS, identified itself as an active political group. The Jana Sangha of Shyamaprasad Mukherjee was active in independent India and formed the foundations for the Bharatitya Janata Party (BJP), established in 1980. Shiv Sena was established in 1966, however its politics with the Hindu Muslim equation is relatively new. There are other organizations such as the Vishwa Hindu Parishad (VHP) and the Bajrang Dal which are active as well. There are numerous studies dealing with Hindu Nationalist politics, see Jaffrelot (1996), Sarkar et al. (1993), Baxter (1971) and Graham (1990), etc.
4. The Shiv Sena has provided snack booths to unemployed Marathi Hindu youth and more recently also established a Shiv *Udyog* Sena (Work) which

is to look into the provision of jobs to Marathi Hindu youth. This is but one example of the promises to the masses.
5. The key text that defines *hindutva* is Vinayak Damodar Savarkar's book entitled *Hindutva* which also has a separate chapter on 'Who is a Hindu'.
6. See Butalia and Sarkar (1995), Jayawardena and Alawis (1995).
7. The RSS and the Swadeshi Jagaran Manch, the ideological forebears of *hindutva* are critical of 'western culture' as a monolith which includes any country to the west of India. Western culture, in their understanding, is characterized primarily by sexual promiscuity and this erodes 'family values' which are seen as central to the well-being of a society.
8. There are innumerable difficulties for the women's movement in India. Particularly the diversity of identities, regional, lingual, religious, caste-based, class-based and the rural–urban divide to just mention a few. This means no effective strategy can be worked out for the 'Indian Woman'. Locally based movements become isolated in the absence of support from outside which can be demoralizing. This is changing today, but so have the techniques of manipulation employed by patriarchal institutions and ideologies such as *hindutva*.
9. This is an example of how comfortably the 'modern' and the non-modern are negotiated in *hindutva* politics.
10. The Sena chief, Bal Thackeray is known to make misogynist public statements. When the state declared 33 per cent reservations for women in local government bodies, he remarked that this would lead to a rise in adultery and corruption. Talking about a senior socialist leader, he once said that, she should stop delivering public speeches as her menstrual clothes were long dry, i.e., he was trying to define her productivity in purely sexual terms, by referring to her age.
11. A coalition government of 13 political parties has come to power in the centre in India following the tenth general elections. A large section of these are socialist parties and they are backed by the left in India. This is the first time the left is effectively a part of the power process, even though it has long been a part of the electoral process.
12. See Joseph Alter, 'Somatic Nationalism: Indian Wrestling and Militant Hinduism', in *Modern Asian Studies* 28(3) (1994); Jahnavi Phalkey, 'The Corporeality of Nationalism: Masculinity in RSS discourse', unpublished dissertation, SOAS, 1996.

REFERENCES

Agnes, F. (1994) 'Women's Movement within a Secular Framework: Redefining the Agenda', *Economic and Political Weekly*. 7 May.
Bacchetta, Paula (1994) 'Communal Property/Sexual Property: On Representations of Muslim Women in a Hindu Nationalist Discourse', in Zoya Hasan (ed.) *Forging Identities: Gender, Communities and the State*, Delhi: Kali for Women.
Basu, A. (1993) 'Feminism Inverted: The Real Women and Gendered Imagery of Hindu Nationalism', *Bulletin of Concerned Asian Scholars* 25(4).

Basu, A. (1995) 'Why Local Riots Are Not Simply Local: Collective Violence and the State in Bijnor, India 1988–93', *Theory and Society* 24: 35–78.
Baxter, C.A. (1971) *Biography of an Indian Political Party – Jana Sangh*, Bombay: Oxford University Press.
Bhaktal, S. (1993) 'Sisterhood and Strife', *Women's Review of Books* 10–11, July.
Bourdieu, Pierre (1977) *Outline of a Theory of Practice*, Cambridge: Cambridge University Press.
Bourdieu, Pierre (1991) *Language and Symbolic Power*. Cambridge: Polity Press.
Butalia, Urvasi and Tanika Sarkar (eds.) (1995) *Women and the Hindu Right*, Delhi: Kali for Women.
Chakravarti, Uma (1989) 'Whatever Happened to the Vedic Dasi?', in Kumkum Sangari and Sudesh Vaid (eds) *Recasting Women: Essays in Colonial History*, Delhi: Kali for Women.
Chatterjee, Partha (1989) 'The Nationalist Resolution of the Women's Question', in Sangari and Vaid (eds) *Recasting Women: Essays in Colonial History*, Delhi: Kali for Women.
Damle, Shridhar and Walter Anderson (1987) *The Brotherhood in Saffron: Rashtriya Swayamsevak Sangha and Hindu Revivalism*, Delhi: Vistaar Publications.
Gledhill, John (1994) *Power and its Disguises: Anthropological Perspectives on Politics*, Delhi: Vistaar Publications.
Gold, Daniel (1991) 'Organised Hinduisms: from Vedic Truth to Hindu Nation', in Marty and Applebly (eds) *Fundamentalisms Observed*, Chicago: University of Chicago Press.
Graham, B. (1990) *Hindu Nationalism and Indian Politics: The Origins and Development of the Bharatiya Jana Sangha*, Cambridge: Cambridge University Press.
Jaffrelot, Christophe (1996) *The Hindu Nationalist Movement and Indian Politics: 1925 to the 1990's: Strategies of Identity-Building, Implantation and Mobilisation*, London: C. Hurst & Co.
Jayawardena, Kumari and Malathi de Alawis (eds.) (1995) *Embodied Violence: Communalising Women's Sexuality in South Asia*, Delhi: Kali for Women.
Kapur, R. and Brenda Crossman (1993) 'Communalising Gender/Engendering Community: Women Legal Discourse and Saffron Agenda', *Economic and Political Weekly*, 24 April.
Kaviraj, Sudipta (1995) 'Religion, Politics and Modernity', in Upendra Baxi and Bikhu Parikh (eds) *Crisis and Change in Contemporary India*. Delhi: Sage India Ltd.
Kishwar, M. (1993) 'Safety is Indivisible – The Warning from Bombay Riots', *Manushi*, special double issue 74–5.
Mazumdar, S. (1995) 'Women on the March: Right Wing Mobilisation in Contemporary India', *Feminist Review* 49, Spring.
Mazumdar, S. (1993) 'Women, Culture and Politics: Engendering the Nation', *South Asia Bulletin* 12(2).
Pandey, Gyanendra (ed.) (1993) *Hindus and Others: The Question of Identity in India Today*, New Delhi: Viking.
Prakash, I. (1938) *A Review of the History and Work of the Hindu Mahasabha and the Hindu Sanghatan Movement*, New Delhi: Akhil Cheratiya Hindu Mahasabha.
Roy, Kumkum (1995) 'Where Women are Worshipped, There the Gods Rejoice: The Mirage of the Ancestress of Hindu Woman', in Tanika Sarkar and Urvashi Butalia (eds) *Women and the Hindu Right*, Delhi: Kali for Women.

Ruddick, S. (1989) *Maternal Thinking: Towards a Politics of Peace*. London: Only Women's Press.
Sangari, Kumkum and Sudesh Vaid (1989) *Recasting Women: Essays on Colonial India*, Delhi: Kali for Women.
Sarkar, Tanika (1993) 'Women's Agency within Authoritarian Communalism: The Rashtrasevika Samiti and Ramjanmabhoomi', in Gyanendra Pandey (ed.) *Hindu and Others: The Question of Identity in India Today*, Delhi: Viking.
Sarkar, Tanika and Urvashi Butalia (1995) *Women and the Hindu Right*, Delhi: Kali for Women.
Sarkar, Tanika et al. (1993) *Khaki Shorts and Saffron Flags: A Critique of the Hindu Right*, Hyderabad: Orient Longman Ltd.
Savarkar, V.D. (1969) *Hindutva: Who is a Hindu?*, Bombay: S.S. Savarkar.
Setalvad, Teesta (1993) Report on *Manushi*, Special double issue.
Strathern, Marilyn (1988) *The Gender of the Gift*, Berkeley, University of California Press.
SunderRajan, Rajeshwari (1992) *Real and Imagined Women: Gender, Postcoloniality and Culture*, London: Routledge.
Thapar, Romila (1989) 'Imagined Religious Communities? Ancient History and Modern Search for a Hindu Identity', in *Modern Asian Studies*, 23.
Van der Veer, Peter (1993) 'Hindu Nationalism and the Discourse of Modernity: The Vishwa Hindu Parishad', in M. Marty and R. Scott Applebly (eds) *Accounting for Fundamentalism*, Chicago: University of Chicago Press.
Yaeger et al. (1992) *Nationalisms and Sexualities*, New York: Routledge.

4 The Impact of Global and the Reconstruction of Local Islamic Ideology, and an Assessment of its Role in Shaping Feminist Politics in Post-revolutionary Iran
Haleh Afshar

In the general analysis of the impact of the global on the local there has been a tendency to concentrate either on the effect of large, world-wide views, such as feminisms or economic liberalism on specific areas, or to consider the effect of specific global politics on groups of peoples such as the dispossessed or impoverished women the world over (Afshar and Dennis 1992; Bakker 1994; Cornion et al. 1987); but there has been rather less work done on the interaction between global policies and the specificities of local circumstances which have altered and changed those policies to benefit groups which would not have been obviously expected to gain. This chapter is concerned with the interaction between specific groups – in this case, Middle Eastern elite women living in Iran and in exile – and general policies – that of Islamification. The intention is to look at the impact that the activities of elite Islamist women in Iran (Moghissi 1996) have had on altering these policies to a point beyond all recognition.

There is a general tendency, particularly at the end of the twentieth century amongst some western intellectuals and economists, to make a blanket assumption that the world is no more than a global village enjoying a considerable degree of homogeneity and integration, and therefore what is required is not so much the premise, but the assessment of the degrees of assimilation. Using the same policies, the same methods of evaluation and the same calculation, it is expected that similar results will emerge. There is, fortunately, a counter-view that refutes such a blanket impression and demands that the specificities of situations be considered. This is a view long advocated by many third world feminists. What this chapter addresses is the interactions between the global and the local and the counteractions that have arisen directly as a reaction to the globalization of cultures, values, moralities and economics. It is the contention of this chapter that Islamism in general and Iranian Islamification in particular are located very much at this juncture.

Despite rising prosperity and undeniable economic growth and rapid modernization in much of the Middle East and Islamic countries in the 1960s and 1970s, there has since been what may be called a 'backlash', but which was seen by its participants as a 'return' and a 'rejection' of global capitalism and consumerism. This rejection, in Egypt, in India, in Turkey and elsewhere, is articulated differently in each case to meet the political and economic contours of place and time, but in all cases it has been formulated by women with a clear understanding of western theories in general and feminism in particular.

Given the rise world-wide of what has been called 'fundamentalism', Iranian women's success in their own country has posed some difficult questions for intellectuals in exile and other western-based academics. Many have found it relatively difficult to contextualize these changes within the mainstream framework of Marxist and/or feminist analysis. It is the contention of this chapter that in the domain of politics the need to legitimize universal positions in terms of particular conditions has enabled women to reconstruct Islamic discourse radically and to carve out not only a place, but a central position within the theory and the practice of Islamic politics in Iran. This specific trajectory, however, does not lend itself easily to mainstream analytical forms and, like much of the more recent fragmented feminist experiences, must be located within its own historical and geographical context.

THE CRITIQUE

Western-based feminists have engaged in a wide-ranging debate as to whether non-secular women seeking and achieving pro-women goals and political measures can in any way be considered to be feminist. I have argued (1994) for a long time that the diversity of feminisms should allow us to accept the differing routes that women take towards similar ends, a view shared by many Iranian feminist scholars (Haeri 1995; Mir-Hosseini 1996; Najmabadi 1995; Paidar 1996), but firmly contested by other luminaries, such as Moghissi (forthcoming) and Kandiyoti (forthcoming).

Arguing against the rapprochement between certain Western and Islamist feminists, Moghissi contends that

> the impact of the similarity of views between activists and feminists outside the country, has been to facilitate the destruction of [the] women's movement inside and outside Iran and has had a lasting effect in curtailing the intellectuals' efforts to set up a democratic system in Iran. (Moghissi forthcoming)

Intellectually, Moghissi is arguing that the act of recognizing the specificities of the Iranian case and respecting it is a product of the postmodernist rejection of the grand narrative. Such a rejection in turn moves towards particularization and carries an inherent conservatism which prevents it from making any kind of ethical evaluation (Callinicos 1989). It thus prevents academics from being judgemental about the actions of others. Moghissi contends that when western-based women academics express 'respect' for the position of women in Iran it reveals their profound ignorance about the conditions of the lives of the mass of Iranian people, and at the same time deprives them of the means of organizing resistance and assisting the oppressed women of Iran.

In addition to their lack of immediate experience of circumstances that they nevertheless support, Moghissi also accuses western-based academics of failing to recognize the dividing line between religion and materialism. The Siren leading them astray is that of populism: ideological strategies formulated by elite Islamist women in Iran which have hoodwinked observers into believing their claims to success.

Kandiyoti's arguments are not so much with Iran, where given the *faits accomplis* of Islamism the choices are limited. Her concern is with the success of Islamism in other Middle Eastern countries. Kandiyoti notes the difficulties of seeking equality for women, given that the Islamists' notions of complementarity of the sexes and the different responsibilities of each gender, render such a quest untenable. However, it is on the policing of women in the name of morality that Kandiyoti focuses her arguments:

> paradoxically, the stress on Islamically appropriate conduct for women may not be due to doctrinal imperatives of fundamentalist impulses but to regimes' pragmatic need to maintain social control. (Kandiyoti forthcoming)

Kandiyoti, like Moghissi, argues that the imposition of social control would have cross-class populist support from men and women, and this in turn would curtail the prospect of women-centred egalitarian political success and the emergence of a pluralist society.

THE RESPONSE

It has never been easy for feminists to find a quick match between grand theories and the experiences of women. Despite repeated efforts for over a decade and a half (Hartman 1981) feminists have had to deal with the gender specificity of women's lives, which are contoured differently at different times and in different places (Elson 1991). Nor has feminism ever sat comfortably with any of the prevailing global narratives; hence the fragmentation of the women's movement over the past decades. It could be argued that Iranian women are merely part of this global process of political separation. The specificities of priorities and issues directing the lives of third world women have long been seen as quite distinct and different from those of western women, and the choices made by them were respected long before postmodernism became fashionable (Afshar 1985). Similarly, those working in western pluralistic societies have persistently demanded that the lives of women of colour not be subsumed by the theories of mainstream, white feminists. It is therefore not easy for some of us to argue that, on the one hand, as non-white feminists living in the West we require that our views, values, cultures, be respected, and on the other hand, and at the same time, refuse to show a like tolerance towards our compatriots who, under difficult circumstances, are doing better than those of us who now live in exile did.

In the absence of a political party structure (Omid 1994) it has not been possible for Iranian women to follow the western forms of democratic electioneering; it is arguable that women such as Faezeh Rafsanjani have used both their power base and the media to cut a populist path towards success. But, at the same time, there are veteran politicians such as Maryam Behruzi and theoreticians such as Zahra Rahnavard who have painstakingly carved a way for the active political participation of women through the mist of Islamification.

Accepting such differing internal and global trajectories is not to deny our own ethical stance (Maynard 1994), nor to avert our eyes and not offer criticisms when necessary. Rather it is to accept the need to use the same yardstick for our compatriots that we use for ourselves. It is in this spirit of conciliation that I would like to offer the following analysis of the impact of women's struggles on the politics of the post-revolutionary state in Iran.

ISLAMISM, WOMEN AND POLITICS IN IRAN

In Iran, as in Afghanistan with the advent of the Taleban, the arrival of Islamism was accompanied by the Draconian exclusion of women from the public domain and a systematic attempt to curtail their progress. The subjugation of women was paraded as the public endorsement and evidence of the continuing supremacy of Islamic law – laws that were to have no room for women. A month after his return to Iran, in March 1979, Khomeini sacked the entire body of women judges and ordered the compulsory veiling of all women. In May of that year co-education was banned, in June married girls were barred from attending school and the government began closing down workplace nurseries. In July sea resorts were sexually segregated and women flogged in public for transgression of these rules. Morality codes were declared and for the first time in Iranian history women were executed on charges of prostitution and moral laxity.

By October the government was dismantling the checks placed on men by revising the personal laws; men regained the right to practise polygamy, to unilateral divorce on demand, and the right to prevent their wives from entering paid employment. The official age of marriage for women was reduced from 18 to 13 and men regained the automatic custody of their children after divorce.

In July 1981, the *Majlis*, parliament, ratified the Islamic *Qassas*, laws of retribution, demanding an eye for an eye and a life for a life. These laws made justice the prerogative of privileged wealthy men and negated women's human rights to justice. Not only are two women's evidence equated with that of one man, as required by the Koran (2: 82), but women's evidence, if uncorroborated by men, is not accepted by the courts. Women who insist on giving uncorroborated evidence are judged to be lying and subject to punishment for slander (article 92 of the *Qassas* laws).

Murder is punished by retribution, but the murderer can opt to pay *diyat*, blood money, to the family of the murdered, in lieu of punishment (Article 1 of *diyat* laws). Whereas killing a man is a capital offence, murdering a women is a lesser crime.

THE VEIL

The most immediately visible change was to make women the principal emblem of Islamification, and their dress code the most significant identifier of revolutionary success. As a result, the veil has become one of the non-negotiable elements governing women's lives.

The imposition of the veil, though articulated in the name of Islam, was very much the result of Khomeini's obsessive fear of women and their sexuality – a fear that has echoed throughout Islamic history and has burdened women with a constructed vision of immorality and disobedience (Mernissi 1991, 1993, 1995; Sabbah 1984). He was convinced that women are the fount of disorder and that their very presence in the public domain disempowers men and prevents them from functioning properly. Therefore not only are women to be secluded, but their oppression is to be the measure of the success of Islam. The imposition of the veil, however, was not merely a matter of personal interpretation by male religious leaders, it was also a means of demonstrating to the world that Islam had succeeded. The global message to the West was the rejection of its values; an additional projection to the Islamic world was the evident desirability of demonstrating the emergence of the rule of the just and deserving Muslims not only over their women, but also over their nation, and in time over the entire peoples of Islam, *umma*, wherever they may be. The best way of demonstrating Islamists' success to the world was the strict imposition of the veil. As the *Guardian* reporter Liz Thurgood has pointed out:

> Women are the barometers of Iranian politics. One look at how much ankle or calf is showing or how much hair can be seen beneath the veil and the colour of the headscarf tell a book about the regime's level of toleration. (*Guardian* 1 July 1989)

A view shared, though expressed differently, by Shahla Habibi, the President's adviser on women's issues:

> Women are the guarantors of culture and education in our country. The enemies of revolution seek to undermine us and rule us through the cultural subversion of our women.
> But our revolutionary women must retain their cultural identity [expressed by donning the veil][1] and must go to men for help. It would be a mistake to assume feminine self-reliance and superiority. (*Kayhan* 3 February 1992)

At the same time zealous revolutionary guards and members of the bourgeoning local *komitehs* have been administering the immediate penalty of 30 to 75 lashes to women they considered poorly veiled.[2] Wealthy women could commute this penalty by paying a 2,000 tuman fine, the equivalent of about 20 per cent of the average monthly salary of a middle-ranking civil servant. Government employees had the additional penalty of dismissal. Over 100,000 women were dismissed in the first decade after the revolution for being poorly veiled (*Peyameh Azadi*, Paris, July 1992).

But even the imposition of the veil had to be contextualized in a global view. Iran viewed in the mirror of the international news media wished to be seen as Islamic and to present itself to the Islamic world as tolerant and supportive of women. Protests, sporadic riots and spontaneous demonstrations against the veil have characterized Iranian summers. But although sometimes the theocrats counsel paternalistic 'guidance', on the whole the regime is merciless; for the post-revolutionary state the issue of the veil is non-negotiable.

PARTICIPATION AND MOTHERHOOD

The veil does not only denote the public separation of gender, but also for the Islamic world it carries connotations of the exclusion of women from the public sphere and their seclusion within the domain of domesticity. In the early days of the revolution women were defined as primarily domestic beings and, under the banner of universal Islamic morality, they were under enormous pressure to withdraw from the public domain and return to the home. They were to become first and foremost wives and mothers, and raise sons for the revolution and subsequently the Iran–Iraq war. Failure to serve the nation as mothers would have led to the destruction of the entire Islamic foundation of the war-torn post-revolutionary land (Omid 1994).

For the entire period of the war with Iraq (1980–8) the government and its myriads of ideology sections did their best to foster the theme of mothering martyrs and make death appear desirable. The discourse is centred on suffering and the willingness to espouse death, to drink the sherbet of martyrdom. Every town and every village had public mourning ceremonies. Black-clad women hurled the traditional wails, *shivan*, at the crowd, tore their hair and offered their remaining sons. Women had become the guardians of the coffin and the cradle, the symbols of suffering and endurance (Afshar 1982). Widows gave long interviews about the wondrous state of martyrdom and the heavenly experience of bereavement for Islam. Many declared their absolute faith in the paradise that is specially made for direct entry by Iranian martyrs to which all should aspire to enter.

Marriage and motherhood were advocated as the sole destiny of women. As men began dying in the war and it was feared that the percentage of women in the population might exceed that of men, the theocracy began advocating the delights of temporary marriages: the Shiia school of Islamic thought allows men and women to marry legitimately for fixed periods; such temporary marriages can last anything between a few moments to 99 years.

By 1987, according to the Statistical Centre of Tehran 96 per cent of urban women of child-bearing age were married and only 1 per cent had never married. A mere 7 per cent of married women used any form of birth control, and the average age for the first birth was 19. On average mothers had four live births, rather more than their stated desired average, which was two in urban areas and three in rural areas. Interestingly, over half the women questioned did not mind whether they had a son or a daughter: 14 per cent expressed a preference for a girl and only 31 per cent had a marked preference for a boy.³

Despite the massacres on the war front, the pro-natalist position of the government and the success of its propaganda machine resulted in a population explosion which was growing at an average annual rate of 3.9 per cent. The population crisis posed a severe dilemma for the Islamic government. It had long since revoked the pre-revolutionary abortion laws and closed the family planning clinics. Now it discovered that families were averaging five or more children and there was no clear policy for halting the momentum. In July 1991 the government decreed that for a fourth birth, working women were not entitled to the statutory three months' paid maternity leave, nor was a fourth child entitled to rations or a ration book. Any family that chose to have a fourth child would have to share their resources, spread them more thinly, with no help from the state.

By 1993 the Ministry of Health had turned to the World Bank and obtained a $300 million loan. This was used by the Ministry's Population Control Bureaux to launch a massive campaign offering free services at national, provincial and rural levels. The loan was backed by a 20 billion rials local budget, 300 per cent higher than that allocated in the previous year. The aim was to follow the World Bank's global view that poverty in the third world is in large part caused by its population explosion and therefore a first essential step for economic development is to cut the birth rate. What is of interest is that although in the public arena, as in the population conference in Cairo, the Iranians joined forces with the Vatican to condemn state intervention in birth control, in practice the situation is quite different. In 1992 the courts decided to reconsider the abortion laws in order to make abortion legal, provided it has been carried out

> 'before the soul enters the body of a being', or if a doctor is of the opinion that it is dangerous to continue with the pregnancy and issues a certificate to that effect; then the pregnancy can be terminated. (*Kayhan*, 1 August 1992)

At the same time the newspapers published a list of 50 hospitals offering free vasectomy and female sterilization. Thus controlling population growth proved to be one of the few cases where the government met its stated goals. The state has been instrumental in reducing population growth to 2.7 per cent per annum (*Kayhan*, 18 April 1993). By 1996 the population was 59.5 million and the growth rate had fallen to 1.8 per cent, reducing the average family size from 5 to 4.8 (*Sarshomariyeh omumiyeh nofus va maskan*, 1996 census).

WOMEN AND POLITICS

If women were not to be prolific mothers, then it was harder to insist that they remain at home for the whole of their lives. Thus, not surprisingly, the Islamic government has had to give way to some of women's political demands. To begin with, the situation seemed desperate indeed; according to the Constitution women are the cornerstone of the home and the hearth. At the same time, they have been given the right to participate fully, at least as an electorate, in national politics (art. 6 of the Constitution and the election and referenda laws). They can be elected to the legislative bodies at both local and national levels (arts 30–32 of the parliamentary election laws and art. 23 of Islamic local councils' organization) to the parliament, *Majlis Shorayeh Eslami*, and the consultative body, *majlis khebregan*, the assembly of experts. But few women have been elected to serve on these bodies. In the *Majlis Shorayeh Eslami*, women are expressly barred from taking the position of leadership. They have not been given high office by the post-revolutionary government; which has never appointed a woman to a ministerial post. Parliament, has had four legislative terms. Yet, although women have formed an active and large part of the electorate, they have gained few seats. In the first *Majlis* of the 270 members only two were women and there were four in the subsequent three *Majlis*. In the fourth *Majlis* their numbers rose to 9 and in the 1996 elections to the fifth *Majlis* 13 women were elected.

SECULAR STRATEGIES

The difficulties that women faced in the wider political context have been exacerbated by the divisions that exist amongst them, particularly between the secularist and the Islamist groups. The leading author, lawyer and feminist campaigner, Mehranguiz Kaar, explains:

> As a result of the contradictions of feminism with their revolutionary belief in the Islamic Republic, the women's movement failed to form a united base... its initial resistance was public but it fragmented and gradually lost its political momentum... (*Zanan*, no. 20, September–October 1994)

However, looking to the future, Kaar is cautiously confident that the gap may be closing:

> General political positioning in terms of anti-imperialism and anti-despotism... has been replaced by specific positions in defence of women's rights... women united, not necessarily on a party political basis, but in order to defend their rights against newly installed parameters. (*Zanan*, no. 20, September–October 1994)

The Islamists themselves are divided between the elite, establishment women who were fighting for the cause within the parameters set out by the post-revolutionary government, and activists such as the Islamist Mojahedin, headed by a woman, Maryam Rajavi, who have relocated their headquarters in Iraq and Paris and run a long-distance oppositional Islamic movement against the regime. Both groups adopted the veil as a mark of their Islamism.

The secularists too are divided between the Marxist revolutionaries and pragmatic professional women. The Marxist groups, including the Fadayan Khalq and other smaller groups, have been driven underground by continuous persecution since the inception of the revolution. So it has fallen to professional secular women to continue the public debate in defence of women's rights. The Islamists formulate their demands in the name of an idyllic Islamist past, *sadre Eslam*, when women were given their rightful dues. The secularists refer to a contemporary global feminist sisterhood. Amongst their leading contenders, the secularists include the feisty lawyer Mehranguiz Kaar, who has consistently and publicly demanded that the Iranian government meets its obligation to abide by UN decisions to which it is a signatory. Kaar singles out the UN's 1979 convention for the removal of inequalities in women's rights and insists that Iranian women should be entitled to the provisions of article 3, which demands that:

> all member countries must in all respects, particularly in terms of political, social, economic and cultural activities ensure that the appropriate legislations are in place to facilitate the extensive and successful development of opportunities for women to participate fully and equally and obtain the maximum benefit from their human rights and liberties, on an equal par with those of men.

Kaar also notes that articles 7 and 8 of the convention demand that member countries ensure that women have the right to vote and be elected in all elections and to all public institutions, the right to be employed in all public posts and to participate in non-governmental organizations (Kaar 1994).

Although, theoretically, Iranian women enjoy all these rights, it is only the right to vote which they have been able to exercise fully since the revolution. Kaar argues that the post-revolutionary 'cultural' context and the animosity of powerful individuals have been responsible for preventing women from exercising their political rights in full. She asks of 'intellectual women' that they use 'logical and rational arguments' to demand that the government fulfils its legal obligation to integrate women in the public sector (Kaar 1994).

The secularists' demands for equality were curtailed by the Iraqi invasion and subsequent war. The paranoic climate created by the war and the American hostage débâcle and subsequent attacks by the US navy against Iranian oil installations and civilian planes (Omid 1994) effectively blocked their internationalist perspectives and hardened the 'cultural barriers'.

After the war, and particularly after Khomeini's death, the situation improved, not least because the Iranian government wanted to prove to the Middle East and the Islamist revivalists that its revolutionary solutions were advantageous to women. The return to the international arena enabled secular and Islamist women gradually to carve out a mutually acceptable political space for themselves. Secular activists came to the conclusion that 'it would be futile to embark on shallow confrontational gestures', and that it was 'essential for intellectual women to organise and...highlight all the positive views and gain support for them to defend women's rights' (Kaar 1994).

The goal for both Islamist and secular women was to make it unacceptable for any public figure openly to oppose women's rights.

Though strategically essential, unity with Islamist women has not been easy to achieve. The problem is that both groups are divided amongst themselves. So, for example, the Islamist concept of the global is directed to the Islamic world and the secularists to the West. As Kaar explains:

> It is virtually impossible to find an agreed definition of women's rights...Their [Islamists'] attempts to place the new interpretations within the context of religion is not well received in the world context and does not sit comfortably with the world view of freedom and liberty. This intensifies the problem. Particularly since they have not discussed their views with other groups...these conflicting views have created a general confusion without any of them gaining the upper hand. (Kaar 1994)

THE ISLAMIST STRATEGIES

The confusion surrounding the definition of rights and the selection of priorities is not confined to the secular/Islamist divide. There was support for Islamification amongst a cross-section of women who denounced the 'non-believer' secularists as belonging to the 'Westoxificated' upper classes, committed to 'western imperialism'. But even amongst the Islamists there is a range of opinions from those like the first Presidential Adviser on Women's Issues, Shahla Habibi, who does no more than voice the state's opinions in the name of women, to radical Islamist campaigners such as Zahra Rahnavard, who openly criticizes the state for failing to meet its obligations to give women their Koranic rights. What this group has in common is that it contests the 'western' definitions of women's rights (Afshar 1994). It is important to note that they too address a global audience, namely the 'West', which they blame for failing to deliver liberation to women. They also target the 'Islamic world', which they suggest should look to Iran as an exemplar of success where the 'West' and the 'rest of the world' have failed. Some of the conservative Islamists such as Soraya Maknun, University Professor and Head of the Research Group on Women, even claim that the post-revolutionary state has solved all women's problems:

> The truth is that our society does not have a women's problem and its just pro-Western critics who have invented such a problem and imposed it on our lives. (*Zaneh Ruz*, 27 January 1990)

Others such as *Majlis* Deputy Maryam Behruzi argue that theirs is an alternative way of looking at gender issues:

> The style of western thinking which posits male and females as opponents has failed and has adversely affected the West. In our view both patriarchy and matriarchy are undesirable and problematic definitions in that they define society in terms of contradictory and oppositional analytical concepts. We must oppose an approach which posits such an oppositional dichotomy between the sexes... (*Zaneh Ruz*, 24 February 1996)

Although this seems to argue for complementarity, in practice Behruzi has systematically pursued egalitarian goals throughout her parliamentary career (Afshar 1998). In fact, frequently, the process of reconstruction of an appropriate Islamic analytical framework has proved hard to achieve. But despite their internal divisions, political exigencies require that Islamist women remain flexible and open to dialogue and bargaining with the male establishment.

The extensive and valuable contribution of women to the war effort and the revolution led them to expect much from their government, and the Islamists in particular feel severely aggrieved about its failure to meet these aspirations. Thus, whereas it is still possible for secularist women to take a relatively optimistic view of the future, the radical Islamist elite women feel despondent. In the early post-revolutionary days the redoubtable politician Maryam Behruzi, who had been imprisoned for her political activities before the revolution and whose son was 'martyred' during the war, went so far as to say that she saw no room for optimism:

> Sadly women have even lost ground... unfortunately at the moment I do not see any room for the development of women in the public sphere... Unfortunately after the revolution women have not been allowed to play a real part in Iranian politics. They are needed to

shout and participate in demonstrations. The most they do is to go to Friday prayers or help out behind the front lines of the war. I think that the absence of a suitable political environment has reduced women to such levels... (Maryam Behruzi, *Zaneh Ruz*, 17 April 1983, no. 861).

A decade after the revolution the well-known author and activist Zahra Rahnavard, who is married to the first long-serving post-revolutionary prime minster, Mir Husein Musavi, could still detect little improvement in women's position:

> Women like myself have continuously campaigned for better conditions. We have made our demands in the *Majlis*, in the press and in the public domain. But no one has taken any notice and our voices are not heard. (*Zaneh Ruz*, 10 February 1990)

These revolutionary women feel that the government owes them far more than they have as yet received. As Rahnavard notes:

> Women have been and continue to be present, at times in larger numbers than men, in our public demonstrations, for the revolution and in its support. But when it comes to public appointments, they are pushed aside... (*Zaneh Ruz*, 10 February 1990)

There has been no room at the top for women despite their continuous struggles. Women like Rahnavard are fiercely critical of the government for failing to reward or even consult them about their political fate:

> There is clear and extensive evidence of absence of women at the planning and decision-making within the government... Why is it that the numbers of female representatives in the *Majlis* are no more than the fingers on our hands? Why do we not have any women in the cabinet? Is it not the case that it was devout women as well as men who together carried the burden of the Islamic revolution? Why is it that now women have been marginalised? Why are they used only when there is need for mass participation, and then they are just used as extras to build up the crowd to give legitimacy to the demonstrations? (Zahra Rahnavard, *Salaam*, 12 September 1994)

There are no satisfactory answers to these questions. As a result, elite Islamist women are often demoralized when it comes to the prospect of success. Jamileh Kadivar, a member of the editorial board of the international information daily, *Etelaateh Binolmelali*, voices their fears:

> It is my personal opinion, which is also reflected clearly in our society, that women are totally marginalized, or are only permitted to just reach the margins. But they have no place in the central decision-making in our society. We only have to look at the absence of women in the three vital areas of legislature, judiciary and administration. (*Salaam*, 12 August 1994)

Even the docile Presidential Adviser, Shahla Habibi, deplores the absence of women in high-ranking political positions. She however attributes this failure to the 'immature and unwise attitude to women'. In an unlikely alliance with secular women, Habibi too resorts to the global perspective and international laws to solve this problem:

> In addition to our own cultural wealth and tradition we must also learn from the world's experience in this respect. (*Akhbar*, 12 November 1995)

POLITICAL PARTICIPATION

When it comes to analysing the causes of women's oppression, elite Islamist women share the secularist criticism of the 'cultural context', the entrenched patriarchal system that has enabled the male hierarchy to use women when it suits the political circumstances and then discard them:

> After the revolution without any discussions on the subject suddenly, particularly amongst the men, the whispering began that the time for women to be part of the public sphere has come and gone and now it's time for women to stay at home and take care of the children and let the men take charge of the government. Men are to rule and women are to obey and follow... Unfortunately this undesirable atmosphere has been allowed to go on and develop... the media and radio and television continuously define women in terms of their maternal duties and do not mention their public obligations. (Maryam Behruzi, *Zaneh Ruz*, 17 April 1983, no. 861)

Islamic Ideology and Feminist Politics 69

The return to political participation for Iranian women has been painfully slow. Those who have achieved a degree of success and positions of some influence have been used to mouth ever-more conservative views about women, as is the case with Shahla Habibi. Those who have refused to do so have, in the long run, been ousted from the public arena. Examples here are Azam Taleqani, who was elected to the first post-revolutionary Parliament, *Majlis*, only and Maryam Behruzi who, in addition to holding the Chair of Islamic Studies at the University of Shaheed Beheshti, served in every *Majlis* after the revolution. Not only was she outspoken, but was also very effective in the fourth *Majlis*. But in the 1996 elections for the fifth *Majlis* she lost her seat. The 'cultural context' has constantly thwarted women's efforts to maintain their tenuous foothold in the legislature. Islamist women have continuously to counter the religious establishment's traditional fear of 'unruly women' who can cause social havoc, *fitna*. Shiia Muslims warily recall the Prophet's wife A'isha, who waged war against the Shiias' revered first imam Ali, cousin and son-in-law of the Prophet. This fear is so deep-rooted that initially Islamist women had considerable difficulty in retaining their right to be *Majlis* representatives or have any political activity at all.

But getting elected has been only the first step; women members of the *Majlis* are severely constrained by the ideological views that designate them as inferior, demand of them to be modest, silent and invisible (Milani, 1992), define them as interlopers in the public domain and decry any form of protest on their part as an act of rebellion. In terms of the general ideological definition of womanhood even the Prophet's daughter, Saint Fatemeh, is best known through the writings of the leading Islamist intellectual Ali Shariati, who is lyrical about her quietude, fortitude and willingness to subsume her own interest to that of her husband (Shariati 1980). In 1983 the then *Majlis* representative Seyed Mohamad Khameneyi was quite clear about women's 'natural irrationality' and feminine wiles:

> in my view women have used women's way to get their rights, that is to say they have screamed and protested... (*Zaneh Ruz*, 17 April 1983, no. 861)

It is hard to counter such deeply held views. As Behruzi explains:

> One of these gentlemen [*Majlis* representatives] came to talk to me in private... He said: 'I thought that you were a learned woman and did not expect you to suddenly claim that women are wise and intelligent.

How could you ever claim that women have brains and that their brain is not partial and deficient?' He was criticizing me for saying that those who think that women's brain in incomplete are wrong and was insisting that in fact they are quite right. He was genuinely amazed at my insistence to the contrary. (Maryam Behruzi, *Zaneh Ruz*, 4 May 1994)

Behruzi has learnt to be philosophical about such attacks. Despite the presence of a vociferous group of *Majlis* representatives who fear the presence of women in the political domain, over the past 19 years Islamist elite women have forged some useful alliances and have made the women's question and the 'defence' of women an important issue for some of the leading male politicians.

FAITH AND POLITICS

In the political arena, as elsewhere in post-revolutionary Iran, the obstacles to women's full participation in politics were erected in the name of Islam. Islamist women have had to counter these views by resorting to Islamic discourse and reconstructing new interpretations that meet their demands – a process that has been going on amongst Islamic feminist throughout the twentieth century[4] and is now firmly rooted in Iran as in the rest of the Middle East.

In the context of the Islamic revolution, it was in the name of Islam and in terms of an idealized past, the *sadre Islam*, the early days of Islamic reign, that Islamist intellectuals and activists posited an alternative pro-woman perspective. The needs of the revolution at the end of the twentieth century to establish its international credibility demanded a reconstruction of the past and setting up standards that the state had to meet if it were to live up to its own propaganda and principles. Women were determined to extract a price for becoming the emblem of Islamification, they wanted to dictate what the Islam that their veiled presence upheld was about: it was something to aspire to and something that accommodated their needs. In a campaigning speech delivered during the 1996 elections, Behruzi presented a cogent defence of political rights in the name of Islam and argued that women's participation in the public domain had been condoned by the Koran and enforced by Islamic teachings and was 'a fundamental matter of creed'. To prove her point Behruzi quoted Khomeini:

According to imam Khomeini women are the very basis and the source of all good deeds and charitable acts and the teachers of mankind; they must be consulted in all national matters, and of course the *Majlis* is the most appropriate place for them to do so. (*Zaneh Ruz*, 24 February 1996)

The defence of rights here is not articulated in the language of liberty or even of equality. What Islamist women demand is entitlements that are balanced by duties. These demands are located firmly within the framework of responsibilities, mutual obligations and complementary roles. There is no mention of the less acceptable western notions of liberty or equality, which are seen as suspect by Islamists. It is interesting to note that Behruzi uses terms such as 'side by side' to demand what is in fact equality presented in the political language of complementarity:

In Islam individuals are valued in terms of the development of their good character and humanity and by all rod measures men and women are side by side and the one who has the greater probity and is better able to fulfil her duties is more valued. (*Zaneh Ruz*, 24 February 1996)

LEGISLATIVE SUCCESSES

By locating their demands firmly within Islamic discourse in the context of a world perspective and by emphasizing the leading role of the Iranian legislature in creating a worthy example for the Islamic world to follow, Iranian women parliamentarians have, despite all the obstacles placed before them, achieved some remarkable successes. The difficulty that Islamist women have is that by embracing the concepts of difference and complementarity they, of necessity, accept some notions of essentialism. For the male hierarchy this essentialism includes the belief that women are 'naturally irrational' and their campaigns are conducted in a hysterical and feminine manner. That is why in his early days as a *Majlis* deputy Khameneyi thought it necessary to advise women to curb their emotionalism:

what they should do is to present their case in a correct and systematic way, that is to say in a logical way that men can understand and not as a demand... (*Zaneh Ruz*, 17 April 1983, no. 861)

But he did not think them beyond redemption:

> It is never too late for women and their organization to try and, with the help of legal advisers, without any emotion and slogans, propose a proper bill to the *Majlis*. (*Zaneh Ruz*, 17 April 1983, no. 861)

Maryam Behruzi shares her male colleagues' view and suggests that over time women have been politically educated:

> despite a couple of failures in the early days when some of the bills that we brought to the *Majlis* were rejected, gradually the *Majlis* has become enlightened and we have been successful with our laws concerning women. We are hoping to bring in better proposals in the future and get them through. (*Zaneh Ruz*, 4 May 1994)

THE CAMPAIGN FOR THE FIFTH *MAJLIS*

The 1996 election saw the culmination of more than a decade of work by elite Islamist women to gain a political foothold. The campaign for the fifth *Majlis* was fought very much along the religious/secular divide. The Islamist women placed their discourse at the heart of Islamic teachings and endorsed women's central role within the family. In return they demanded greater participation in the public domain to meet the specificities of female demands. Of the total of 5359 applicants to the *Majlis* 305 were women; of these the candidature of 187 was ratified. In the absence of a formal party system, some stood as independents, others were adopted by various political groups.

During the election campaign Behruzi was far more outspoken than all the other women candidates; years of experience and recent success had made her confident and she firmly advocated the need to include women in the public domain:

> In the world today the link between the situation of men and women is becoming ever more apparent and clearly society needs the intellectual and political powers of its women as much as it needs those of its men. (*Zaneh Ruz*, 24 February 1996)

Throughout, the language of political discourse has been couched in Islamic terms. Every woman candidate had to begin her campaign speech by reaffirming her right to be a politician and to assert that she could represent both men and women.

Despite their extensive campaign and remarkable efforts only 13 women were elected to the fifth *Majlis*. Surprisingly Behruzi did not get in. It is difficult to explain her failure in terms of her outspoken defence of women since the second highest vote in Tehran was cast for the newcomer, Faezeh Hashemi. (Decorum demanded that the speaker should gain the highest vote in the capital.) Daughter of the President and Deputy Director of the national Olympics committee, head of the council of collaboration of women's sport in Islamic countries, *Shorayeh hambastegi varsheshe banovan keshvarhsayeh Eslami*, Hashemi is the nearest thing to a feminist in Islamist Iranian politics. She ran a high-profile campaign, arguing not only that there should be more women in *Majlis*, but that they should set about altering things:

> We need to have more women representatives in the Fifth *Majlis* and they must...change some of the laws and alter them quite radically... as an example we can take the labour laws. If these are fully implemented then the employers would prefer to employ men rather than women and employment opportunities for women would decrease. (*Zaneh Ruz*, 27 January 1996)

Although the labour laws are yet to be changed the new women representatives have finally managed to set up a parliamentary committee to consider women's issues and have amended the divorce laws to include a clause which links women's *mehre* (marriage payment usually made on divorce) to the rate of inflation. These are small steps, but they may be indicative of greater successes to come.

CONCLUSION

Though not numerous, the women representatives intended to be effective and succeeded by combining their Islamic position with a global one. Iranian politics is continuously posited in terms of its impact on the Muslim world and its image in the western media. What this has meant is the pursuit of many mainstream feminist demands, including those for equal rights, articulated in terms of a reconstructed Islamic discourse. The global helped to shape the local by presenting a framework of human rights which cannot easily be flouted. At the same time the local has determined the regional, particularly the Middle Eastern, and to some extent an international position of Islamist women. But the position is refracted through the specific experiences of women in particular countries and specific histories and the results are fragmented policies that echo an idealized notion of Islam, but offer different solutions to the problems they face within the localities. What remains more difficult to resolve is the analysis offered of these measures by western academics. The impact of Islamification on the ideologies of secular white feminism is yet to be evaluated. As a researcher I cannot but admire what has been achieved by Iranian women in very difficult circumstances. As a feminist, however, what I find unacceptable is the denial of choice[5] to those who do not wish to frame their demands in Islamic terms and would prefer openly to flout Islamic values. Whether it is the theocracy, Islamism or Islamic women that are to blame remains an open question.

ACKNOWLEDGEMENTS

The author would like to thank the Humanities Research Board of the British Academy for funding the research leave which enabled her to carry out the preliminary preparations for this chapter. She would also like to thank Stephanie Barrientos for her detailed comments on an earlier draft of this paper. The author is responsible for all mistakes and misrepresentations.

An earlier draft of this chapter will be published as part of the proceedings of the *Colloque interdisciplinaire 'L'Islam et l'espace euro-meditérranéen'*, held at Luxembourg in September 1997.

NOTES

1. Author's addition.
2. Amnesty International report, quoted by the communiqué of the World Organization of Iranian Women Solidarity, Paris, 25 July 1992.
3. 1978 sample survey of child-bearing women, carried out by the Statistical Centre and reported in *Kayhan*, 26 February 1987.
4. Already in the 1840s scholars such as Qoratolayn in Iran were embarking on the process of reinterpretation. By the 1920s scholars such as Nazira Zin-al-Din in Lebanon and in the 1940s Zeinab Al-Ghazali in Egypt had developed the process to present an alternative Islamic vision which offered women high visibility and leading roles both in the religious and political establishments.
5. I am grateful to Ruth Pearson for pointing this out to me many years ago.

REFERENCES

Afshar, H. (1982) 'Khomeini's Teachings and their Implications for Women', pp. 79–90 in A. Tabari and N. Yeganeh (compilers) *In the Shadow of Islam*, London: Zed Press.

Afshar, H. (1985) *Women, Work and Ideology In The Third World*, London: Tavistock.

Afshar, H. (1994) *Why Fundamentalism? Iranian Women and Their Support for Islam*, Department of Politics Working Paper no. 2, York.

Afshar, H. (1998) *Islam and Feminisms: an Iranian Experience*, Basingstoke: Macmillan.

Afshar, H. and Dennis, C. (eds) (1992) *Women and Adjustment in The Third World*, Basingstoke: Macmillan.

Amuzegar, J. (1993) *Iran's Economy under the Islamic Republic*, London: I.B. Tauris.

Bakker, I. (ed.) (1994) *The Strategic Silence*, London: Zed Press.

Callinicos, Alex (1989) *Against Post-Modernism: A Marxist Critique*, Cambridge: Polity Press.

Cornion, A. et al. (eds) (1987) *Adjustments with a Human Face*, Oxford: Clarendon Press.

Elson, Diane (ed.) (1991) *Male Bias in the Development Process*, Manchester: Manchester University Press.

Haeri, Shahla (1995) 'Of Feminism and Fundamentalism', *Contention* vol. 4, no. 3, Spring.

Hartmann (1981) 'The Unhappy Marriage of Marxism and Feminism' in Lydia Sargent (ed.) *Women and Revolution*, London: Pluto Press.

Kaar, Mehrangiz (1994) 'Hoquqeh Siassi Zan dar Iran, as Bahman 57 ta emruz' [Iranian Women's Political Activities February 1979 till today], *Zanan*, no. 20, Sept–Oct.

Kandyoti, M. (1997) 'Beyond Beijing: Obstacles and Prospects for the Middle East', in M. Afkhami and E. Friedle (eds) *Muslim Women and the Politics of Participation, Implementing the Beijing Platform*, Syracuse, NY: Syracus University Press.

Maynard, Mary (1994, 1995) '"Race", Gender and the Concept of "Difference" in Feminist Thought' in H. Afshar and M. Maynard (eds) *The Dynamics of Race and Gender: Some Feminist Interventions*, London: Taylor and Francis.

Mernissi, Fatima (1991) *Women and Islam; an Historical and Theological Enquiry*, Oxford: Blackwell.

Mernissi, Fatima (1993) *The Forgotten Queens of Islam*, Minneapolis: University of Minneapolis Press.

Mernissi, Fatima, (1995) 'Arab Women's Rights and the Muslim State in the Twenty-first Century: Reflection on Islam as Religion and State' in M. Afkhami (ed.) *Faith and Freedom: Women's Human Rights in the Muslim World*, London: I.B. Tauris.

Milani, Farzaneh (1992) *Veils and Words, the Emerging Voices of Iranian Women Writers*, London: I.B. Tauris.

Mir-Hosseini, Ziba (1996) 'Stretching the Limits: a Feminist Reading of the *Sharia* in post-Khomeini Iran', in Mai Yamani (ed.) *Feminism and Islam*,

Legal and Literary Perspectives, Reading, Mass.: Ithaca Press Garnet Publishing.
Moghissi, Haideh (1996) "Factionalism and Muslim Feminine Elite in Iran" in Saeed Rahnema and Sohrab Behdad (eds) *Iran after the Revolution*, London: I.B. Tauris.
Moghissi, Haideh (forthcoming) 'Feminsimeh populismy va "feminsimeh Eslami"', *Kenskash*.
Najmabadi, A. (1995) 'Salhayeh osrat, salhayeh ruyesh' [The Era of Hardship and the Era of Development], *Kenkash*, no. 12, autumn.
Omid, Homa (1994) *Islam and the Post Revolutionary State in Iran*, Basingstoke: Macmillan.
Paidar, P. (1996) 'Feminism and Islam in Iran', in D. Kandiyoti (ed.) *Gendering the Middle East*, Syracuse, New York: Syracuse University Press.
Sabbah, Fatna A. (1984) *Women in the Muslim Unconscious*, New York and Oxford: Pergamon Press.
Shariati, Ali (1980) *Fatima is Fatima* (translated by Leila Bakhtiar), Teheran: Hamdami Foundation.
Shariati, Ali (n.d.) *Tashiiyeh Alavi va Tashiiyeh Safavi* [Alavi and Safavid Forms of Shiism] Hoseiniyeh Ershad publication.
Zin al-Din, Nazrina (1929) *al-Fatat wa'l-shiukh*, Beirut; quoted by Shaaban, Bouthaina, 'The Muted Voices of Women Interpreters', in Mahnaz Afkhami (ed.) (1995) *Faith and Freedom; Women's Human Rights in the Muslim World*, London and New York: I.B. Tauris.

5 The Informal Sector and the Conservative Consensus: a Case of Fragmentation in Egypt
Noha El-Mikawy

INTRODUCTION

Globalization as a primarily economic phenomenon has had its social, political and philosophical manifestations. With globalization, capital, labour and ideas have been moving round the globe with unprecedented speed, creating hope for a more homogeneous world. There is talk of waves of democratization and discussions of the universal ability of liberal thought to offer guiding principles for social and political systems.

However, experience has shown that the free and rapid movement of capital and labour does not always produce equal economic prosperity for all. With globalization we have come to know the phenomenon of growth without employment, or at least employment as we knew it: formal, contractual, regulated, within bureaucratized and rational structures. Many economies have come to depend instead on seasonal and informal employment. While some optimists celebrate that development, others warn that it could lead to fragmented markets, fragmented state power and exploitation. Nor has globalization resulted in a global village of liberal, democratic citizens, equally believing and practising such principles. Experience has shown that globalization can produce strong cultural and social reactions against the liberal way of life.

Women have been affected by globalization and its spin-offs. As much as some women have come to enjoy the benefits of growth and foreign capital investment in their own countries, more women have found no place to earn a living other than in the informal sector. Furthermore, while some women have enjoyed improved living conditions, thanks to the concerted effort of international and non-governmental agencies, many more have become victims of the conservative reactions to globalization. This chapter addresses the manifestations of globalization in Egypt first with regard to the issue of women's presence in the informal sector, and second with regards to the increasingly conservative consensus about women's identity and proper social role.

FRAGMENTATION IN THE INFORMAL SECTOR

Globalization and the Informal Sector

In the face of economic and political crises by the mid-1970s, Egypt opened up its economy to private enterprise and reinstated a mutli-party system. Since the early 1990s, it has been implementing IMF and World Bank recommendations for structural adjustment. The government has been trying to orient the economy away from import-substitution industrialization (the 1960s) and beyond a dependence on rentier revenue (the 1970s and 1980s) towards NIC-like export-oriented production. Thus restructuring has been accompanied by high rates of unemployment – the result of decreasing investment in the public sector and slow growth in the private sector.

Typically, the informal sector has gained in importance, accounting in 1986 for 65.3 per cent of all urban and non-agricultural employment (Forum 1996: 1). Studies of poor women in Cairo by E. Early, D. Singerman and J. Gertel attest to the rising significance of women as breadwinners through informal means. Most working women in Egypt are in the informal sectors of agriculture and services, where work is characterized by long hours, bad pay and non-existent organization.

The Significance of the Informal Sector

To appreciate the impact of the informal sector on women, one needs to remember that Egyptian women entered the formal public sector only to be hindered by two main biases, and the participation of working women in the manufacturing sector has remained weak compared to other Middle Eastern countries (12 per cent of the labour force in manufacturing). Within that sector, most Egyptian women have been excluded from the production line and managerial jobs (Moghadam 1993: 31–40). This is exacerbated by a class bias. Professional women in managerial positions have predominantly come from the middle and upper classes, and have enjoyed family connections and education privileges (Papps 1993).

In other words, the formal sector has not enabled women's integration in the job market or massive social mobility. Furthermore, whereas women in the informal sector depend mainly on household production units, women in the formal sector depend on family connections and family-dependent educational privileges. Hence, any improvements regarding job creation, job conditions or organization in the professions have been experienced by a few, who have often been far removed from the experiences of the majority. Therefore, whether in the formal or the informal sector, women whose gains depend on family connections, privileges or household economic units remain barely touched by the process of public interest aggregation and articulation.

The Informal Sector Debate

Some reject this argument and assert that the informal sector has many advantages that could redress market biases against women. It can become the engine of growth replacing the public sector. Its flexibility can be advantageous to women who often lack skills and have to juggle work and family responsibilities. As Nickolas Hopkins points out, there are those who regard the informal sector as a nascent manifestation of private initiative, an 'incipient or actual small business sector... [which] includes people who have successfully resisted integration into the hierarchical control of work characteristic of the formal sector, and there is thus an element of personal liberation and fulfillment, albeit at some monetary cost' (Hopkins 1991: 121). In a sense, some regard the informal sector as liberalism in the making.

Others are more pessimistic. On a factual level, argues Suad Kamel of Cairo University, the informal sector offers jobs that are accompanied by low levels of education and lack of social welfare, even if in some cases it offers higher levels of financial compensation than the formal sector does (Forum 1996: 1, 7, 8). According to world system theorists, the informal sector 'represents a marginal class of people who are subordinated to the domination of international capitalism... who are exploited in the sense of being paid substandard wages... or no wages at all... and who therefore concretize the industrial reserve army' (Hopkins 1991: 121). Georg Stauth saw the informal sector as a form of unequal accumulation and exploitation typical of peripheral modes of capitalist resource utilization (Stauth 1991: 78–103).

Stauth also pointed to a significant disadvantage of the informal sector. Not only does it utilize resources, both material and human inefficiently; it also threatens to produce retarded civic consciousness. He argued that local interests in the informal sector of peripheral capitalist systems mobilize social and economic community relations up to a point which helps advance the cause of capital accumulation. Beyond that, however, local interests 'prevent stable communal action on a higher level of responsibility' (Stauth 1991: 99–100).

Years after Stauth published his work, Nazih Ayubi described the social experience in the informal sector as one of 'symbolic display, of interaction rituals and personal ties, of physical proximity coexisting with social distance,' underlining the limited public experience involved in the informal sector (Ayubi 1995: 440). According to this assessment, women could not function in the civic domain of citizenship, public debate and conscious collective action.

The Informal Sector and Women's Fragmentation

If we add to this the fact that Egyptian women in general have a weak participation level, we end up with a picture of dismal marginalization from the political process and serious social fragmentation into family / household units. The data collected by Amani Qandil on non-governmental organizations in Egypt since the 1960s attests to the marginality of women's participation in civil society and, thus, to the weakness of their sense of individualism outside the family and of belonging to a collective entity bigger than the family. Less than 1 per cent of all registered organizations in 1992 were women's organizations. The highest representation of women has been in organizations devoted to family support and planning where they represent 44 per cent of the members and 41 per cent of the managers. In child care organizations, they represent 30 per cent of the members and 37.5 per cent of managers, whereas in charity organizations, they represent 26 per cent and 13 per cent respectively. In cultural, scientific and religious organizations, their representation drops to 14 per cent of total membership and 8 per cent of total managerial posts (Qandil 1995: 95–101).

Hence it may be important to reassess the liberalizing role of the informal sector as far as women are concerned. Is it necessary that we look for the influence of the informal sector as a social experience over women's public consciousness and identity? The guess is that women active in the informal sector develop no faith in individual initiative because of the insecure nature of the work and income; they also develop no sense of individualism, for the family remains the locus of activity and the focus of trust.

The Informal Sector and the Family

The increasing relevance of the family as a productive unit in the informal sector has led many social scientists to reintroduce the family as a social and political unit of participation and to accept the fact that the family/household can function as a political unit. This was the thrust of Diane Singerman's recent work on *Avenues of Participation* (Singerman 1995).

Others, however, warn against bringing the family into politics. They draw attention to the fragmenting potential of confining one's private and public experience to the the family/household unit. Suad Joseph argued that family-based civil society is like family-based politics; both perpetuate patron–client relationships that 'foster a notion of cititzen rights as charity or gifts. Citizens come to have rights in such systems of distribution not because they are accorded and entitled to equality by virtue of their individualized citizenship but because of specific sets of personalized relationships of unequal exchange' (Joseph 1996: 4–10). Val Moghadam also doubted the liberalizing nature of family-based politics. She warned of the all too frequent alliance between patriarchy and conservative social forces (Moghadam 1993: 24). This alliance looms large in Egypt today as a reaction to Egypt's latest thrust into the international phenomenon of globalization. That is the subject of the following section.

FRAGMENTATION IN THE GENDER DEBATE

Movements calling for some celebration of the heritage emerge in response to the increasing pressure imposed by globalization on local cultures. In the case of Egypt, a strong movement has taken root, advocating the shedding of western culture and a return to the superior principles of Islamic culture. This movement, as observers note, has managed to create a consensus in the discourse over the identity and proper role of women. While attempts to shape the reality of women according to secular, liberal standards set by the international community do exist, they are shy in the face of the hegemonic conservative consensus.

Discourse

The discourse on women takes its principles from three sources: (1) the Islamic tradition, history and jurisprudence (Bint al-Shati, Zaynab al-Ghazali, Mohamad al-Ghazali, Yousef al-Qaradawi, Mitwali al-Sha' raw-i); (2) liberal principles of equality (Qasim Amin); and (3) the Marxist analysis of infrastructural relationships of exploitation and superstructural control (Nawal al-Sa'dawi, Amina Shafik Latifa al-Zayyat). There is an increasing amount of research, however, that argues that the gender debate has come to rely on a combination of all these principles, making it difficult to find exclusionary and antagonistic camps (Cynthia Nelson and Nadia al-Ali).

The Islamic agenda on women in Egypt ranges from dogmatic (Yousef al-Qaradawi) to pragmatic (Mohamad al-Ghazali) and progressive (Adel Hussein and Heba Rauf). The main issues on this agenda are: (a) the status of women and their rights; (b) the issue of equality and differences between the sexes; (c) the conduct and attire of women in public; and (d) women's private and public roles.

All Islamic thinkers, and most secular ones, affirm that Islam contributed in a revolutionary manner to the status of women and their rights. As to equality between the sexes, the pragmatic and progressive camps insist on the equal status of both sexes as guaranteed by the Koran. Mohamad al-Ghazali said, 'Islam equates man and woman with regards to all rights and duties. If there are differences, they are to respect human nature' (al-Ghazali 1996: 15). Adel Hussein stressed that 'Islam asserts very clearly the principle of total equality between men and women in everything related to human dignity and responsibility.' Hussein explained that Islam does not disagree with equality in principle, but it refuses to adopt western views on equality and gender (Hussein 1990: 35).

While pragmatic and progressive Islamic thinkers stress equality, dogmatic ones often speak out loudly about the differences between men and women. Yousef al-Qaradawi said, 'whoever disobeys Allah's laws of inheritance has deviated from the just course made plain by Him, transgressing His limits, and must expect the punishment promised him...' (al-Qaradawi 1992: 232). The pragmatic camp, in comparison, offers a more qualified albeit sometimes inconsistent approach. Pragmatic thinkers differentiate between gender differences ordained by Islam and others inherited from centuries of intermingling between local tradition and imported values. Mohamad al-Ghazali, for example criticized fellow Islamists who seem, in his mind, to uphold principles ordained by socio-economic, cultural and often imperialist traditions, rather than by God or his Prophet. In disagreement with those Islamists, he insisted on the woman's right to choose her husband, to unveil her face, to speak out, to have her husband called to account if he beats her, to insist on divorce if she so desires. He set men and women on an equal footing, arguing that men would learn to respect these rights if they only imagined what life would be like without them. What seems to be lacking, in an argument that is otherwise quite provocative, is consistency. When it came to the right to travel, al-Ghazali sacrificed it for the sake of guarding *al-'ird* (honour) from anything that would be a temptation or threat. Al-Ghazali failed to see the concept of *al-'ird* as an artifact of culture and tradition (al-Ghazali 160–1).

The dogmatic–pragmatic spectrum is also reflected in stands on the proper role of women. Some dogmatic thinkers emphasize the woman's 'natural and God-given domesticity... and predict certain doom to befall the Islamic world if the woman abandons or is lured away from her traditional place in society...' (Stowasser 1987: 276 and 1994: 129). Others allow women a public role under specific circumstances. Al-Qaradawi has been known to allow women a presence in public life provided it does not result in the 'intermingling with men in such a way that their bodies come in contact, as happens so often in... auditoriums and buses'. He wrote, 'Islam does not require, as some people claim, that a woman should remain confined to her house... On the contrary, she may go out for prayer, for her studies, and for her other lawful needs, both religious and secular' (al-Qaradawi 1992: 164–7).

More pragmatic thinkers and more development-oriented ones have developed a model that allows for women's participation in public life, basing their arguments on developmental needs. Adel Hussein's argument defines progress using cultural and materialistic indicators. Progress in his model is not only measured in terms of growth and GNP. Progress has a human, cultural dimension which determines the woman's major mission as one of raising disciplined and industrious children to contribute indirectly to growth and production. Within that model, women are welcome to work if they are needed or if they have special expertise; one need not blindly support the principle of work for its own sake, degrading in the process the civilizing role of wives and mothers (Hussein 1990: 34–5).

The young but increasingly celebrated scholar in the intellectual world of Islamic thought, Heba Rauf, went many steps further in acknowledging and advocating a public role for women. In her MA thesis, presented to Cairo University and later published as a book, Rauf defends the equality of men and women as civic beings. Both are entitled to education, political consciousness, political competence and participation. She contributes to the literature on the role of women by taking the woman's public role beyond that of raising good citizens within the family. Hers is an audacious argument, basing women's entitlement to public participation on the cardinal Islamic principles of *tawhid* (the unity of God) *istikhlaf* (human responsiblity for life on Earth), *wajib* (duty) and '*amal* (toil) (Rauf 1995).

The Conservative Consensus

However, it still remains to be seen how her attitude, based partly on the encouragement of pragmatic Islamic thinkers such as Tarik al-Bishry, Abdel Fattah Ismail and Abdel Halim Abu Shuqqah, will affect the mainstream, which still lauds the supremacy of motherhood. Such a tendency is found in all genres of Islamic writing on the role of women, and seems to find a willing audience among the majority of women. Surveys of Egyptian women's attitudes towards their work indicate that the maternal role always comes first (Papps 1993: 108).

Some may argue that this perception of the role of women is not unique to Islamic thinkers. In fact similar views were common in the early days of the liberal age. For instance, during the French revolution, women were accepted and hailed as demonstrators but after the revolution were sent back to the homes to fulfil their duty, namely raising citizens for the nation. Furthermore, Rousseau, Hegel and de Tocqueville gave women some rights, yet deprived them of others. Particularly curious was the exclusion of women from political rights. The woman was the mother who taught male citizens the requisites for civic virtue, namely affection, empathy and selfless love. But it was those very same qualities which disqualified her, in Rousseau's eyes, as an active participant in public life. Hegel, too, relegated women to the private sphere on the grounds that women possessed qualities that were good for the male citizen but disqualified them from participating in politics, making them unable to rationalize and abstract from personal welfare to the general interest (Coole 1993: 78–91 and 139–43). De Tocqueville could not conceive of a public role for women despite his support of equality in principle. Describing the virtues of American life he said, 'American women never manage the outward concerns of the family ... or take part in political life ... Nor have the Americans ever supposed that one consequence of democratic principles is the subversion of marital power or the confusion of the natural authorities in families' (de Tocqueville 1994: 201–12)

However, there is one distinct feature to the Islamic argument: the narrowness of the concept 'private'. Glorifying her domesticity, Islamic thinkers such as al-Qaradawi think it proper to regulate many of women's affairs, such as the do's and don'ts of wearing jewellery, plucking eyebrows, dyeing hair and painting fingernails (al-Qaradawi 1992: 70–94 and 165–8). That underlines the shrinking of the private sphere in the face of public, authoritative and prescriptive utterances. This encroachment on the definition and scope of what is private exists within a context that calls for an organic society, where neighbour cares for neighbour, and all see to it that mores are upheld in the home and on the street: 'an Islamic street is one where all passersby and people sitting outside cooperate to prevent profane language, immodest gaze and those who do not uphold the norms of decency and conservatism' (al-Ghazali 1996: 43).

The shrinking of what is private is not only promulgated by the intrusiveness of some Islamic thinkers. It has become a fact of life within the current socio-economic conditions of Egypt. Many Egyptians do not experience privacy in their daily lives – a daily problem in poorer neighbourhoods where every inch of space is shared with other family members and neighbours. Al-Ghazali has noted the lack of decent utilities and facilities in the lives of average Egyptians. He gave Egyptians the right to aspire to a comfortable life and to resent their government for not providing proper facilities (al-Ghazali 1996: 112–15 and 125–8). But his note was to assure his readers that Islam is not a religion of austerity, but one of worldly comfort. He did not mean to point out, as the author of this chapter does, that lack of decent facilities reduces the Egyptian's sense of privacy and encroaches on his/her identity.

When al-Ghazali describes the comfortable life Moslems should aspire to, he almost reminds us of Qasim Amin's description of the ideal bourgeois family in *The Liberation of Women*, which was influenced by Amin's knowledge of European bourgeois ideals (Amin 1992). However, the globalization of bourgeois ideals could ironically underline, as it does in the Egyptian context, a limitation of individuality and of privacy. When Amin defends the rights of women, alluding to the bourgeois ideals of Europe, he wanted to improve the status of women as mothers to bring up better, industrious citizens and offer men better companionship. When al-Ghazali evokes bourgeois images of the family he did so to criticize the government. Neither he nor Amin use the bourgeois ideal of the good family life to defend the principle and rights of individuality. It is certainly part of the globalization effect to talk of families and facilities in ways that resemble the bourgeois ideal of well-being. However, the globalization effect which makes bourgeois standards of living everybody's aspiration has its limits: conservative bourgeois ideals are used to support conservative values and principles.

Action

In bourgeois Europe and America, action went beyond the limits of the conservaitve bourgeois discourse. How is that to be compared to the Egyptian case? Has there been any counter-pressure among secular activists, both liberal and Marxist, to the conservative consensus described above? Secular activists reaped the fruits of globalization, often being supported by data collection and reality assessment studies guided by the internationally acclaimed gender agenda. However, secular activists continue to manifest an Egyptian specificity, namely shyness in the face of the conservative consensus. Summarizing this specific feature, Inas Taha lists the major points of the secular, liberal agenda: (a) reforming the personal status laws and criminal punishment; (b) reforming working relations and conditions; (c) redressing the negative impact of liberalization and structural adjustment on women; and (d) educational reform to stress democracy and human rights. She argues that such a list hides a non-assertive attitude regarding freedoms and liberties which could be criticized by Islamists as being in violation of Islamic tenets (Taha 1995).

Another feature of secular, liberal action concerning women is its focus on formal equality. Activists are noticeably present and active in the field of legal reform. They demand revising the marriage contract to give women more leverage over divorce, travel and work decisions. They want nationality and children custody laws to be changed, as well as criminal law concerning female offenders. The formal nature of those demands, focusing on the legal dimension of equality, is not matched by action to liberalize the family structure, and raise awareness regarding the individual identity of family members and the harmful effect on women's consciousness of persistent male chauvinism (Khalifa 1995: 8). Efforts to go beyond formal equality have either been demobilized (in the case of Nawal al-Sadawi), ostracized (in the case of Saad Eddin Ibrahim) or confined to limited circles (in the case of al-Mar'ah al-Jadida group).

A third feature characterizing secular, liberal action is a structural naiveté which leaves the populist tendency of the discourse on women unchallenged. Responding to fears and frustrations created by unemployment, the Islamic discourse perpetuates the patriarchal family which assigns to males the function of earning the family's living, making it unnecessary for women to seek work. This family is so idealized that it does not correspond to any socio-economic reality, level of education or professional achievements. Women are often ideal types who take as their guide the wives and daughters of the Prophet, who in turn are idealized (Baron 1994: 115). The veil, too, is idealized and presented as a symbol devoid of class connotations: a symbol of anti-globalization (Ahmad 1988). Liberal, secular action does not qualify the idealized images with equally public campaigns that stress structural differences, status differences, etc. Turning a blind eye to the facts of women's reality, liberal, secular activists forget that it is such socio-economic differences that defy legal equality. It is precisely this bias towards formality in liberal thought that Carole Pateman warned against in Almond's and Verba's *Civic Culture Revisted*. The bias towards formal equality all too often goes hand in hand with liberal neglect of social and economic inequality (Pateman 1980).

A fourth feature of secular action is the neglect of women's role as civic agents. Whereas the mainstream comes under the influence of populist action, the secular agenda works in limited contexts and does not organize women. The populist tendency manifests itself in the mobilization of women in amorphous crowds that defend contentious causes such as religion or culture. As women become active in such crowds, they raise their female consciousness but not their civic responsibility. Women become, in other words, aware of the private affairs of womanhood and they seek to make a public cause out of them. They do not, however, become aware of public matters and do not seek to make public matters their private responsibility (Drew 1995: 1–33). Secular action in Egypt does not seek in any effective way to redress this picture and empower women as active and equal participants, boosting women's civic consciousness. In its failure to nurture civic consciousness among women, the secular agenda in Egypt resembles the conservative bourgeois tradition which, according to Carole Pateman, only assumed civic consciousness as a cardinal element of bourgeois, liberal democratic culture, but did not explain it (Pateman 1980).

In sum, the conservative reaction to globalization regarding women has faced a timid secular counteraction. The secular action has failed to counterbalance the conservative consensus by opting for a conservative understanding of liberal, bourgeois equality.

CONCLUSION

The discussion points to legitimate doubts regarding the liberating impact of globalization. Our work has pointed to the reality of fragmentation, not liberation, in the Egyptian context. Fragmentation here is used to mean political isolation and disempowerment within a social framework that reifies female identity at the cost of civic identity and brings the family/household as an economic unit back into public life at the expense of other civic institutions.

Two domains of globalization have been discussed: one economic and the other political. Economically, it is often said that globalization will connect an economy to the international market, bring in capital and increase employment. Some economists celebrate the development of an informal sector as a sign of economic vitality and capital formation/accumulation. Some liberals celebrate the same phenomenon as a sign of the revival of civil life and autonomy from the state. In so doing, both ignore the potential fragmentation that can result from increasing dependency on the informal sector. Earning a living informally may be liberation from the exploitation and control exercised in modern structures of bureaucratized and rationalized work institutions. But the informal sector may equally well end up making the household the site of socio-economic exploitation and control untroubled by public regulation. Optimists also fail to consider the effect of fragmentation on women of households as economic units, especially in the context of women's increasing exclusion from political participation.

Politically, it is often assumed that globalization will herald the triumph of liberal thought and action, an assumption that has proved precarious in the Egyptian context. Experience has shown that globalization of the economy does not automatically produce staunch liberals and defenders of freedom of investment as well as of movement, expression and organization. Globalization has produced conservative, populist movements which express their fear of the market and their distrust of the massive free movement of capital and ideas.

Hence the Egyptian case demonstrates two limitations of globalization. First, globalization produces strong counter-reactions. The counter-reaction to globalization in Egypt has been conservative and populist, idealizing women, reifying their private role as mothers and undermining their public role as civic partners. The problem with this conservative, populist consensus is not that it opposes globalization, but rather that it can isolate women. Most Islamic activists focus on the family as the highest civil unit and intrude on that unit with authoritarian utterances which reduce women to their biological function and their social role to that of pedagogical agents perpetuating the conservative message.

Second, the globalization of ideas cannot guarantee the final version in which these ideas will be received in any one socio-economic context. Although the secular agenda in Egypt has been guided by the international agenda on women, it seems to have absorbed more of the conservative bourgeois definition of equality. Equality has been defined formally, with less regard for socio-economic differences. Individuality and liberty have been hailed in speeches and only assumed in action, partly to avoid confrontation with the Islamic camp. Civic identity has been assumed but not nurtured, making civic consciousness an easy target of the rising tide of populist thought and action. Hence, the acceptance of the universal rights of women by most secular activists in Egypt has been accompanied by an increasing lack of civic, participative competence among women.

REFERENCES

Ahmad, L. (1988) 'Arab Women 1995', in H. Sharabi (ed.) *The Next Arab Decade*, Boulder: Westview Press, 208–20.
al-Ghazali, M. (1996) *Qadaya al-Mar'ah Bayn al-Taqaleed al-Raqidah wa al-Wafidah* [Women Issues: Imported and Existing Traditions], 6th edition. Cairo: Dar al-Shuruk.
al-Qaradawi, Y. (1992) *The Lawful and the Prohibited in Islam*, International Islamic Federation of Student Organisations. Kuwait: Al-Faisal Press.
Amin, Q. (1992) *The Liberation of Women: A Document in the History of Egyptian Feminism*, Cairo: American University in Cairo Press.
Ayubi, N. (1995) *Over-stating the Arab State*, London: I.B. Tauris.
Baron, B. (1994) *The Women's Awakening in Egypt*, New Haven: Yale University Press.
Coole, D. (1993) *Women in Political Theory*, London: Harvester-Wheatsheaf.
De Tocqueville, A. (1994) *Democracy in America*, Book 3, Chapter 9, New York: Everyman's Library.
Drew, N. (1995) 'Female Consciousness and Feminism in Africa', *Theory and Society* 24.
Gertel, Joerg and Said Samir (1995) 'The Search for Security: Informal Sector Food Vendors in Matariya', in J. Gertel (ed.) *The Metropolitan Food System of Cairo*, Verlag für Entwicklungspolitik, Saarbrücken.
Ghannam, Farha (1995) 'Gender and Food in Everyday Life: An Ethnographic Study of a Neighborhood', in Cairo in J. Gertel (ed.) *The Metropolitan Food System of Cairo*, Verlag für Entwicklungspolitik, Saarbrücken.
Hopkins, N. (1991) 'Markets, Marketing the Market: Informal Egypt', *Cairo Papers in Social Sciences* 14(4), Winter, Cairo: American University in Cairo Press.
Hussein, A. (1990) *al-Islam: Din wa Hadharah* [Islam: A Religion and a Civilization], Cairo: Matab' al-Manar al-Arabi.
Joseph, S. (1996) 'Gender and Citizenship in Middle Eastern States', *Middle East Report* 26(1), January.

Khalifa, A. (1995) 'The Withering Youth of Egypt', *Ru'ya*. Spring.
Moghadam, V. (1993) *Modernizing Women*, Boulder, Colorado: Rienner.
Anon. (1996) 'Informal Sector in the MENA Region', *Forum* 3(1), March, 1 and 7–8.
Papps, I. (1993) 'Attitudes to Female Employment in Four Middle Eastern Countries', in H. Afshar (ed.) *Women in the Middle East*, London: Macmillan Press.
Pateman, C. (1980) 'The Civic Culture: a Philosophical Critique', in G. Almond and S. Verba. (eds) *Civic Culture Revisited*. Boston: Little, Brown, 57–102.
Qandil, A. (1995) *al-Jam'iyat al-Ahliyya fi Misr*. [Civil Organisations in Egypt], Cairo: Markaz al-Dirasat al-Siyasiyya wa al-Istratijiyya.
Rauf, H. (1995) *al-Mar'ah wa al-'Amal al-Siyasi: Ru'ya Islamiyya* [Woman and Political Action: An Islamic View], Cairo: al-Ma'had al-'Ali lil Fikr al-Islami.
Singerman, D. (1995) *Avenues of Participation*, Princeton: Princeton University Press.
Stauth, G. (1991) 'Gamaliyya: Informal Economy and Social Life in a Popular Quarter of Cairo', *Cairo Papers in Social Sciences*, 14(4), Winter. Cairo: American University in Cairo Press.
Stowasser, B. (1987) 'Liberated Equal or Protected Dependant? Comtemporary Religious Paradigms on Women's Status in Islam', *Arab Studies Quarterly* 9(3).
Stowasser, B. (1994) *Women in the Quran, Tradition and Interpretation*, New York: Oxford University Press.
Taha, I. (1995) 'Mu'tamar al-Mar'ah fi Bekin'. *Kurasat Istratijiyya* [Strategic Notes]. Cairo: Markaz al-Dirasat al-Siyasiyya wa al-Istratijiyya.

6 Women-headed Households: Global Orthodoxies and Grassroots Realities
Sylvia Chant

INTRODUCTION[1]

Recent increases in the number of women-headed households in most parts of the world have provoked growing public discussion, especially on lone motherhood. Debates have taken place in a wide range of arenas on both sides of the North–South divide – in political and governmental circles, in development institutions and NGOs, in academia, in religious organizations and in the mass media. A persistent thread running through discussions on lone mother households is that they are something of a 'problem', whether in terms of how they themselves fare in society or the difficulties they present for others (be these 'close others' such as their own offspring, or 'distant others' such as the state and policymakers). Wittingly or otherwise, these debates have often drawn on, as well as reproduced, a variety of negative stereotypes about their economic, social and psychological corollaries. Some stereotypes are found so frequently, and with such little substantiation by place- (and people-) specific evidence, that they seem to have assumed the status of 'global orthodoxies'. Prominent among these stereotypes are that women-headed households are the 'poorest of the poor' and that they are 'bad for children'.[2] Yet how accurately do such epithets reflect or represent the circumstances of lone mother households at the grassroots? On the basis of my work in low-income communities in Mexico and Costa Rica there appears to be considerable evidence to challenge indiscriminately negative portrayals.[3] In light of the sustained (and growing) presence of lone mother households in these two countries and elsewhere, there are important reasons for exposing disjunctures between discourses and realities and bringing contrasting experiences more squarely into the public arena. Highlighting diversity may not only help to produce a more balanced picture of the circumstances surrounding lone motherhood, but

92 *Sylvia Chant*

create greater tolerance towards a group who, virtually everywhere in the world, are regarded as an 'undesirable minority'. In turn, movement towards popular acceptance of multiple forms of household and parenting arrangements could make life considerably easier for many lone mothers, and afford them a greater sense of personal and civil legitimacy in contexts where male-headed households have traditionally been perceived, and promoted, as a societal ideal.

Although space does not allow for the detailed discussion of survey data, I hope to provide sufficient glimpses of case study research in Mexico and Costa Rica to underline the need for more concerted efforts to dispense with blanket negativity about lone mother households.[4] Given the pervasiveness of stereotypes linking lone motherhood with poverty and child disadvantage across the world, the first section of this chapter locates these within discussions on lone motherhood at a global level. Section two examines how closely 'global stereotypes' depict low-income households headed by female lone parents in Mexico and Costa Rica, while the third section addresses the ways in which stereotyping impacts on the lives of households headed by lone mothers at the grass roots. The fourth and final part of the chapter summarizes the findings and considers some of their implications for conceptualizing households. Although the term 'women-headed households' encompasses a wide range of domestic arrangements, it will be used here only to refer to units headed by lone mothers. Lone mothers are women with co-resident children who live without the father of their offspring or a male partner. In the case of Mexico and Costa Rica, most lone mothers are separated or widowed rather than never-married women.

PUBLIC DEBATES ON LONE MOTHERHOOD:
GLOBAL PERSPECTIVES

The diverse range of 'sites' in which discussions on lone mothers are taking place in different parts of the world reflect a variety of reasons for mounting interest in this group. Academics, for example, have focused on reasons for their expanding numbers, the significance of female household headship for social change, and how constraints affecting 'minority' households might be addressed by policymakers (see for example, Bortolaia Silva 1996; Folbre 1991; Kumari 1989; Moore 1994; Shanthi 1994). Concern with many of these issues is shared by non-governmental organizations, charitable agencies and feminist groups committed to practical and political struggles for greater social, economic and legal rights for lone mothers (see Burghes 1994; Hewitt and Leach 1993; NCOPF 1991, 1994). In contrast, governments and other sections of the establishment in several countries are more often concerned with stemming the growth of lone parent units as a means of protecting institutions deemed to be socially desirable (such as marriage), and with alleviating the 'burden' that rising numbers of lone mothers place on state welfare (see Duncan and Edwards 1994, 1996; Grosh 1994: 84–5; Laws 1996; McIntosh 1996; Millar 1992; Rosemblatt 1997; Safa 1995: 166).

These latter considerations have been particularly marked in the North where the spotlight on lone mothers has intensified in the context of moves to scale down public expenditure and to increase personal responsibility for children at a time of rising divorce rates, increasingly visible levels of juvenile crime and the perceived growth of a threatening 'underclass' (see, for example, Laws 1996; Phoenix 1996; Roseneil and Mann 1996; Sarre 1996; Smart 1996; Waldfogel 1996; Westwood 1996). Indeed, while lone mothers are present in all socio-economic groups, those targeted in public discussion are usually working-class, unmarried mothers who, as Smart (1996: 47) contends, are regarded as most likely to 'disrupt the carefully calibrated norms of motherhood'.[5] This is echoed by Bortolaia Silva's (1996: 4) observation that:

> The legal institution of motherhood prescribes rules that are secured by stigmas and impositions placed upon those who disregard the rules. In the context of 'normalizing motherhood', working class unmarried mothers are perceived as the most disruptive of the norms. They are presumed to be 'bad mothers' in opposition to the married 'good mother'.

Despite the multiplicity of issues embedded in resistance to lone motherhood (Baylies 1996: 94), and the varied forms resistance takes, categorical pathologizing has been especially marked in the US and the UK (particularly in the last years of the Major administration), and has led to an overriding construction of lone mothers as a negative 'other'. At one end of the spectrum, lone mothers have been depicted as weak and vulnerable, at the other, they have been portrayed as a social aberration, linked with the 'breakdown' of 'family values'. Such portrayals seem to have maintained a powerful grip on the popular imagination despite opposition from feminist scholars and pressure groups, and the challenge posed to 'traditional' norms of household life by the sheer numbers of lone mother households *per se* (see, for example, McIntosh 1996; Phoenix, 1996).[6,7] Establishment commentators have either dismissed feminist challenges as products of political correctness (see Dennis 1993; Dennis and Erdos 1992; Parker 1995), or have hijacked and subverted well-intentioned concern about the problems faced by lone mothers into justifications for their non-viability and/or unworthiness for state support (Duncan and Edwards 1994; Moore 1996: 59). While debates on lone mothers elsewhere in the world have not been as heated nor the focus of such intense media attention (as discussed in greater detail later), concern about these women and their 'problematic' households is discernible in a number of countries on both sides of the North–South divide. As Moore (1996: 59) has pointed out, increases in lone motherhood in the wake of globalization and market integration have been associated with a 'general perception of disequilibrium and unsought-for change in family life'. Thus while it 'would certainly be more than foolish to make global generalizations...anxieties about a "crisis in the family" have found fertile ground in many places, albeit for rather different reasons' (ibid.). Such anxieties may also be reflected (if not intensified) by the pronouncements and/or actions of international organizations. Baylies (1996: 76) draws attention to the fact that in their 1994 *Human Development Report*, the United Nations Development Programme includes a column on the incidence of lone motherhood (alongside statistics on intentional homicides and juvenile prisoners), in a table entitled 'weakening social fabric'. Aside from the fact that only OECD countries[8] appear in the female lone parent column, Baylies argues that the inclusion of these data in itself 'suggests some curious presumptions about the directions of social change and the nature of idealized norms' (ibid.). Indeed, when lone motherhood and its implied 'disintegration' of family life are presented in this way, an obvious inference is that male household headship is both positive and universal.

The concept of 'weakening social fabric' is closely interwoven with a series of negative stereotypes about different aspects of lone motherhood. Of the two identified earlier, the 'poorest of the poor' stereotype is possibly the more ubiquitous, and has given rise to statements containing little room for difference or agency. Examples here include Bullock's (1994: 17–18) assertion that 'women-headed households are overrepresented among the poor in rural and urban, developing and industrial societies', and Tinker's (1990: 5) charge that 'the global economic downturn has pressed most heavily on women-headed households, which are everywhere in the world, the poorest of the poor.' (For similar pronouncements, see Acosta-Belén and Bose, 1995: 25; Buvinic 1995; Buvinic and Gupta 1993; Graham 1987; INSTRAW 1992: 237; UNDAW 1991: 45.) The second, and related, stereotype, that lone motherhood results in the inter-generational transmission of disadvantage to children – material, emotional and/or psychological – tends to be more (although not exclusively) confined to state and policy discourses (see Burghes 1994; Graham, 1993; Kennedy 1994; Legum 1996; Shanthi 1994). None the less, both notions have assumed the status of what we might call 'globalized stereotypes', despite the fact that their applicability is questionable in practice.

One reason for remaining circumspect about dominant representations of lone mothers is that substantive empirical analysis of female household headship remains relatively scant. Another is that the political and policy agendas implicit in public debates on the subject (for example, removing incentives for lone motherhood or strengthening the two-parent family) may have acted to mask diversity and deny the existence of countervailing evidence. Phoenix (1996: 181) draws attention to the pattern in which discussions of lone motherhood commonly fit a 'normalized absence/pathologized presence couplet, where those lone mothers who are faring well are not discussed while those who are problematic make headlines' (see also later). Moreover, even where attempts to undermine the legitimacy of women-headed households are less transparent, the fact that contributions to the debate are rarely solicited from lone mothers themselves raises doubts about representation and accuracy. As Moore points out in a paper prepared for the World Social Summit in Copenhagen (*Is There a Crisis in the Family?*), since public discourses are often produced and domained by the state or élite groups, 'it is not clear how well they correspond to local understandings and experiences of family life' (Moore 1994: 6).

The exclusion of lone mothers' views from centre stage in discourses on household change is even more conspicuous when the South is considered. Despite exhortations by feminist postmodernists to eliminate ethnocentrism and universalism from theorization about households, and to incorporate 'other voices' (Rathgeber 1995: 220; see also Mohanty 1991; Parpart and Marchand 1995: 7; Udaygiri 1995: 164), most publications which claim by their titles to consist of generic discussions of 'the changing family' refer only (or primarily) to advanced economies. Beyond this, even if unease about, or antipathy towards, lone mothers have strong bases in local cultures, one is tempted to speculate whether the (negative) manner in which they are presented would be the same without influence from the North, especially given their historical presence in many parts of the developing world. Recognizing that pejorative constructions may owe to the fact that 'mainstream' theory has consistently posited nuclear households as a 'characteristic of modernity, at the very pinnacle of the development process' (Baylies 1996: 77), it is perhaps no surprise that the general literature on family structure among the urban poor in the South (especially from a Northern vantage-point) 'paints a picture of instability, magnifying the plight of female-headed households and deploring high fertility rates and illegitimacy' (Scott 1994: 86).

With these considerations in mind, how far do 'women-headed households are the poorest of the poor', and 'lone mother households are bad for children' fit grassroots 'realities' in Mexico and Costa Rica, bearing in mind that 'representations' might be a better term than 'realities' given that my analysis is based on personally constructed impressions from long-standing contact and interviews with low-income women in Mexico and Costa Rica?[9] In the following sections, discussion of case study evidence is preceded by brief synopses of salient factors in the wider debates surrounding the two stereotypes.

GLOBAL STEREOTYPES AND GRASSROOTS EXPERIENCES. 1: 'POOREST OF THE POOR'

In the literature on both developing and developed economies, women-headed households are regarded as the 'poorest of the poor' because their incidence is assumed to be higher among low-income groups, and because they are thought to experience greater extremes of poverty than male-headed units (Moghadam 1996: 31; Paolisso and Gammage 1996: 23–5). These beliefs are interwoven with two further notions. First, women-headed households are thought more likely to *emerge* in conditions of poverty; second, various features of female household headship are deemed likely to *exacerbate* poverty. Key reasons offered for the putatively greater formation of female-headed households among the poor (particularly in the South) include labour migration (and its effect on fragmenting family units), absence of formal marriage (through lack of guaranteed/future financial security) and conjugal breakdown due to economic stress (see Boyden and Holden 1991: 18; Bullock 1994: 17; Cleves Mosse 1993: 45; Kumari 1989: 31; Legum 1996: 3; Lewis 1993: 28; López Barajas and Izazola Conde 1995: 23; Shanthi 1994: 19). As for the ways in which female household headship exacerbates poverty, reasons commonly given include first, that they have less (adult) labour supply than two-parent households. This is especially important at a time when the 'family wage' has all but disappeared in most countries and has required the majority of households to rely on multiple sources of income. A second reason is that women with children face particular disadvantage in the labour market due to discrimination by employers and the need to reconcile employment with childcare, domestic responsibilities, and so on. Indeed, as labour markets worldwide have become informalized, women's exclusion from protected, full-time employment seems to have become more pronounced. A third and final reason linking female headship with poverty is that lone mothers tend to receive limited income from sources external to their households (principally the [absent] fathers of the children and/or the state). (For discussions and references, see Chant 1997b; Folbre 1991: 110 *et seq*; Merrick and Schmink 1983; de Oliveira et al., 1995: 15–16; Safa 1995; UNDAW 1991: 38.)

Notwithstanding that many of these factors undoubtedly put female-headed households at an above-average risk of poverty, we can by no means automatically assume that they are the 'poorest of the poor'. In respect of incomes, for example, there is scant evidence that women-headed households are disproportionately represented among the ranks of the indigent and destitute, whether from micro-level case studies (see Hackenberg et al. 1981: 20, Kumari 1989: 31, Lewis 1993: 23, Moser 1996: 50, Weekes-Vagliani 1992: 42, Willis 1994: 79 and 142), or from macro-sources such as census data (see, for example, Chant 1997a: 48 *et seq*; Kennedy 1994; Menjívar and Trejos 1992, Moghadam 1996: 32). Beyond this, a range of qualifications deriving from my own field experience, and parallelling the findings and arguments of studies based in other places, is that we need to think much more closely about how poverty is defined and measured, and what poverty means to people in a personal sense. While more comprehensive reviews of these issues are given elsewhere (see Chant 1997a: Chapters 2 and 7, 1997b), three interrelated points which merit emphasis are as follows.

Conceptualizing Poverty

First, total current earnings of household members are often the basis on which conventional poverty assessments are made, especially in national and international data sources. However, amongst others, Sen (1981, 1985, 1987a) and Chambers (1983, 1989) argue that broader conceptualizations of poverty, which look beyond incomes and consumption to encompass notions of well-being, vulnerability, assets and entitlements, are more relevant to people's lives. Assets, for example, not only include material resources at a household's disposal (for example, labour, tools, land and savings), but encompass 'human capital' such as education and skills, or 'social capital' such as kin and friendship networks and community organizations (see also Baulch 1996; Beall 1996; Chambers 1995; Moser 1996; Moser et al. 1996a, b; Moser and McIlwaine 1997; Wratten 1995). These, in turn, may be crucial in mediating vulnerability and arresting and/or exacerbating poverty-inducing processes. Integral to this more holistic approach to poverty is the question not only of how the poor obtain resources, but how they command them. The latter plugs into Sen's concept of households as sites of 'cooperative conflict' (Sen 1987b, 1990), which has been widely endorsed by feminist research on gendered dimensions of poverty, and has emphasized the indispensability of disaggregating households in order to analyse competing claims, rights, power, interests and resources between constituent members (Moore 1994: 87; see also Baden and Milward, 1995; Beall 1997: Chapter 3; Bradshaw 1996; Chant 1985; Dwyer and Bruce 1988; Kabeer 1994: Chapter 5, 1996; Molyneux 1996: 35).

Although the above perspectives have only relatively recently come to occupy a prominent place in the poverty literature (and, significantly, are now encroaching into the work of major development institutions),[10] even my initial field experience in Querétaro in the early 1980s indicated that the need to look inside households was paramount in adjudging levels of personal well-being. For example, although aggregate earnings are usually higher in male-headed households (especially when heads themselves are the main earners),[11] women-headed households are usually smaller, so that, on average, per capita incomes are either the same or higher (see Chant 1997a: 209; also Selby et al. 1990: 95 on Oaxaca, Mexico; Bradshaw 1996 on Honduras; Paolisso and Gammage 1996: 21 on Chile; Shanthi 1994: 23 on India).[12] Moreover, aside from the fact that households may receive remittances, state transfer payments, and so on, earnings themselves convey little about the money allocated to expenditure that benefits the household as a whole. Indeed, whereas male household heads may retain significant amounts of their wage for discretionary personal expenditure, what we might call 'disposable household income' is usually greater in female-headed households because women tend to relinquish all their earnings to household needs. In turn, larger amounts of disposable income in female-headed households are frequently invested in goods which benefit the household in its entirety, and which, in themselves, can become assets. One example is housing, with many Mexican respondents reporting that they were only able to consolidate their dwellings once their husbands had died or deserted. Thereafter, women's houses were often used more profitably as settings for home-based production, petty landlordism and other commercial ventures (Chant 1997a: 208–13; see also Larsson 1989: 95 on Botswana).

The Visibility of Poverty among Female Household Heads

Related to the above, because the poverty of female-headed households may in some cases, and according to some criteria, be more visible (especially in macro-level data sources based on interviews with 'household heads'), this can lead to neglect of the fact that poverty may also affect women and children in male-headed units. This point has been argued by several feminist researchers, including Muthwa (1993: 8), who, with reference to South Africa, contends:

> within the household, there is much exploitation of women by men which goes unnoticed when we use poverty measures which simply treat households as units and ignore intra-households aspects of exploitation. When we measure poverty, for example, we need measures which illuminate unequal access to resources between men and women in the household.

(See also Blanc-Szanton 1990; Graham 1987: 57; Kabeer 1991: 14; UNDAW 1991: 41; Young 1992.)

While respondents in the case study communities in Mexico and Costa Rica frequently complain of scant resources, female spouses in male-headed units often have the additional burden of 'secondary poverty' if husbands fail to contribute adequate amounts of their earnings to household subsistence. This can have serious implications, with a widowed respondent, Ana María (Puerto Vallarta), reporting that when her husband was alive, her 12–member family lived a hand-to-mouth existence due to his drinking. On numerous occasions, her husband would not come home the night he was paid, but would show up the following morning declaring '*no hay para comer*' ('there's no money for food'). This information was gleaned in the course of in-depth interview and life history work with Ana María over a number of occasions; the likelihood of its being picked up in a one-off macro-survey is more remote. Indeed, if varying combinations of pride, shame and resignation prevent many women from revealing the extent of their poverty to friends and kin, then we have to acknowledge that this is even more likely to apply in the case of official/census enumerators and should be borne in mind when it comes to reading accounts of poverty based on secondary sources.

Perceptions of Poverty

A third and final point under the heading of poverty is the fact that even if in quantitative material terms women *are* worse-off heading their own households, they may *feel* they are better-off or at least less vulnerable (see also Chant 1985; Sen 1985). The vast majority of female heads I have interviewed, in both Mexico and Costa Rica, say that although male incomes can clearly be useful (especially when their families are young), as lone mothers they do not necessarily perceive their position as weaker. Indeed, many women claim to manage better on their own because their ex-partners did not share much of their money with the household, or because, on their own, women are freer to decide which type of employment to do and what to spend their earnings on. In short, the 'poverty of powerlessness' that can accompany a partnership with a man may, in some cases, be deemed less desirable than having *more* power, as lone women, over a smaller material resource base. These findings are not confined to the case study communities. González de la Rocha (1994a: 210) observed in relation to her work on Guadalajara that, despite lower total *and* per capita incomes, the women who head lone parent units 'are not under the same violent oppression and are not as powerless as female heads with partners' (see also Bradshaw 1996 on Honduras).

Among many women in the case study communities who asserted that they were better-off economically (and in other ways) on their own was Layla, a mother of four, in Cañas, Costa Rica. Layla told me that both her former partners had been poor providers, and *'no se puede enamorarse de hambre'* ('you can't fall in love with hunger'). Aside from the fact that there were few financial incentives to stay with either spouse, Layla's personal suffering in both relationships added to her motivation to terminate the unions. Both spouses were drug dealers whose skirmishes with the law placed her and her children in the vulnerable position of not knowing when the men might have to 'disappear' for a few weeks, or even when they themselves might need to uproot and/or change their circumstances. With her first spouse, for example, Layla had only a few days' notice that their ten-year relationship was to become a marriage (her husband thought that the 'respectability' of being married and having a 'proper family' might aid his case in court). On top of this, violence and infidelity were habitual problems with both men. Her second partner came out of jail after seven months on a marijuana charge and, despite Layla's warnings against 'behaving badly', slept with another woman within the first fortnight of his release. Layla attributed the catalyst in the breakdown of both relationships as adultery. Although in the early stages she had wondered whether it might be worth putting up with infidelity so as not to deprive her children of financial support, she now claims to feel *'poderosa'* ('powerful') for having taken the initiative in both instances, not to mention *'orgullosa'* ('proud') for having successfully raised her children single-handedly (see Chant 1997a: 202–4). Similar sentiments were expressed by a Mexican respondent, Socorro (Querétaro), who declared *'me siento a gusto'* ('I feel good') now that most of her nine children are grown-up and have jobs and a good education. Although Socorro has had a total of three co-resident partners in her life, and was forbidden to work by the first one (with whom she lived for seven years), she has always preferred having her own money to relying on men, especially given her experience of dwindling support as each relationship wore on, and given that her second and third spouses were rather resentful of sharing their income with step-children.

While most women who were heads of household claimed to feel better-off alone than they had been with men in their homes, this is not to suggest that women readily left their spouses. In fact, more often than not they are the victims of desertion rather than the primary decision-takers in separation (see also Safa 1995: 121 on the Dominican Republic; Schlyter 1989: 189 on Zimbabwe).[13] Yet it is also interesting that most women who become female heads in the case study communities in Mexico and Costa Rica prefer to stay alone once they end up in this position.[14, 15] This is especially so where they have teenage or adult sons to make up the shortfall of a lack of spouse's earnings (see also Bradshaw 1996 on Honduras; Fonseca 1991 on Brazil). While beyond the scope of the present chapter, stage in the life-course and interrelated factors such as household composition, the nature of female headship (*de jure* or *de facto*) and levels of remittances all play a critical part in affecting the relative poverty of different women-headed households (for discussions see Chant 1997a: Chapters 6–8; Jackson 1996: 491–3; also Chalita, 1992; González de la Rocha 1994b: 8 on Mexico; Thomas 1995: 82 on Chile; Brydon and Legge, 1996: 49 and 69; Lloyd and Gage-Brandon 1993: 121 and 123 on Ghana). These factors are also important in mediating the so-called 'inter-generational transmission of disadvantage' in lone mother units. However, their routine eclipse by global stereotypes tends again to perpetuate a picture of unmitigated misery, with Moore (1996: 61) arguing that:

> The straightforward assumption that poverty is always associated with female-headed households is dangerous, both because it leaves the causes and nature of poverty unexamined and because it rests on a

prior assumption that children will be consistently worse-off in such households because they represent incomplete families.

GLOBAL STEREOTYPES AND GRASSROOTS EXPERIENCES. 2: 'THE INTER-GENERATIONAL TRANSMISSION OF DISADVANTAGE'

Aside from discernible moral undercurrents embedded in the 'transmission of disadvantage' stereotype,[16] it is hardly surprising to find that poverty features prominently as a deleterious outcome for children of growing up in lone mother households. On one hand, the poverty projection revolves around the disadvantage children are likely to face in material terms. In both the advanced and developing economies, for example, lone motherhood has been associated with residence in marginal or substandard housing and poor health, both of which can prejudice the life-chances of children (see, for example, Hardey and Crow 1991: 1; also Graham 1993: Chapter 3; Pothukuchi 1993: 288; Shanthi 1994: 20; Winchester, 1980: 81 *et seq*). Another factor linked to the poverty of female-headed households is the idea that children have to take part-time work at a young age or leave school prematurely in order to help out with family finances – the latter, in turn, contributing to an inter-generational 'poverty trap' (see Lewis 1993: 35; Momsen 1991: 26). A second set of problems wedded to the inter-generational transmission of disadvantage stereotype is that of 'father absence', especially for sons, who are deemed to be deprived of an 'adequate' male role model (see Collier 1995: 201; Collins 1991: 160–1; Edwards and Duncan 1996). As Laws (1996: 65) summarizes with reference to the UK:

> Lone mothers are ... regarded as bad mothers, especially in relation to discipline for their sons. Perceptions that young men in areas of high unemployment are increasingly 'out of control' are attributed to lack of proper patriarchal authority in the family. Women are seen as inherently unable to exert parental authority.

Related to the above, a third set of problems is linked with the idea that employed mothers will be over-burdened by their 'triple burdens' as parents, housewives and workers, and will have insufficient time to devote to child-rearing (see Moser 1992: 108–9; Rogers 1980: 23–4). A fourth idea about the inter-generational transmission of disadvantage (and which ties in with all the above-mentioned factors), can be traced back to

Oscar Lewis's work on the 'culture of poverty', whereby 'dissolute' or 'incomplete' households are regarded as prone to replicate themselves among younger generations (see Lewis 1966). A fifth notion is that children growing up in female-headed households suffer social stigmatization (Shanthi 1994: 27). This may have negative implications for future marriage alliances, as noted by David Lewis (1993) for Bangladesh. It may also mean isolation of children within lone mother households where it is perceived that their socialization differs from that in 'mainstream' (couple-headed) households (see, for example, Valentine 1996: 596–7, 1997a: 74).

While these arguments have some relevance in some contexts, a growing number of analyses have called for extreme caution in interpreting accounts of the inter-generational implications of lone parenthood. One qualification is that the empirical bases of many assertions on the topic may be dubious. Large-scale studies tend to be based on 'snapshot' samples at different points in time, with little in-depth knowledge of intervening changes (Burghes 1994: 13–19). This makes it difficult to evaluate with any degree of accuracy whether the problems some children may have (for example, delinquency, low educational achievement, emotional/psychological difficulties) are due to lone parenthood *per se*, or the disruption and/or trauma caused by divorce or relationships between parents prior to divorce (unhappy marriages often persist for long periods before they actually dissolve) (ibid.: 40). Another, related, problem is the *a priori* assumption that intact marriages must be coherent and that couple-based parenting is better, when it is clear that 'father absence' may be just as much a problem in male-headed households (Hewitt and Leach 1993: 15).[17] Other reasons to remain circumspect relate first, to the diffficulties of disentangling lone parenthood from other phenomena such as poverty, unemployment, and poor health and education (Bortolaia-Silva 1996: 8; Collins 1991: 160–1), and second, to the fact that people themselves are rarely asked directly about how they perceive the outcomes for their lives and well-being of growing up in different types of household.

My research in Mexico and Costa Rica can only provide insights to this debate since although I have interviewed some women, men and children on growing up in different family circumstances, I have not yet conducted what I would call a large or 'systematic' sample survey. However, discussions with a variety of respondents have indicated a number of features which challenge the overriding negativity of 'mainstream' stereotypes.

As indicated earlier, more income may end up invested in housing in female-headed than in male-headed households, and, echoing other studies from a range of developing countries, infant and child mortality is not notably greater in female-headed households. Indeed, most female heads of household in the case study localities who had lost children had done so when they were still partnered by men, and blamed their men's 'irresponsibility' as a contributory factor (see Chant 1997a: 228-30).

Despite charges that the children of lone mothers will achieve less educationally, they actually fare rather well, especially daughters. One reason for the latter is that lone mothers seem to be highly motivated to equip their female children with the means of being able to *'defenderse'*, another being that they do not have to fight husbands who may feel threatened by daughters becoming more educated than they are (Chant 1997a: Chapter 8). For example, while concerned that her 17-year-old daughter Rosalba should finish *preparatoria* and proceed to a university education, María Asunción (Querétaro) has been locked in constant battle with her husband, Antonio, a primary school graduate, to allow Rosalba to continue studying. Whereas María Asunción desires her daughter to become a professional and to earn an independent income, Antonio does not believe women need further education because they will 'only get married and have children'. While content to spend money on the schooling of their three sons (his young twin boys are actually in a private institution), Antonio resents the fact that Rosalba's studies prevent her from working in the family grocery store on a full-time basis. Amongst the conditions he has laid down for his daughter's continued study are that she helps out in the shop after school and at weekends (which clearly cuts down the time she can spend on homework), and that she does not mix with the opposite sex. Rosalba's education is accordingly being achieved at the cost of heavy personal constraints, as well as at the expense of on-going tension between her parents. In female-headed households, by contrast, daughters seem to be encouraged to pursue an education as much, if not more, than their brothers. In the case of Lupe (Puerto Vallarta), for example, her only daughter, 25-year-old Giovana, who is presently reading for a degree in business studies at the University of Guadalajara, is the most educated member of the family. This is partly because Lupe's greatest desire is that her daughter will become a professional and be able to fend for herself, and partly because housework was always shared equally between Giovana and her two brothers so that she was never overburdened with domestic chores in the way that applies to some daughters in male-headed households,

On the question of 'father absence', the idea that this leads to delinquent or anti-social behaviour among boys in particular is again something that seems to hold little water in the Mexican and Costa Rican contexts. In fact, I have been consistently struck at the way in which sons in long-term female-headed households are remarkably responsible, not only in standing by their mothers but in having exemplary relations with their own wives, including respectful conduct, spending time at home and sharing family responsibilities. Forty-six-year-old Tereso (Querétaro), for instance, is described by his family as a 'wonderful' husband and father. For the 15 years I have known the family, he has always participated as much, if not more, in domestic and childcare responsibilities as his wife Paula (who works full-time as a school cleaner-cum-dinner lady). Tereso has consistently impressed upon me how lucky he feels to have a family like his and has also stressed that his desire to create a happy and loving household is probably a reaction to the misery of his own childhood. Tereso's father became an alcoholic, beat his mother and the children, and eventually abandoned the household. This came as a relief to Tereso who, enjoying the prospect of peace in the family at long last, thereafter tried to fill his father's shoes. Committed to keeping the family together, Tereso determined from an early age that he would never make his children suffer in the way that he had.

María Cruz (Querétaro) suggests that her two sons, Rodolfo and Ramiro, have probably grown into responsible and caring young men because they were forced to mature at an early age, and because their father, Armando, was not around to 'teach them bad ways' (Armando was an inveterate womanizer and left home when the boys were 6 and 8 years old respectively). Since Armando severed all contact and gave no economic support, the boys rallied round their mother and ran errands after school to supplement her earnings from a breakfast stall. They also helped out with domestic chores, and Rodolfo, now aged 20, who is studying for an accountancy degree, continues to do so when he is not at college or doing his part-time job in a pizzería. Ramiro, 22, has a spouse and child and works as a taxi-driver. Ramiro professes to adore all the three women in his life – María, his wife and his three-year-old daughter – and that he is delighted that this wife regards María as a '*segunda mamá*' (second mother). They live a few doors down from María and spend considerable amounts of time in each other's homes. Both Ramiro and Rodolfo also help María out financially.

Sons' attempts to maintain the cohesiveness of their natal (and own) families appear to derive from their efforts to compensate for their fathers' behaviour and to create greater security for themselves and close kin. Their apparently greater willingness to share domestic tasks may be due to the fact that in female-headed households, divisions of labour along lines of gender are something of a luxury – everyone has to pitch in and help, and this early experience seems to carry on into later life. On top of this, lone mothers often say they do their best to cultivate 'better men' out of their sons, which echoes an idea discussed in wider studies of masculinity that, in a variety of ways and through a variety of relationships, women have a critically important part to play in shaping male identities and behaviour (see for example, Gutmann 1996; Heward 1996). Another important point is that although children clearly experience pain at not having fathers, and many were abandoned before they were even born, this does not mean they do not have masculine figures in their lives – grandfathers, maternal uncles and so on – with whom relationships are often close and supportive (see also Fonseca 1991 on Brazil; Pulsipher 1993 on the Caribbean).

As for the idea that 'working mothers' will have less time for their children, we have to acknowledge that it is increasingly the case that mothers in two-parent households work too,[18] besides which lone mothers commonly try to accommodate proximity to children by working near or within home. Where women have 'outside jobs', they usually attempt to spend as much of their free time with their children as possible. Lidia, for example, a 30–year-old Nicaraguan lone parent residing in Cañas, Guanacaste, has been on her own with her 10-year-old son Elwin since her husband (also Nicaraguan) abandoned her seven years ago. Lidia works hard as a domestic servant and supplements her income selling lottery tickets ('*la rifa*'), but ensures that she spends all her free time with her son, either at home, or in the homes of her relatives. Partly as a means of protecting her relationship with her child, she has desisted all offers to date men since her husband left her (see Chant 1997a: Chapters 7 and 8). Indeed, without a man to 'look after' (and/or to quarrel with or worry over), many women feel they have more patience, emotional capacity and time to devote to their children. Lupe, a one-time victim of repeated infidelity in Puerto Vallarta, became so guilty about the way she took out her angst on the children that she decided to leave her partner (a second spouse, who was step-father to her oldest son and daughter) to allow her to give her children priority in her life (see also Ford 1996a: 117 on the UK).

As for the notion that lone motherhood leads to unstable unions among offspring, this is not borne out by my case study material. One factor is that the pursuit of education (and a career) among children from female-headed households (see earlier) often dissuades them from embarking on an early marriage or partnership which may stand a slim chance of long-term survival. Moreover, a strong preference tends to be shown by lone mothers for their children (especially daughters) to *marry* rather than enter consensual unions, particularly in Mexico. This often arises as a reaction to the kind of treatment lone mothers get from others: as one respondent, Lupe (Puerto Vallarta), put it: *'La mujer se ve mal si tiene hijos sin casarse'* ('Women look bad if they have children out of wedlock'). Indeed lone mothers are often rather restrictive with their daughters, knowing that men may be more 'predatory' than usual when young women do not have a 'male protector' (Chant 1997a: Chapter 8; see also Shanthi 1994: 26 on India).

This latter point brings to light the fact that one of the biggest crosses lone mother households have to bear is the attitudes of others in their communities, and prevailing stereotypes about women without partners.

THE IMPACTS OF STEREOTYPES ON LONE MOTHER HOUSEHOLDS AT THE GRASSROOTS IN MEXICO AND COSTA RICA

Discussions with female heads of household and other residents of low-income communities in Mexico and Costa Rica suggest that lone mothers are especially likely to suffer stigmatization (and antipathy) from people outside their immediate circles of friends and relatives. In some senses this hostility seems odd given that there has not been the same level of public debate (or vitriol) about lone motherhood in Mexico or Costa Rica as there has been in, say, the UK and US. While both the tabloid and right-wing press in Britain have routinely presented lone mothers as 'selfish', 'wilful', 'irresponsible' individuals with little regard for their children's well-being, media and government sources in Mexico and Costa Rica seem to adopt a more sympathetic standpoint, emphasizing instead an image of lone mothers as 'victims' to be pitied for their plight, and/or reluctant casualties of male desertion.[19] While these depictions are by no means free of stereotypical assumptions either, the Costa Rican state in particular appears to be genuinely concerned to help female household heads, especially in respect of material well-being.

State Constructions of Female Household Headship

Unlike many countries in Latin America (or elsewhere in the South), the Costa Rican state has remained committed to providing basic social welfare for its citizens, even during serious economic crises in the 1980s and 1990s (Sojo 1994). The majority of poor families have long been entitled to public health care, a range of pensions for disability, retirement, old age, widowhood, and so on (collectively known as *'pensiones familiares'*), and benefits such as free milk for under-fives.[20] In the wake of increased poverty in the early 1990s, President Rafael Calderón's administration (1990–4), complemented existing provisions with a system of vouchers for housing as well as education and food (Lara et al. 1995: 63). Although lone mothers with children under 15 have technically been entitled to pensions throughout this period (see Folbre 1994: 227–8),[21] in 1995 lone mothers were targeted for special assistance under a major new poverty alleviation initiative (*Plan Nacional de Combate a la Pobreza*) launched by President José María Figueres (1994–8).

Women (denominated as *'Promujeres'*) represent one of the five major components of the National Poverty Plan, the others being children and youth (*'Proinfancia y Juventud'*), employment (*'Protrabajo'*), the elderly and infirm (*'Solidaridad'*), and local development, housing and quality of life (*'Desarrollo Local: Vivienda y Calidad de Vida'*) (Presidencia de la República 1996). The *'Promujeres'* segment comprises two target groups: (1) female household heads, and (2) young adolescent mothers. Interventions for female household heads are oriented in the first instance to the 16 most vulnerable zones of the country, and comprise five interrelated programmes: education and training, labour force insertion and income-generation, health, housing, and 'resocialization of roles' (encompassing advice and education geared to gender sensitization, self-esteem building, and consciousness raising). One of the most significant interventions thus far is a scheme to enable female heads to undertake adult education and/or skills training via a state stipend or 'temporary family allocation' (*'Asignación Familiar Temporal'*) for a maximum of six months. Although the monthly stipend is only 10,000 colones ($51 US about half the minimum wage), it provides some means of helping households to subsist until their head is able to enter the labour force with a higher level of human capital (Chant 1997a: 151).

Female heads are further assisted in their pursuit of training and/or labour force participation by an expanded number of childcare places in 'community homes' (*'hogares comunitarios'*).[22,23] Administered by the Social Welfare Institute (IMAS/*Instituto Mixto de Ayuda Social*), and concentrated primarily in low-income settlements, women running 'community homes' are given training in childcare and paid a small subvention by the state for looking after the children of neighbours. Parents availing themselves of the service pay what they can as a token gesture and lone mothers are technically entitled to priority access (see Sancho Montero 1995).[24] Even if state support for lone mothers in Costa Rica, whether directly (through targeted social programmes) or indirectly (through legislation for women's rights), appears unlikely (due to limited coverage, inadequate enforcement and so on) to add significantly to women's own attempts to combat poverty, the situation compares favourably with Mexico. Despite calls for attention to the special needs of female lone parents in the Beijing documentation on the family (de Oliveira et al. 1995: 29), and a specification in the National Women's Programme to prioritize female heads in income-generating programmes and to eliminate their barriers to social interest housing (see Secretaría de Gobernacíon 1996: 96), there has been little practical support to date.[25] None the less, the Costa Rican state (like Mexico), continues to operate the bulk of its social, family and anti-poverty programmes on the basis of a couple-headed household model, and is concerned to stress within the National Poverty Plan that it by no means wishes to provide incentives for an increase in lone parenthood (Presidencia de la República 1996: 45).[26]

Constructions of Female Household Headship in Low-income Communities

The fact that neither the Mexican nor Costa Rican state has positively endorsed female household headship is undoubtedly important in contributing to a pattern whereby, in both countries, motherhood within the context of marriage and a male-headed household is widely felt to be a norm and ideal for women at the grassroots (see Facio 1989; Fernández 1992; Goldenberg 1994 on Costa Rica; Benería 1991; Benería and Roldan 1987; González de la Rocha 1995; LeVine 1993 on Mexico). In contrast, lone parenthood remains stigmatized, although sexual and moral stereotypes grounded in religion and culture tend to figure more prominently than those emanating from policy discourses, one popular belief being that a woman without a man to protect her is potentially sexually available (Goldenburg 1994: 221), not to mention 'libertine' (PANI 1990: 4–5). Moreover, in both countries the Catholic Church plays an important ideological and pragmatic role in encouraging women to marry and to remain with their spouses in spite of difficulties (see Chant 1997a: Chapters 3–5). As such, while notions about the poverty of female-headed households and disadvantage for children are present in the case study communities, the most obvious and/or powerful stereotypes about lone mothers tend to centre on the ways in which lesser moral and/or spiritual rectitude sets them apart from 'decent' married women.

Such stereotypes provoke a variety of reactions towards lone mothers, but common ones include imposing isolation through speculative gossip and/or restricted social contact. Female neighbours, for example, may distance themselves from lone mothers, whether because their husbands get suspicious about them fraternizing with women who, theoretically at least, have more freedom, or because the women themselves are worried about women on their own posing a threat to their marriages. As one respondent in Puerto Vallarta put it: *'no tiene marido, y tengo que cuidar el mío'* ('she doesn't have a husband, so I'd better look after mine') (see also Chant and McIlwaine 1995 on the Philippines; Morrison 1995 on Malaysia).

Although in reality many lone mothers in Mexico and Costa Rica end up heading their own households due to male abandonment, the notion that women are 'at fault' in provoking this predicament seems rather pervasive. For example, one married interviewee in Mexico, Rosa (Puerto Vallarta), declared *'madres solteras no me caen bién'* ('I don't like single mothers'), adding that it would be better for them and their children if they got married. Glossing over the fact that the decision to marry or to stay married is usually out of women's hands, another respondent in Costa Rica, Concepción (Liberia), declared that a lot of women brought separation upon themselves by 'behaving badly': 'They go out and sometimes they leave the children. Some of them drink with their friends as well. There's always conflict when this happens and the men usually leave.' An important underlying theme here is that household dissolution is especially likely to occur when women contravene idealized norms of wife and motherhood.

Intimations of moral and sexual deviance are also linked with reactions to the economic circumstances of lone parents. Prevailing assumptions about the poverty of women-headed households (and possibly the belief that women should endure exiguous circumstances as 'penance' for their 'sins'), means that signs of upward mobility have to be carefully concealed so as not to evoke suspicions about 'immoral earnings'. For example, one widowed respondent, Dolores, in Puerto Vallarta reported that new clothing would often be commented upon by neighbours in a way that implied it had been obtained by money from men.

Another aspect of the poverty projection is the way in which lone mothers are frequently subject to unsolicited sexual propositions. One disabled respondent, Emilia (Puerto Vallarta), reported numerous instances of being offered money for 'favours' by taxi-drivers, her fellow market workers and her neighbours' husbands. Although this particular woman was not sure whether her disability was a factor in this, predation by men is viewed as a fairly routine 'hazard' by women on their own in Mexico (and Costa Rica). At the same time, the reality is that lone mothers usually have to work and therefore have resources at their disposal. Lidia in Costa Rica (see earlier, for example), had turned down as many as five suitors because she felt they were not only after her for sex but her money as well.

In order to fend off charges of promiscuity or 'loose morals', many lone parents tend to lead extremely restricted social lives. This, in turn, could be construed as cutting off links which might be helpful financially, socially and psychologically. Layla (Cañas) has now built up a considerable network of trust and support with neighbours, but fears she may lose their sympathy if she were to take up with another man. Thus, while at a personal level some female heads develop positive self-images and have no wish to change their domestic arrangements, their resistance to stereotyping (not to mention their subjection to community surveillance) may simultaneously circumscribe their gains and prevent them transcending the household domain (see also Chant and McIlwaine 1995: Chapter 7 on the Philippines). In turn, the mutually reinforcing interactions between social stigma and economic disadvantage can act as powerful deterrents to women 'choosing' to head their own households. As summarized by Hobson (1994: 279) in the context of comparative research on family policy:

> Solo motherhood is the reflector or rearview mirror for the dynamics of power and dependency – the more difficult and stigmatised solo motherhood is in a society, the greater the barriers against opting out of a bad marriage.

FROM THE GRASSROOTS TO THE GLOBAL: CONCLUDING COMMENTS

The aim of this chapter has been to demonstrate that assumptions about female-headed households – whether at community, national or global levels – are often misplaced, and that greater knowledge of personal circumstances and the diversity that exists within the group at the grassroots is essential in breaking down unhelpful, not to mention harmful, stereotypes. In the interests of illustrating this argument, I have drawn attention to evidence that suggests that for some women, heading their own household may be preferable to living in a male-headed unit. In turn, their children do not seem to be markedly disadvantaged. These readings are not just based on women's own opinions (which clearly may be couched within positive terms as a means of justifying their socially marginal status), but on the basis of more 'objective' indicators as well. This adds weight to the idea that 'the social pathology of the lone mother is just as imaginary as the social desirability of the nuclear family' (McIntosh 1996: 150). While evidence of this nature is important and needs wide and substantiated exposure if we are to check tendencies to homogenize the negative experiences of lone mother households, I am equally concerned to stress that this should not lead to oppositional counter stereotypes.

Little, for example, is to be gained by denying that women suffer social or economic inequalities as heads of household when they can clearly benefit from greater assistance from the state and other constituencies in their roles as lone parents, nor when greater societal support of motherhood in general and committed promotion of gender equality, could greatly expand women's options and livelihood capacities. Indeed, it is undeniable that female heads of household face an above-average risk of poverty and that children are disadvantaged (amongst other things) by competing demands on their mothers' time (especially where there are limited childcare facilities). Yet, as Roseneil and Mann (1996: 205) point out, while the material deprivation suffered by many lone mothers and their children might conceivably be regarded as a social problem in need of policy attention, it is more usually the case (especially in government circles and the media) that lone mothers themselves become 'the problem' (see also Phoenix 1996: 174). Aside from the fact that focusing on lone mothers reinforces assumptions that women are accountable for child welfare in a way in which men are not (Moore 1996: 63), 'problem mothers' are regarded as bad for society, with concern centring 'far more on what are seen as dangers to *others* of lone parenthood' (Laws 1996: 64, emphasis in original). This not only extends to children and the state, as already discussed, but also to the 'supposed effects of men cut loose from family responsibilities' (ibid., see below).[27] Taken collectively, these responses scapegoat women and shift emphasis away from wider structures of gender inequality (Moore 1996: 74). They also feed into the notion that motherhood is only acceptable in the context of a male-headed household, preferably based around a first and only marriage (see Collins 1991: 159; Hewitt and Leach 1993).

Leading on from this, another potential counter-stereotype is that male-headed households are bad for women, but I see no reason to undermine male household headship or couple-based parenting when this clearly works in several cases. As Gutmann (1996: 256), amongst others, has observed, diversity is as much a feature of male- as female-headed households. This point is as critical for men as it is for women, since even if 'responsible and respected family man' may be a less than accurate description of many husbands/fathers (McIntosh 1996: 151), an unproblematized ideal of the heterosexual two-parent family means that men who visibly fall outside this arrangement are subject to charges of personal failure or deviancy. With reference to the UK, Westwood (1996: 27) observes that part and parcel of the 'vilification' of lone mothers is the construction of men who abandon their (material) responsibilities to their offspring as 'feckless fathers'. While in Britain these discussions have mainly been grounded in moves to cut the welfare bill, parallel observations can be found in the literature on Latin America, where Lehmann (1994) notes that the frequent pathologization of poor urban men as 'violent and drunken' means that the 'analysis of household dynamics is too often side-tracked into the denunciation of the consequences of male misbehaviour' (see also Gutmann 1996). Such constructions fail to acknowledge the immense constraints men face in fulfilling normative (and sometimes legally specified) familial roles as 'breadwinners',[28] and might conceivably push men further away from taking an active responsibility for their children, whether as members of households or as non-resident fathers. In turn, this may simply increase risk for, and isolation of, (lone) mothers.

Aside from a discernible need to move towards more flexible ideals of gender and parenthood in light of contemporary realities, finding ways to equalize the status, legitimacy and rights of different households is critical when lone mother units are usually regarded as a 'mutant form of the so-called "normal" two-parent family' (Hardey and Crow 1991: 2). As Westwood (1996: 26) argues of Britain under the Conservative Party: 'The suggestion from government rhetoric is that single parents with children are a category apart from "the family" rather than one instance of the increasing diversity of family forms...' Whether or not a shift towards wholehearted acceptance of the coexistence of a plurality of household types is possible remains questionable, however. As Smart (1996: 47) has argued with reference to Foucauldian notions of 'normalizing discourse' (see earlier):

> For there to be a normative ideal of motherhood, it is perhaps self-evident that there must be those who 'fall' outside the norm. These two are in a symbiotic relationship and, although the boundaries between them are redrawn according to fashions in motherhood, without the one, the other could not have a social existence.

One possible strategy to break down this binary pairing of empty stereotypes is to pinpoint the contradictions characterizing state and societal attitudes towards gender, parenthood and family life. McIntosh (1996: 150) has pointed up the irony in the fact that critics 'bewail the "culture of dependency"' of lone mothers on the state, yet do not deplore the dependency of women within male-headed households (see also Duncan and Edwards 1997). Another mechanism might be to find ways to create more equitable legal and social frameworks for male- and female-headed households. One suggestion offered in the background document prepared on Mexican families for the Fourth Women's World Conference is to incorporate a (re)definition of family in the country's civil codes that encompasses diversity and heterogeneity (de Oliveira et al. 1995: 27). Another initiative, specified in the National Poverty Plan in Costa Rica (see earlier), is to foster greater self-esteem among female household heads by means of group and community consciousness-raising initiatives (Presidencia de la República 1996: 46). Whether or not these plans will materialize into concerted action and effect changes in attitudes in society at large, at the very least, lone mothers in Mexico and Costa Rica have been spared the anti-lone mother rhetoric espoused by some governments in the North. While this, in part, is because state support for lone mothers in Mexico and Costa Rica is not as costly as it is in the UK, for example, it is clearly an issue here.[29] However, the fact that governments under greater economic pressure to reduce social expenditure are taking a more benign stance to female household headship than their economically advantaged counterparts (and in Costa Rica are going as far as to target eroding public funds to female household heads) suggests that greater acknowledgement of what is going on in these countries might be salutary for Northern governments. Aside from the value of lessons to be learned from the comparative analysis of social policy, particularly in respect of how children are affected as well as mothers,[30] acknowledging experiences from the South could also help to challenge the intellectual grip of Northern perspectives on 'global' phenomena, which women-headed households are rapidly in the process of becoming.

NOTES

1. This chapter draws heavily from comparative research on female-headed households in Mexico, Costa Rica and the Philippines conducted during 1994–5 under the auspices of a Nuffield Foundation Social Science Research Fellowship. An earlier version of the paper entitled 'Women-headed Households in Mexico and Costa Rica: Grassroots and Global Perspectives on Lone Motherhood' was presented in the panel session 'Poverty, Gender and Inequality: Female Household Headship in Urban Latin America' at the XX meeting of the Latin American Studies Association in Guadalajara, Mexico, 17–19 April 1997. This will be published in Spanish in a volume of proceedings edited by the panel organizer, Dr Mercedes González de la Rocha, CIESAS del Occidente, Guadalajara. I would like to record my thanks to the Nuffield Foundation for funding the research, and to the British Academy for assisting my participation in the LASA conference. Gratitude also goes to Dr Cathy McIlwaine, Queen Mary and Westfield College, University of London, Dr David Lewis, London School of Economics, and Dr Stephanie Barrientos, University of Hertfordshire, for their helpful comments on previous drafts.
2. These are by no means the only 'global orthodoxies' attached to female household headship. One extremely widespread and fundamental one noted by Varley (1996) is the tendency to overstate the proportion of female-headed households on a world scale.
3. My work in low-income communities has taken place over a number of years. In Mexico, interviews have been held with a cumulative total of over 400 low-income households in the cities of Querétaro, León and Puerto Vallarta during 1982–3, 1986, 1992 and 1994. In Costa Rica, a total of 350 households were interviewed in the towns of Cañas, Liberia and Santa Cruz in the north-west province of Guanacaste in 1989, 1992, 1994 and 1996 (see Chant 1997a: Chapter 6, also Chant 1991a, b for methodological details).
4. More detailed reviews of case study material relating to stereotypes of lone mother households can be found in Chant (1997a: Chapters 7 and 8, 1997b).
5. Many discussions omit to point up the fact that there are also many lone mothers who have been married and that they are also found in large numbers among middle-class and elite groups. Bortolaia Silva (1996: 3), for example, highlights the irony of focusing on working class lone parents in Britain, when, in late 1992, all six of Queen Elizabeth's grandchildren were living in lone mother families!
6. I put 'traditional' in inverted commas here to signal the use of the term within discourses which have 'naturalized' two-parent household life and ignored its cultural and historical specificity.
7. In the UK in 1991, as many as 19 per cent of households were lone-parent units (92 per cent of which were headed by women), compared with 13 per cent in 1981, and 8 per cent in 1971 (Burghes 1994: 7 and 50; Duncan and Edwards 1994).
8. Member countries of the OECD (Organization for Economic Co-operation and Development) are Australia, Austria, Belgium, Canada,

Denmark, Finland, France, Germany, Ireland, Italy, Japan, New Zealand, the Netherlands, Norway, Sweden, Switzerland, the UK and the USA (Baylies 1996: 95n).
9. Feminist debate on research methods and epistemology has drawn attention to the difficulties of 'recovering women's knowledge and voices' (Parpart and Marchand 1995: 18), and to the need for dedicated scrutiny of interview procedures and analyses. For example, the nature of interviews (location, content, mode of questioning, etc.), connections between researcher and 'researched' (relations of power, language differences, and so on), and characteristics and standpoints of the interviewer (colour, class, politics, research agenda, personal experiences) all affect what is said, what is revealed, what information is used in the research account, and how it is presented. In short, 'truths' are 'constructed' and cannot be read off dialogue as realities (see Maynard 1994; Phoenix 1994; Thompson 1992). As Maynard and Purvis (1994: 6) sum up: 'There is no such thing as "raw" or authentic experience which is unmediated by interpretation', and this applies as much to the researcher as the researched. Other considerations include the fact that female heads do not necessarily identify themselves solely in this manner, but have multiple subject positions and identities (affected by where they live, their marital status, stage in the life course, and so on). A final issue, of particular relevance to the present work, is that the in-depth semi-structured interviews from which I draw most of the qualitative material were carried out with relatively small numbers of respondents, so cannot be argued to be 'representative' as much as indicative (see note 3).
10. Embracing the need to find more meaningful instruments to measure poverty, for example, the UNDP has recently developed a 'Capability Poverty Measure', latterly translated into the Human Poverty Index. The CPM is assessed on the basis of the proportions of people lacking basic or minimally essential capabilities. Although the measure is relatively crude thus far, it comprises three indicators which go beyond the more narrow criteria conventionally used in poverty assessments:

(a) 'health capability' – represented by children under 5 years of age who are underweight,
(b) 'the capability for healthy reproduction' – represented by the proportion of births unattended by trained personnel,
(c) 'the capability to be educated and knowledgeable' – represented by female rather than male or general illiteracy as a means of recognizing that women's deprivation seriously undermines the human development of families and societies (see UNDP 1996: 27).

11. In the case study settlements in both Mexico and Costa Rica, for example, male household heads are likely to earn twice as much as their female counterparts (Chant 1997a: Chapter 6). See also Ghigliazza et al. (1995: 18) for national data pertaining to Mexico, and Gindling (1993) and UNDP (1995: 36) on Costa Rica.
12. A study of 1990 Mexican census data by Cortés and Rubalcava (1994) cited in the background report on Mexican families prepared for Beijing by de Oliveira et al. (1995) showed that at national level, the poorest households

in Mexico (as defined by per capita incomes), are male-headed households with exclusively female wage-earners (2.5 per cent of all households), female-headed households with exclusively male incomes (3.8 per cent), and households headed by men with exclusively male earnings (64.7 per cent). In contrast, the intermediate strata comprises female-headed households with exclusively female earnings (6.7 per cent of total households), women-headed households with predominantly male earnings (2 per cent), and households headed by women with predominantly female earnings (1.4 per cent of the total) (de Oliveira *et al*. 1995: 17). In other words, on the basis of per capita incomes, women-headed households would not appear to be a disproportionate number of the poorest households in Mexico (see also Acosta Díaz 1992: 3; González de la Rocha 1997).

13. This is hardly surprising given that women in most societies have fewer survival opportunities than men. Taking Sen as her starting point, Wilson (1991: 31) points out that 'the less power people have to order their lives satisfactorily outside the household, the more likely they are to remain within it' (see also Kandiyoti 1991).

14. While some studies in other places indicate similar findings (for example, that of Bradshaw 1996 on Honduras; Fonseca 1991 on Brazil; Safa 1995: 83 on Puerto Rico), work on Guadalajara, Mexico by González de la Rocha (1988) reveals that low earnings may force some women to stay in male-headed households or to return to former partners.

15. In a related vein, it is interesting that a panel study of 950 UK lone parents conducted by the Policy Studies Institute over the years 1991–6 showed that lone parents were just as likely to improve their economic condition by getting a job as they were by setting up home with a new partner. The study also indicated that around half the respondents were not concerned about finding someone else to live with. The reasons given included a preference for living independently, the fact that they had not met anyone they liked sufficiently since the termination of their previous relationship, the fact that a new 'father' would not be good for the children and, among widows, concern about losing social security benefits (Ford 1996b).

16. Echoing Bortolaia Silva's (1996: 3) assertion that 'Poverty and moral stigmatisation are recurrent aspects of lone motherhood', non-marriage and/or illegitimacy appear to be implicit in constructing a picture of disadvantage for the offspring of lone mother households given that, technically speaking, family law in most countries upholds the principle of paternal maintenance. Indeed, one popular conventional wisdom is that most lone mothers are young, unmarried women, where as, in reality, the proportion of lone mothers they constitute is a small minority in most countries (see, for example, Bradshaw 1996 on Honduras; Chant 1997a on Mexico, Costa Rica and the Philippines; Laws 1996; McIntosh 1996 on the UK; but for an exception see Safa 1995: 138 on Cuba). Beyond this, it is also the case that in societies where marriage is a normative ideal, women without what Lewis (1993: 32) calls 'male guardians' are likely to be treated as a suspicious moral and sexual category (see also Buitelaar 1995: 8–11; Chandler 1991: 6; Gordon 1994: 3–4, Morrison 1995).

17. 'Father absence' is clearly a complex and multi-dimensional concept, and depending on context and vantage point is not intrinsically problematic. On the basis of his work in Mexico City, Gutmann (1996: 76) makes the observation that the comparatively greater absence of fathers from the home than mothers can lead men to 'indulge their children when they are with them', and also points out that absence is used by some fathers, especially from older age groups, as a means of maintaining an emotional distance deemed necessary to exercise authority in the household (ibid.). See also Burgess (1997: 22–34) on the interrelations of changing constructions of fatherhood and levels of contact/intimacy with children in the UK.

18. As Valentine (1997b) notes for the UK, although mothers are still idealized as having principal responsibility for children's welfare, lone mothers and working mothers alike find it very difficult to live up to this prescription.

19. Laws (1996: 61) points out that UK newspaper articles on the Conservative Party's 'Back to Basics'/'Family Values' campaigns of the 1990s were overwhelmingly negative, usually focusing on individual women and their motives. For example, typical headlines include those in *The Times* (9 July 1993): 'Where daddies are a myth. Low-life Britain today – by the no-hope single mums and their fatherless children', and the *Sunday Express* (26 September 1993): 'Britain can no longer afford these mothers'. Such captions, in turn, derived from numerous pronouncements by Cabinet ministers on the undesirability of lone motherhood, one symptomatic speech being that by John Redwood (then Secretary of State for Wales) at the Conservative Summer School in Cardiff in July 1993:

> One of the biggest social problems of our day is the surge in single parent families. Everyone would wish to help the young family that has suddenly lost a father through death, or if the mother has been abused or badly treated by the father and the relationship has broken down. What is more worrying is the trend in some places for young women to have babies with no apparent intention of even trying a marriage or stable relationship with the father of the child. (cited in Laws 1996: 61)

In Costa Rica and Mexico, by contrast, more sympathetic appreciation of women's difficulties as lone mothers is apparent. As examples, one article in the Costa Rican newspaper, *La República* (4 October 1994) considering the rising numbers of lone mothers in the country ran: '*este tipo de mujer se coloca en una posición de desventaja. Su autoestima es muy baja y por una cuestión de socialización se le enseñó desde niña a ser madre y a depender del hombre, lo cual le impide colocarse laboralmente*' ('this type of woman [female head] finds herself disadvantaged. Her self-esteem is very low, and for reasons of socialization she is brought up to be a mother and to depend on a man, which then makes it difficult to find a foothold in the labour force'). A similar example from Mexico lies in the section on women's issues from Enrique Burgos's electoral campaign for the state governorship of Querétaro in 1991: '*Las mujeres que en forma despectiva se las señala con la marca de "madres solteras", normalmente y por esta triste condición social, pierden la oportunidad de seguir preparando para poder alcanzar las metas que solo la preparación admite*' ('Women who are contemptuously labelled

"single mothers", normally, due to this wretched social condition, lose the opportunity of pursuing and attaining the goals that only education/training permit').
20. Coverage of these provisions 'on the ground' may be less than comprehensive, however. For example, in my survey of 350 households in low-income communities in Liberia, Cañas and Santa Cruz in 1989, only 37.5 per cent of widows were in receipt of an old age or widow's pension, and a mere 15 per cent of households received child allowances or free milk (Chant 1997a: 175).
21. I say 'technically', because no lone mother in the communities in Guanacaste has ever reported receiving a lone mother pension.
22. The '*hogares comunitarios*' system dates back to President Calderón's administration, but remained extremely limited until Figueres took office in 1994 (Chant 1997a: 51).
23. Greater state support for childcare in Costa Rica during the present decade is also due to the passing of the Law Promoting Social Equality for Women in 1990 which called for increased funding for daycare centres in rural areas and state institutions. Although lone mothers were not specified as primary beneficiaries, this prescription was clearly relevant to the potential viability of women-headed households. Clauses with comparable implications in the Social Equality Law included the compulsory joint registration of property in marriage (or in non-formalized unions, registration in the woman's name), prohibition of dismissal from employment on grounds of pregnancy, and greater rights for victims of domestic violence summarily to evict the perpetrators from their homes (see IJSA 1990; also Badilla and Blanco 1996; Chant 1997a: 136; Facio 1989; Vincenzi 1991).
24. Some daycare in Costa Rica has also been provided as part of the 'CEN-CINAI' programme (*Centros Infantiles de Nutrición y Atención Integral*) which is oriented to children under seven years of age at high nutritional and psycho-social risk. Entry to the scheme is based on the calculation of points attributed to different risk factors such as mothers being out at work (10 points), mothers under the age of 18 (20 points), mothers with no more than primary education (10 points), presence of 'social pathology' in the family (15 points), and elements such as insecure employment and informal housing being accorded 5 points apiece. Within this schema, single motherhood is attributed a high risk value of 15 points, although this has by no means guaranteed their children's eligibility to date (see Grosh 1994: 89–91).
25. One of the few forms of state support for lone mothers in Mexico is the priority technically given to those in employment for subsidized childcare in the nurseries of the DIF (*Desarrollo Integral Familiar*/Integrated Family Services). However, competition for places is extremely high (see Chant 1997a: 124, Gutmann 1996: 76).
26. This parallels policy discourses on lone mothers in many other parts of the world (especially the North), in which it is assumed that state welfare will provide perverse incentives for increased numbers and thereby contribute to a growing 'underclass' of citizens reliant on government handouts (see Duncan and Edwards 1994, 1997; Folbre 1991: 111; Kamerman and Kahn

1988: 27; Laws 1996: 64–5; Millar 1992: 156, Safa 1995: 166). The fact is, however, that in most societies welfare payments are so limited that they are hardly likely to provide an incentive for the formation of women-headed households. This is certainly applicable to Costa Rica where, as noted in the context of education and training schemes, government support arguably remains more symbolic than substantive. Having said this, it is conceivable that greater tolerance on the part of the state to lone motherhood (through varying combinations of social programmes, gender-aware legislation and backing for women's organizations) may help to create a more sympathetic environment for the existence of women-headed households and thereby help to diminish some of the social opprobrium which restrains their emergence in so many countries (see Chant 1997a: Chapters 3–5 for fuller discussions of the wide range of economic, social, cultural and other factors affecting female headship in different parts of the world).

27. Smart (1996: 56) citing the work of Patricia Morgan (1995) notes the existence of a popular belief that lone motherhood is not only bad for children, but for men and wider society, insofar as men are 'civilised' through marriage and by assuming responsibilities for wives and offspring (see also Laws 1996: 65). See also Giddens (1992) for a more general discussion of men's and women's relations to marriage and sexuality.

28. For example, Article 35 of the Costa Rican Family Code specifies that husbands should be the principal economic providers for their families (Vincenzi 1991: 262).

29. In 1989, 43 per cent of all expenditure by the UK Department of Social Security was accounted for by lone parent households (see Hardey and Glover 1991: 93). This gave rise to criticisms that government subsidies were making single parenthood more attractive than two-parent families. Writing in a publication of the right-wing think tank, the Institute of Economic Affairs, for example, Parker (1995: 88) argued: 'Whether or not one takes a moral view about lone parent families, there is no doubt that under present arrangements they impose a costly burden on the rest of society – hence reason enough, from an economist's point of view, for changes that will strengthen the traditional two-parent family.'

30. Laws (1996) and Waldfogel (1996) point out for the UK and USA respectively, that punitive policies towards lone mothers are often remarkably silent on the prospective outcomes for children. See also Bruce and Lloyd (1992).

REFERENCES

Acosta-Belen, E. and C. Bose (1995) 'Colonialism, Structural Subordination and Empowerment: Women in the Development Process in Latin America and the Caribbean'. pp. 15–36 in C. Bose and E. Acosta-Belen (eds) *Women in the Latin American Development Process*, Philadelphia: Temple University Press.

Acosta Diaz, F. (1992) 'Hogares Más Pobres con Jefaturas Femeninas', *Demos*, 2, 30–1.

Baden, S. with K. Milward (1995) *Gender and Poverty*, Sussex: Institute of Development Studies, Bridge Report No. 30.
Badilla, A. and L. Blanco (1996) *Código de la Mujer*, San José: Editorial Porvenir S.A./CECADE.
Baulch, B. (1996) Editorial. 'The New Poverty Agenda: a Disputed Consensus', *IDS Bulletin*, 27 (1), 1–10.
Baylies, C. (1996) 'Diversity in Patterns of Parenting and Household Formation' pp. 76–96 in E. Bortolaia Silva (ed.) *Good Enough Mothering? Feminist Perspectives on Lone Motherhood*, London: Routledge.
Beall, J. (1996) 'Social Security and Social Networks among the Urban Poor in Pakistan', *Habitat International*, 19 (4), 427–45.
Beall, J. (1997) 'Households, Livelihood and the Urban Environment: Social Development Perspectives on Solid Waste Disposal in Faisalabad City, Pakistan'. Unpublished PhD thesis, Department of Geography, London School of Economics.
Benavides, B. (1996) *Total de Hogares Comunitarios por Provincia, Cantón, Distrito, Según: Madre Comunitaria, Número de Hogar, Niñas y Niños Beneficiarios, Marzo 1996*, San José: Instituto Mixto de Ayuda Social, Dirección Programa Hogares Comunitarios, Departamento Ejecución Técnico.
Beneria, L. (1991) 'Structural Adjustment, the Labour Market and the Household: The Case of Mexico' pp. 161–83 in G. Standing and V. Tokman (eds) *Towards Social Adjustment: Labour Market Issues in Structural Adjustment*, Geneva: International Labour Office.
Beneria, L. and M. Roldan (1987) *The Crossroads of Class and Gender: Industrial Homework, Subcontracting and Household Dynamics in Mexico City*, Chicago: University of Chicago Press.
Blanc-Szanton, C. (1990) 'Gender and Inter-generational Resource Allocation among Thai and Sino-Thai Households' pp. 79–102 in: L. Dube and R. Palriwala (eds) *Structures and Strategies: Women, Work and Family*, New Delhi: Sage.
Bortolaia Silva, E. (1996) 'Introduction' pp. 1–9 in E. Bortolaia Silva (ed.) *Good Enough Mothering? Feminist Perspectives on Lone Motherhood*, London: Routledge.
Bortolaia Silva, E. (ed.) (1996) *Good Enough Mothering? Feminist Perspectives on Lone Motherhood*, London: Routledge.
Boyden, J. with P. Holden (1991) *Children of the Cities*, London: Zed Books.
Bradshaw, J. and J. Millar, 1991. *Lone-parent Families in the UK*, London: HMSO.
Bradshaw, S. (1996) 'Female-headed Households in Honduras: a Study of their Formation and Survival in Low-income Communities'. Unpublished PhD thesis, Department of Geography, London School of Economics.
Bruce, J. and C. Lloyd (1992) *Finding the Ties that Bind: Beyond Headship and the Household*, New York: Population Council/Washington DC: International Center for Research on Women.
Brydon, L. and K. Legge (1996) *Adjusting Society: The IMF, the World Bank and Ghana*, London: I.B. Tauris.
Buitelaar, M. (1995) 'Widows' Worlds: Representations and Realities' pp. 1–18 in J. Bremmer and L. Van den Bosch (eds) *Between Poverty and the Pyre: Moments in the History of Widowhood*, London: Routledge.

Bullock, S. (1994) *Women and Work*, London: Zed Books.
Burgess, A. (1997) *Fatherhood Reclaimed: The Making of the Modern Father*, Vermilion: London.
Burghes, L. (1994) *Lone Parenthood and Family Disruption: the Outcomes for Children*, London: Family Policy Studies Centre, Occasional Paper No. 18.
Burgos, E. (1991) *Encuentros de Análisis y Propuestas de la Sociedad Civil: Campaña Política*, Querétaro: Editorial Mazar.
Buvinic, M. (1990) 'The Vulnerability of Women-headed Households: Policy Questions and Options for Latin America and the Caribbean'. Paper presented at the Economic Commission for Latin America and the Caribbean Meeting on 'Vulnerable Women', Vienna, 26–30 November.
Buvinic, M. (1995) *Investing in Women*,Washington DC: International Center for Research on Women, Policy Series.
Buvinic, M. and Gupta, G.R. (1993) 'Responding to Insecurity in the 1990s: Targeting Woman-headed Households and Woman-maintained Families in Developing Countries'. Paper presented at the International Workshop 'Insecurity in the 1990s: Gender and Social Policy in an International Perspective', London School of Economics and European Association of Development Institutes, London, 5–6 April.
Chalita, P. (1992) 'Sobrevivencia en la Ciudad: Una Conceptualización de las Unidades Domésticas Encabezadas por Mujeres en América Latina' pp. 271–97 in A. Massolo (ed.) *Mujeres y Ciudades: Participación Social, Vivienda y Vida Cotidiana*, México DF: El Colegio de México.
Chambers, R. (1983) *Rural Development: Putting the Last First*, Harlow: Longman.
Chambers, R. (1989) 'Vulnerability: How the Poor Cope', *IDS Bulletin*, 20(2) 1–9.
Chambers, R. (1995) 'Poverty and Livelihoods: Whose Reality Counts?', *Environment and Urbanisation*, 7(1), 173–204.
Chandler, J. (1991) *Women Without Husbands: an Exploration of the Margins of Marriage*, Houndmills, Basingstoke: Macmillan.
Chant, S. (1985) 'Single-parent Families: Choice or Constraint? The Formation of Female-headed Households in Mexican Shanty Towns', *Development and Change*, 16(4), 635–56.
Chant, S. (1991a) *Women and Survival in Mexican Cities: Perspectives on Gender, Labour Markets and Low-income Households*, Manchester: Manchester University Press.
Chant, S. (1991b) 'Gender, Households and Seasonal Migration in Guanacaste, Costa Rica', *European Review of Latin American and Caribbean Studies*, 50, 51–85.
Chant, S. (1997a) *Women-headed Households: Diversity and Dynamics in the Developing World*, Houndmills, Basingstoke: Macmillan.
Chant, S. (1997b) 'Women-headed Households: Poorest of the Poor? Perspectives from Mexico, Costa Rica and the Philippines', *IDS Bulletin*, 28(3), 26–48.
Chant, S. and C. McIlwaine (1995) *Women of a Lesser Cost: Female Labour, Foreign Exchange and Philippine Development*, London: Pluto Press.
Cleves Mosse, J. (1993) *Half the World, Half a Chance*, Oxford: Oxfam.
Collier, R. (1995) *Masculinity, Law and the Family*, London: Routledge.

Collins, S. (1991) 'The Transition from Lone-Parent Family to Step-Family' pp. 156–75 in M. Hardey and G. Crow (eds) *Lone-Parenthood: Coping with Constraints and Making Opportunities*, Hemel Hempstead: Harvester Wheatsheaf.
Cortes, F. and R.M. Rubalcava (1994) 'Monografía Censal Sobre el Ingreso de los Hogares, Proyecto MOCAMEX 1990', México DF: INEGI-SSA (mimeo).
Dennis, N. (1993) *Rising Crime and the Dismembered Family: How Conformist Intellectuals Have Campaigned against Common Sense*, London: Institute of Economic Affairs, Health and Welfare Unit.
Dennis, N. and Erdos, G. (1992) *Families without Fatherhood*, London: Institute of Economic Affairs, Health and Welfare Unit.
Duncan, S. and R. Edwards (1994) 'Lone Mothers and Paid Work: State Policies, Social Discourses and Neighbourhood Processes', Gender Institute, London School of Economics (mimeo).
Duncan, S. and R. Edwards (1996) 'Lone Mothers and Paid Work: Neighbourhoods, Local Labour Markets and Welfare State Régimes', *Social Politics: International Studies in Gender, State and Society*, 3 (4).
Duncan, S. and R. Edwards (1997) 'Lone Mothers and Paid Work: Human Capital or Gendered Moral Rationalities', Gender Institute Research Seminar Series, London School of Economics, 5 March.
Dwyer, D. and J. Bruce (eds) (1998) *A Home Divided: Women and Income in the Third World*, Stanford: Stanford University Press.
Edwards, R. and Duncan, S. (1996) 'Lone Mothers and Economic Activity', in F. Williams (ed.) *Social Policy: A Reader*, Cambridge: Polity Press.
Facio, A. (1989) 'La Igualdad Entre Hombres y Mujeres y las Relaciones Familiares en la Legislación Centroamericana', *Estudios Sociales Centroamericanos*, 50, 55–75.
Fernandez, O. (1992) '¿Qué Valores Valen Hoy en Costa Rica?' in J.M. Villasuso (ed.) *El Nuevo Rostro de Costa Rica*, Heredia: Centro de Estudios Democráticos de América Latina.
Folbre, N. (1991) 'Women on their Own: Global Patterns of Female Headship' pp. 69–126 in R. Gallin and A. Ferguson (eds) *The Women and International Development Annual Vol.2*, Boulder: Westview.
Folbre, N. (1994) *Who Pays for the Kids? Gender and the Structures of Constraint*, London: Routledge.
Fonseca, C. (1991) 'Spouses, Siblings and Sex-linked Bonding: a Look at Kinship Organisation in a Brazilian Slum' pp. 133–60 in E. Jelin (ed.) *Family, Household and Gender Relations in Latin America*, London: Kegan Paul International/ Paris: UNESCO.
Ford, R. (1996a) *Childcare in the Balance: How Lone Parents Make Decisions About Work*, London: Policy Studies Institute.
Ford, R. (1996b) 'What Happens to Lone Parents?', Population Studies Seminar, Department of Social Policy and Administration, London School of Economics, 5 December.
Ghigliazza, A. with M. Aguilar and D. Arriage (1995) *Mujer, Desarrollo Sustentable y Combate a la Pobreza*, México DF: CONAPO, Comité Nacional Coordinadora para la IV Conferencia Mundial Sobre la Mujer.
Giddens A. (1992) *The Transformation of Intimacy: Sexuality, Love and Eroticism in Modern Societies*, Cambridge: Polity Press.

Gindling, T.H. (1993) 'Women's Wages and Economic Crisis in Costa Rica', *Economic Development and Cultural Change*, 41(2), 277–97.
Goldenberg, O. (1994) 'En Clave de Género', pp. 185–233 in O. Goldenberg and V. Acuña, *Género y la Informalidad*, San José: FLACSO.
Gonzalez de la Rocha, M. (1988) 'De Por Qué las Mujeres Aguantan Golpes y Cuernos: Un Análsis de Hogares sin Varón en Guadalajara' pp. 205–27 in L. Gabayet et al. (eds) *Mujeres y Sociedad: Salario, Hogar y Acción Social en el Occidente de México*, Guadalajara: El Colegio de Jalisco/CIESAS del Occidente.
González de la Rocha, M. (1994a) *The Resources of Poverty: Women and Survival in a Mexican City*, Oxford: Blackwell.
Gonzalez de la Rocha, M. (1994b) 'Household Headship and Occupational Position in Mexico', pp. 1–24 in E. Kennedy and M. González de la Rocha, *Poverty and Well-Being in the Household: Case Studies of the Developing World*, San Diego: Center for Iberian and Latin American Studies, University of California San Diego.
González de la Rocha, M. (1995) 'Social Restructuring in Two Mexican Cities: an Analysis of Domestic Groups in Guadalajara and Monterrey', *European Journal of Development Research*, 7(2), 389–406.
González de la Rocha, M. (1997) 'Hogares de Jefatura Femenina en México: Patrones y Formas de Vida'. Paper presented at the session 'Pobreza, Género y Desigualdad: Jefatura Femenina en Hogares Urbanos Latino-americanos', XX International Congress of the Latin American Studies Association, Guadalajara, Mexico, 17–19 April.
Gordon, T. (1994) *Single Women*, Houndmills, Basingstoke: Macmillan.
Graham, H. (1987) 'Being Poor: Perceptions and Coping Strategies of Lone Mothers' pp. 56–74 in J. Brannen and G. Wilson (eds) *Give and Take in Families: Studies in Resource Distribution*, London: Allen and Unwin.
Graham, H. (1993) *Hardship and Health in Women's Lives*, Hemel Hempstead: Harvester Wheatsheaf.
Grosh, M. (1994) *Administering Targeted Social Programs in Latin America: From Platitudes to Practice*, Washington DC: World Bank.
Gutmann, M. (1996) *The Meanings of Macho: Being a Man in Mexico City*, Berkeley: University of California Press.
Hackenberg, R., A. Murphy and H. Selby (1981) 'The Household in the Secondary Cities of the Third World'. Paper prepared in advance for the Wenner-Gren Foundation Symposium 'Households: Changing Form and Function', New York, 8–15 October.
Hardey, M. and G. Crow (1991) 'Introduction' pp. 1–18 in M. Hardey and G. Crow (eds) *Lone Parenthood: Coping with Constraints and Making Opportunities*, Hemel Hempstead: Harvester Wheatsheaf.
Hardey, M. and J. Glover (1991) 'Income, Employment, Daycare and Lone Parenthood' pp. 88–109 in M. Hardey and G. Crow (eds) *Lone Parenthood: Coping with Constraints and Making Opportunities*, Hemel Hempstead: Harvester Wheatsheaf.
Heward, C. (1996) 'Masculinities and Families' pp. 35–48 in M. Mac an Ghaill (ed.) *Understanding Masculinities: Social Relations and Cultural Arenas*, Buckingham: Open University Press.
Hewitt, P. and P. Leach (1993) *Social Justice, Children and Families*, London: Institute for Public Policy Research.

Hobson, B. (1994) 'Solo Mothers, Social Policy Regimes and the Logics of Gender' pp. 170–88 in D. Sainsbury (ed.) *Gendering Welfare States*, London: Sage.
IJSA (Investigaciones Juridicicas, A.) (1990) *Ley de Promoción de la Igualdad de la Mujer*, San José: IJSA.
Instraw (1992) 'Women and the Household' pp. 185–201 in K. Saradamoni (ed.) *Finding the Household: Methodological and Empirical Issues*, New Delhi: Sage.
Jackson, C. (1996) 'Rescuing Gender From the Poverty Trap', *World Development*, 24(3), 489–504.
Kabeer, N. (1994) *Reversed Realities: Gender Hierarchies in Development Thought*, London: Verso.
Kabeer, N. (1996) 'Agency, Well-being and Inequality: Reflections on the Gender Dimensions of Poverty', *IDS Bulletin*, 27(1), 11–21.
Kamerman, S. and A. Kahn (1988) *Mothers Alone, Strategies for a Time of Change*, Dover, Mass.: Auburn Publishing House Company.
Kandiyoti, D. (1991) 'Bargaining with Patriarchy' pp. 104–18 in J. Lorber and S. Farrell (eds) *The Social Construction of Gender*, Newbury Park: Sage.
Kennedy, E. (1994) 'Development Policy, Gender of Head of Household, and Nutrition' pp. 25–42 in E. Kennedy and M. González de la Rocha, *Poverty and Well-Being in the Household: Case Studies of the Developing World*, San Diego: Center for Iberian and Latin American Studies, University of California San Diego.
Kumari, R. (1989) *Women-headed Households in Rural India*, New Delhi: Radiant Publishers.
Lara, S. with T. Barry and P. Simonson (1995) *Inside Costa Rica*, Albuquerque: Resource Center Press.
Larsson, A. (1989) *Women Householders and Housing Strategies: The Case of Gaborone, Botswana*, Gävle: The National Swedish Institute for Building Research.
Laws, S. (1996) 'The Single Mothers Debate: a Children's Rights Perspective' pp. 60–77 in J. Holland and L. Adkins (eds) *Sex, Sensibility and the Gendered Body*, Houndmills, Basingstoke: Macmillan.
Legum, M. (1996) 'The Right Time to Institutionalise Gender', *Social Development Newsletter* (ODA, London), 4(2), 2–5.
Lehmann, D. (1994) 'Bringing Society Back in: Latin America in a Post-Development World'. Draft application for British Academy Research Fellowship, Centre for Latin American Studies, University of Cambridge.
LeVine, S. in collaboration with C. Sunderland Correa (1993) *Dolor y Alegría: Women and Social Change in Urban Mexico*, Madison, Wisc.: University of Wisconsin.
Lewis, D. (1993) 'Going it Alone: Female-Headed Households, Rights and Resources in Rural Bangladesh', *European Journal of Development Research*, 5(2), 23–42.
Lewis, O. (1966) 'The Culture of Poverty', *Scientific American* (October), 19–25.
Lloyd, C. and A. Gage-Brandon (1993) 'Women's Role in Maintaining Households: Family Welfare and Sexual Inequality in Ghana', *Population Studies*, 47, 115–31.

López Barajas, M. and H. Izazola Conde (1995) *El Perfil Censal de los Hogares y las Familias en México*, Aguascalientes: Instituto Nacional de Estadística, Geografía e Informática.
Mädge, E. and Neusüss, C. (1994) 'Lone Mothers on Welfare in West Berlin: Disadvantaged Citizens or Women Avoiding Patriarchy?', *Environment and Planning, A*, 26, 1419–33.
Maynard, M. (1994) 'Methods, Practice and Epistemology: the Debate about Feminism and Research' pp. 10–26 in M. Maynard and J. Purvis (eds) *Researching Women's Lives From a Feminist Perspective*, London: Taylor and Francis.
Maynard, M. and J. Purvis (1994) 'Doing Feminist Research' pp. 1–9 in M. Maynard and J. Purvis (eds) *Researching Women's Lives From a Feminist Perspective*, London: Taylor and Francis.
McIlwaine, C. (1996) 'Ethnicity and Vulnerability: the Case of Afro-Caribbeans in Limón, Costa Rica.' Paper presented at the symposium 'Vulnerable Groups in Latin American Cities', Annual Conference of the Society of Latin American Studies, University of Leeds, 29–31 March.
McIntosh, M. (1996) 'Social Anxieties about Lone Motherhood and Ideologies of the Family: Two Sides of the Same Coin' pp. 148–56 in E. Bortolaia Silva (ed.) *Good Enough Mothering? Feminist Perspectives on Lone Motherhood*, London: Routledge.
Menjívar, R. and J. Trejos (1992) *La Pobreza en América Central*, 2nd edition. San José: FLACSO.
Merrick, T. and Schmink, M. (1983) 'Households Headed by Women and Urban Poverty in Brazil' pp. 244–71 in M. Buvinic, M. Lycette and W. McGreevey (eds) *Women and Poverty in the Third World*, Baltimore: Johns Hopkins University Press.
Millar, J. (1992) 'Lone Mothers and Poverty' pp. 149–61 in C. Glendinning and J. Millar (eds). *Women and Poverty in Britain in the 1990s*, Hemel Hempstead: Harvester Wheatsheaf.
Moghadam, V. (1996) 'The Feminisation of Poverty: Notes on a Concept and Trends'. Report prepared for United Nations Development Programme, Human Development Report, September.
Mohanty, C. (1991) 'Under Western Eyes: Feminist Scholarship and Colonial Discourses' pp. 51–80 in C. Mohanty, A. Russo and L. Torres, (eds) *Third World Women and the Politics of Feminism*, Bloomington: Indiana University Press.
Molyneux, M. (1996) *State, Gender and Institutional Change in Cuba's 'Special Period': The Federación de Mujeres Cubanas*, London: University of London, Institute of Latin American Studies, Research Papers No. 43.
Momsen, J. (1991) *Women and Development in the Third World*, London: Routledge.
Moore, H. (1994) *Is There a Crisis in the Family?*, Geneva: World Summit for Social Development, Occasional Paper No. 3.
Moore, H. (1996) 'Mothering and Social Responsibilities in a Cross-cultural Perspective' pp. 58–75 in E. Bortolaia Silva (ed.) *Good Enough Mothering? Feminist Perspectives on Lone Motherhood*, London: Routledge.
Morgan, P. (1995) *Farewell to the Family: Public Policy and Family Breakdown in Britain and the USA*, London: Institute for Economic Affairs, Health and Welfare Unit.

Morrison, J. (1995) 'The Circulation of Men: Marriage Practices and Gender Relations among the Bajou of Sabah, East Malaysia'. Paper presented at the 15th annual conference of the Association of Southeast Asian Studies in the United Kingdom, 'Gender and the Sexes in Southeast Asia', University of Durham, 29–31 March.
Moser, C. (1996) *Confronting Crisis: A Comparative Study of Household Responses to Poverty in Four Poor Urban Communities*, Washington DC: Environmentally Sustainable Development Studies and Monographs Series No. 8.
Moser, C., M. Gatehouse and H. Garcia (1996a) *Urban Poverty Research Sourcebook. Module I: Sub-city Level Household Survey*, Washington DC: UNDP/UNCHS/World Bank – Urban Management Program, Working Paper Series 5.
Moser, C., M. Gatehouse and H. Garcia (1996b) *Urban Poverty Research Sourcebook. Module II: Indicators of Urban Poverty*, Washington DC: UNDP/UNCHS/World Bank – Urban Management Program, Working Paper Series 5.
Moser, C. and C. McIlwaine (1997) *Household Responses to Poverty and Vulnerability Volume 3: Confronting Crisis in Commonwealth, Metro Manila, the Philippines*, Washington DC: World Bank, Urban Management Program.
Muthwa, S. (1993) 'Household Survival, Urban Poverty and Female Household Headship in Soweto: Some Key Issues for Further Policy Research'. Paper given in seminar series 'The Societies of Southern Africa in the 19th and 20th Centuries: Women, Colonialism and Commonwealth', Institute of Commonwealth Studies, University of London, 19 November.
National Council for One Parent Families (NCOPF) (1991) *Legal Rights of Single Mothers*, London: NCOPF.
National Council for One Parent Families (NCOPF) (1994) *Maintenance and the Child Support Agency*, London: NCOPF.
De Oliveira, O. with M. Eternod, M. De la Paz and A. Monroy (1995) *Las Familias Mexicanas*, México DF: CONAPO, Comité Nacional Coordinadora para la IV Conferencia Mundial Sobre la Mujer.
PANI (Patronato Nacional De la Infancia) (1990) *Características de la Mujer Agredida Atendida en el PANI*, San José: PANI.
Paolisso, M. and S. Gammage (1996) *Women's Responses to Environmental Degradation: Case Studies from Latin America*, Washington DC: International Center for Research on Women.
Parker, H. (1995) *Taxes, Benefits and Family Life: The Seven Deadly Traps*, London: Institute of Economic Affairs.
Parpart, J. and M. Marchand (1995) 'Exploding the Canon: An Introduction/Conclusion' pp. 1–22 in M. Marchand and J. Parpart (eds) *Feminism/Postmodernism/Development*, London: Routledge.
Phoenix, A. (1994) 'Practising Feminist Research: the Intersection of Gender and "Race" in the Research Process' pp. 49–71 in M. Maynard and J. Purvis (eds) *Researching Women's Lives from a Feminist Perspective*, London: Taylor and Francis.
Phoenix, A. (1996) 'Social Constructions of Lone Motherhood: a Case of Competing Discourses' pp. 175–90 in E. Bortolaia Silva (ed.) *Good Enough Mothering? Feminist Perspectives on Lone Motherhood*, London: Routledge.
Pothukuchi, K. (1993) 'Non-traditional Living Arrangements: Beyond the Nuclear Family' pp. 286–94 in H. Dandekar (ed.) *Shelter, Women and Development:*

First and Third World Perspectives, Ann Arbor, Mich.: George Wahr Publishing Company.

Presidencia de la República (1996) *Consejo del Sector Social*, San José: Instituto Mixto de Ayuda Social.

Pulsipher, L. (1993) ' "He Won't Let She Stretch She Foot": Gender Relations in Traditional West Indian Houseyards' pp. 107–21 in C. Katz and J. Monk (eds) *Full Circles: Geographies of Women over the Life Course*, London: Routledge.

Rathgeber, E. (1995) 'Gender and Development in Action' pp. 204–20 in M. Marchand and J. Parpart (eds) *Feminism/Postmodernism/Development*, London: Routledge.

Rogers, B. (1980) *The Domestication of Women: Discrimination in Developing Societies*, London: Tavistock.

Rosemblatt, K. (1997) 'She's Not a Libertine, He Doesn't Drink. Popular Morality and the State in Twentieth Century Chile'. Paper delivered at the XX International Congress of the Latin American Studies Association, Guadalajara, Mexico, 17–19 April.

Roseneil, S. and K. Mann (1996) 'Unpalatable Choices and Inadequate Families: Lone Mothers and the Underclass Debate' pp. 191–210 in E. Bortolaia Silva (ed.) *Good Enough Mothering? Feminist Perspectives on Lone Motherhood*, London: Routledge.

Safa, H. (1995) *The Myth of the Male Breadwinner: Women and Industrialisation in the Caribbean*, Boulder: Westview.

Safa, H. and P. Antrobus (1992) 'Women and the Economic Crisis in the Caribbean' pp. 49–82 in L. Benería and S. Feldman (eds) *Unequal Burden: Economic Crises, Persistent Poverty and Women's Work*, Boulder, Col.: Westview Press.

Sancho Montero, S. (1995) *El Programa Hogares Comunitarios en Costa Rica, Sus Primeros Pasos. Primera Parte*, San José: Instituto Mixto de Ayuda Social, Dirección Hogares Comunitarios.

Sarre, S. (1996) *A Place for Fathers: Fathers and Social Policy in the Post-War Period*, London: London School of Economics, Suntory and Toyota International Centre for Economics and Related Disciplines, Welfare State Programme Paper No. 125.

Schlyter, A. (1989) *Women Householders and Housing Strategies: The Case of Harare, Zimbabwe*, Gävle: The National Swedish Institute for Building Research.

Scott, A.M. (1994) *Divisions and Solidarities: Gender, Class and Employment in Latin America*, London: Routledge.

Secretaría de Gobernación (1996) *Alianza par la Igualdad: Programa Nacional de la Mujer, 1995–2000*, México DF: Secretaría de Gobernación.

Selby, H., A. Murphy and S. Lorenzen (1990) *The Mexican Urban Household: Organising for Self-Defence*, Austin: University of Texas Press.

Sen, A.K. (1981) *Poverty and Famines*, Oxford: Clarendon Press.

Sen, A.K. (1985) *Commodities and Capabilities*, Helsinki: United Nations University, World Institute for Development Economics Research.

Sen, A.K. (1987a) *Hunger and Entitlements*, Amsterdam: North-Holland Press.

Sen, A.K. (1987b) *Gender and Cooperative Conflicts*, Helsinki: World Institute for Development Economics Research, Working Paper No. 18.

Sen, A.K. (1990) 'Gender and Cooperative Conflicts' pp. 123–49 in I. Tinker (ed.) *Persistent Inequalities: Women and World Development*, New York: Oxford University Press.

Shanthi, K. (1994) 'Growing Incidence of Female Household Headship: Causes and Cure', *Social Action* (New Delhi), 44, 17–33.
Smart, C. (1996) 'Deconstructing Motherhood' pp. 37–57 in E. Bortolaia Silva (ed.) *Good Enough Mothering? Feminist Perspectives on Lone Motherhood*, London: Routledge.
Sojo, A. (1994) *Política Social en Costa Rica: Reformas Recientes*, San José: FLACSO, Programa de Costa Rica, Cuadernos de Ciencias Sociales No. 67.
Tacoli, C. (1996) 'Gender, Life Course and International Migration: The Case of Filipino Labour Migrants in Rome'. Unpublished PhD dissertation, Department of Geography, London School of Economics.
Thomas, J.J. (1995) *Surviving in the City: The Urban Informal Sector in Latin America*, London: Pluto Press.
Thompson, L. (1992) 'Feminist Methodology for Family Studies', *Journal of Marriage and the Family*, 54, 3–18.
Tinker, I. (1990) 'A Context for the Field and for the Book' pp. 3–13 in I. Tinker (ed.) *Persistent Inequalities: Women and World Development*, New York: Oxford University Press.
Udaygiri, M. (1995) 'Challenging Modernisation: Gender and Development, Postmodern Feminism and Activism' pp. 159–77 in M. Marchand and J. Parpart (eds) *Feminism/Postmodernism/Development*, London: Routledge.
UNDAW (United Nations Division for the Advancement of Women) (1991) 'Women and Households in a Changing World' pp. 30–52 in E. Masini and S. Stratigos (eds) *Women, Households and Change*, Tokyo: United Nations University Press.
UNDP (United Nations Development Programme) (1995) *Human Development Report 1995*, Oxford: Oxford University Press.
UNDP (United Nations Development Programme) (1996) *Human Development Report 1996*, Oxford: Oxford University Press.
Valentine, G. (1996) 'Angels and Devils: Moral Landscapes of Childhood', *Environment and Planning D: Society and Space*, 14, 581–99.
Valentine, G. (1997a) '"Oh Yes I Can". "Oh No You Can't". Children and Parents' Understandings of Kids' Competence to Negotiate Public Space Safely', *Antipode*, 29(1), 65–89.
Valentine, G. (1997b) 'Gender, Children and Cultures of Parenting'. Geography and Urban and Regional Planning Seminar, Department of Geography, London School of Economics, 30 January.
Varley, A. (1996) 'Women Heading Households: Some More Equal Than Others?', *World Development*, 24(3), 505–20.
Vincenzi, A. (1991) *Código Civil y Código de la Familia*, San José: Lehmann Editores.
Waldfogel, J. (1996) *What Do We Expect Lone Mothers to Do? Competing Agendas for Welfare Reform in the United States*, London: London School of Economics, Suntory and Toyota International Centre for Economics and Related Disciplines, Welfare State Programme Paper No. 124.
Weekes-Vagliani, W. (1992) 'Structural Adjustment and Gender in the Côte d'Ivoire' pp. 117–49 in H. Afshar and C. Dennis (eds) *Women and Adjustment Policies in the Third World*, Basingstoke: Macmillan.
Westwood, S. (1996) '"Feckless Fathers": Masculinities and the British State' pp. 21–34 in M. Mac an Ghaill (ed.) *Understanding Masculinities: Social Relations and Cultural Arenas*, Buckingham: Open University Press.

Willis, K. (1994) 'Women's Work and Social Network use in Oaxaca City, Mexico'. Unpublished DPhil dissertation, Nuffield College, Oxford.
Wilson, G. (1991) 'Thoughts on the Cooperative Conflict Model of the Household in Relation to Economic Method', *IDS Bulletin*, 22(1), 31–6.
Winchester, H. (1990) 'Women and Children Last: the Poverty and Marginalisation of One-parent Families', *Transactions, Institute of British Geographers*, NS, 15(1), 70–86.
Wratten, E. (1995) 'Conceptualising Urban Poverty', *Environment and Urbanisation*, 7(1), 11–36.
Young, K. (1992) 'Household Resource Management' pp. 135–64 in L. Østergaard (ed.) *Gender and Development: a Practical Guide*, London: Routledge.

7 Women, Industrialization and the Environment in Indonesia
Ines Smyth

> The impact of environmental degradation is often greater on women because of ... gender divisions of labour within households which allocate work such as firewood and water collection to women, precisely tasks which become more difficult with deforestation and falling water tables. However, from a gender analysis standpoint the costs of degradation cannot be assumed to fall predominantly on women without investigating how gender divisions of labour are contested and change under environmental stress ... (Jackson 1993: 405)

INTRODUCTION

The entrance into global markets through the acceleration of the industrialization process is considered to be the driving force of Indonesia's economic development. This process relies predominantly on the utilization of natural resources. Indonesia is endowed with an extraordinary richness of natural resources, including 10 per cent of the earth's tropical forests. But the ecology in both the rural and urban areas is seriously threatened by a variety of factors (World Bank 1994), especially on the island of Java. Industrialization is undoubtedly among the factors that affect the natural environment most directly, in both urban and rural communities.

Thus, while the exploitation of natural resources is the key to this industrialization, their conservation is essential to its sustainability (World Bank 1994). The challenge is, according to the Second Long Term Development Pan (*Pembangunan Jangka Panjang Tahap* II [PJPT II]), to continue accelerating industrialization, while at the same time reducing its negative environmental impact. A central part of this challenge must be to monitor how industrialization affects people's life style and quality of life, both directly and through the impact that manufacturing has on natural resources, either when the latter are plundered as inputs or when they are polluted by outputs.

This chapter considers the impact that rapid and widespread industrialization is having on the gender division of labour that prevails in peri-urban Java. It reveals that the impact on the natural environment has been unmitigatedly negative, but the effects on the community have been complex and contradictory. Globalization is creating new patterns of integration and exclusion, which are reproducing, and in some cases exacerbating, pre-existing patterns of social differentiation. The impact of this process on gender relations is equally uneven, but by no means as totally deleterious to women as some of the literature argues.

This chapter is based on a research project sponsored by the Overseas Development Administration (UK) as part of the research programme on 'Links Between Population and the Environment'. The research was carried out between October 1994 and April 1996, in collaboration with two Indonesian non-governmental organizations. It used a variety of research methods:[1] participant observation, unstructured interviews, a survey, focus group discussions and in-depth case studies. The broad aim of the research was to study the impact of industrialization on the availability – in quantity and quality – of water, fuel and animal fodder and, consequently, on the established practices through which households ensure access to these resources. The aim of the research project was to reflect on the equity and sustainability of the apparent gains of industralization.

The literature linking gender to environmental issues is relatively recent, but is already rich in debates and insights. The position which draws on the special relationship women are said to have with the natural environment – in particular those in the South (Shiva 1988; Jiggins 1994) – posits them as the principal victims of environmental depletion and degradation because of their responsibilities for reproductive activities on the one hand, and because they are the most effective environmental managers, on the other (Martin 1994). This position has been challenged on many counts (Agarwal 1989; Joekes, Leach and Green 1995) with arguments which rely on one, or several, of the strands of gender and development analysis which have evolved in recent years (van den Hombergh 1993). This chapter explores some of these critiques, and uses the research to illustrate the following two points:

1. That it is not possible to state in abstract and absolute terms what the nature of the involvement of men or women (or children) with natural resources in a given social context is. This must be a subject for research, because any generalization relies on a simplistic and essentialist identification between women with nature (Plumwood 1993; Agarwal 1997).

2. That changes in resource availability do not take place where the division of labour is fixed (Jackson 1993; Joekes et al. 1995). This notion is central to this chapter, which tries to document the changes that problems in the availability and access to natural resources have brought to the gender division of labour which is dominant in the region.

This discussion is only possible by rejecting the notion of the household as monolithic and undifferentiated (Dwyer and Bruce 1988; Folbre 1994). The 'household strategies' devised to adapt to environmental changes have to be understood as the different contributions made by each household member to the daily activities through which such resources are obtained and put to use. Furthermore, such considerations must be placed in the context of the impact that the same processes have on the socio-economic configuration of the community.

The following sections reflect this logic. First, we explore the different contributions made by household members to the activities related to natural resources. Second, we concentrate on the changes brought to the local community by globalization. Third, we examine more closely how the impact of industrialization on the three key natural resources is leading to contradictory changes in the lives of local women, especially in relation to their workload.

GENDER AND NATURAL RESOURCE USE

Social norms in Java dictate that women, men and children are responsible in different ways for the collection of water and fuel for household needs and fodder for cattle, as well as for other productive and reproductive tasks (Smyth 1986; Locher-Scholten and Niehof 1987).

This section describes some of the central features of the gender division of labour dominant in Java and other parts of Indonesia, in those tasks that are directly related to the collection and utilization of these three natural resources. It should be pointed out that while the literature[2] on environmental conditions and changes at the macro-level in Indonesia is large and growing, less appears to be available about practices at the micro-level.

Water

In Indonesia water is extremely important for agriculture, aquaculture, commercial and industrial purposes, hydroelectric power, navigation and for religious and domestic uses. Despite the abundant rainfall, per capita resources are low and access to clean water is limited to a minority of the population (World Bank 1990). For these reasons water in the household has to be carefully managed.

Drawing and carrying water for domestic use is often – though not exclusively – the responsibility of women, usually adult women, helped by their daughters or other young female relatives. This is extremely time-consuming and exhausting work from which there can be no respite, since water is indispensable to the smooth running of any household, and its quantity and quality have a serious and immediate impact on the health and wellbeing of its members. A study by Aripurnami (n.d.) shows that women in Sumatra may walk more than 5 km a day to fetch water and to bathe. Women's responsibility for tasks related to water extends to irrigation and other productive uses. But their role in water management is ignored by extension workers and other officials, as well as by men in their communities (van Dok 1991; Smyth 1992).

Fodder

In the work associated with tending and feeding domestic animals the division of labour is quite flexible. Some gender-based rules, as well as generational ones, apply nonetheless. Large animals, such as cows and buffaloes, are herded by men and boys. In Java, small boys herding and bathing water buffaloes are a common sight. Animal fodder is also collected mostly by males. Smaller animals, on the other hand, are tended by women (Berninghausen and Kerstan 1992). This is particularly the case with chickens, which women keep in coops, or free-range in their *pekarangan* (home-yard), for family consumption, for barter and for other uses related to religious and community rituals, as well as for cash sales (this also applies to eggs). The labour of own children is often used for the care of goats (Peluso 1992). This too is very time-consuming, since the work has to be carried out daily (Palte 1989) to ensure that the fodder is fresh.

Wood Fuel

In Java, the work associated with the collection of wood and other fuel material is shared by most household members. Women often collect bundles of wood – as well as animal fodder – while engaged in other work, for example, when returning from the fields or from taking food to their husbands at work (Smyth 1986; Peluso 1992). Women tend to be more active in gathering domestic fuel from areas close to their home and village, while men venture further afield. Though greatly ignored by the literature, the casual observer cannot fail to notice that it is often older women who carry heavy bundles of wood, demonstrating the contribution women make throughout their lives. Even when helped by male household members, women have the principal responsibility for household fuel supplies. This is a consequence of their reproductive duties, many of which involve fuel: cooking, processing food for sale, boiling water for drinking, bathing small children. Dankelman and Davidson (1993) claim that this leads to women bearing most of the burden for the fuelwood crisis. Whether this is true in the Javanese context, or whether households devise new patterns of responsibility in the face of a fuel crisis, is one of the question examined in this chapter.

INDUSTRIALIZATION AND ENVIRONMENTAL CHANGE

Since the mid-1980s Indonesian industrialization policies have undergone important changes in direction. While the structure of industry used to reflect the twin features of import substitution and reliance on the country's resource base, now there is a sustained move towards foreign trade and investment; liberalization and non-oil exports and revenue are strongly encouraged. Though these policies have encouraged the production of intermediate goods, resource-based industries still dominate manufacturing in both output and employment. Light industry such as textiles, garments, footwear, toys and electronics are acquiring increasing importance, especially as a consequence of the relocation of many labour-intensive, manufacturing industries from Japan, South Korea and Taiwan (Saptari 1994). A fairly narrow range of goods, among which textiles and garments are the most important, represent the bulk of Indonesian manufacturing export (Hill 1989: 22).

Industrialization in Indonesia is characterized by marked regional concentration, with the capital, Jakarta, and West Java attracting 40 per cent of foreign and domestic investment. Here manufacturing is concentrated in and *around* major cities (Manning 1992), and this process is parallel to the growth of urban centres, since the possibility of work in factories encourages migration (Soegijoko 1992). The importance of the growth of peri-urban areas is often ignored, perhaps obscured by a focus on metropolitan centres; but in West Java population growth has been greater in rural subdistricts, which are now showing characteristics of urban settlements. This should be put in the context of the regional decline in the importance of agriculture in the structure of the labour force in comparison with the national average (Sasyogyo and Wahyni 1992). Unlike the trends reported for many countries of the region, female workers do not comprise the majority of the labour force. However, their numbers are growing, with different industries showing different degrees of interest in female employment (Saptari 1995). Studies on female migrants or commuters in Java have stressed the fact that the women engaged in this work form links between the industrial, urban (or semi-urban) sector and the rural, agricultural sector (Mather 1985; Wolf 1992, 1993; Saptari 1994). The links they create are through their mobility, the remittances they send and the support – material and otherwise – they receive from their community and families of origin. Though large numbers of migrant workers are employed in the research site, the focus of this chapter is local women. Their situation differs from that of industrial workers in Thailand (Kurian, this volume) and of fruit pickers in Chile (Barrientos and Perrons, this volume), in that industrial penetration has completely eliminated the possibility of combining manufacturing work with agricultural production. This process is discussed in more detail in the following section.

Industrialization in the Research Site

Part of the research on which this chapter is based was carried out in a village in the province of West Java, in the district of Sumedang. West Java was chosen because a large proportion of foreign and domestic investments is centred here (Bappeda 1988). The impact on the physical, cultural and economic environments of these two regions has been dramatic. One feature is the transformation of rural into urban or semi-urban communities, reflecting the influx of migrants (Sayogyo and Wahyuni 1992).

Cintamulya is a village located on the road from Bandung to the eastern end of the island; it is densely populated, with 3316 people/km^2 (nowhere matching that of Jakarta, which has a population density of 13,964 [Biro Pusat Statistik 1992: 282]). Cintamulya has a total population of 4311 people, and an unspecified number of temporary inhabitants who work in nearby factories.

Because of its position adjacent to a main road, the village has been slowly urbanizing for a number of years. The most dramatic transformations date from the late 1980s, when several textiles factories began setting up their plants virtually on its doorstep. The most immediate and visible consequence has been on land use: from agricultural to industrial.

This is as a consequence of the large amount of land acquired by factory owners. According to local statistics, in 1986 the land area (within the village boundaries) occupied by irrigated rice fields was 87.6 ha, and land for industrial use was only 10 ha. By 1995 the area occupied by rice fields had declined to 20.75 ha and that given over to factories had risen to 55.2 ha (or 42.3 per cent of the total village land). A similar decline was found in home-yards. Among the households surveyed for the research only 45 per cent still owned a home-yard, a very low percentage in an environment where the gardens surrounding the house are prevalent and contribute valuable resources such as shade, space, edible fruits and plants.

The survey confirmed this shift, and showed that of all households in the sample only 19 per cent own any rice fields, while another 26 per cent rent. Of those who own land, the majority have very small plots, less than 0.26 square ha. Many have sold land during the last ten years: this amounts to 19 per cent of those interviewed for our survey. According to informants, the first to sell their plots were the larger landowners, usually from outside the area. Local farmers were encouraged to sell their much smaller plots once they became marooned among vast expanses of land already surrendered to the factories. The effect on employment is shown in Table 7.1, which illustrates the relatively low involvement of local people in agricultural work.

What Table 7.1 cannot reveal, but was clearly expressed in discussions with local informants, is what these changes mean to the socio-economic structure of the community, because of the integrated nature of agrarian systems. Here the changes brought about by industrialization are reproducing the social divisions which already existed. Those who owned land are able to maintain their economic and social position by selling it and reinvesting their profits either in land (in other locations) or in building accommodation to be rented out to migrant workers (see below). On the other hand, those who were landless and relied on the earning opportunities that agriculture offered, find themselves deprived of their principal source of income, while often unable to benefit from the new employment opportunities created by the factories. In Java both men and women take part in agricultural work, in rice cultivation as well as in the cultivation of other crops. While the recent changes have had repercussions for both male and female labourers, it is older people who have suffered most, since they do not have the education or flexibility of younger people. One of the effects of industrialization is thus to increase social fragmentation, not only along lines of landownership and wealth, but also according to age.

Patterns of inclusion and exclusion are also peculiar to specific sectors of manufacturing, thus it is necessary to describe the nature of industrial production in the area. The five factories closest to the village all produce cloth and yarn, 60 per cent of which is destined for external markets. They vary in size; the largest employs nearly 9000 workers, the smallest just over 60. Workers come from the nearby villages but also, and in greater numbers, they are migrants from other parts of Java and beyond. Among both migrants and local people, a great majority of the workers are women. It is often repeated – in the relevant literature and by local respondents – that employers prefer younger, unmarried women. However, of the female workers included in our survey, the largest group was in the age range 21–30 years, and were generally married. To satisfy themselves that prospective workers are single, employers require a letter of confirmation of civil status (*Surat Keterangan Belum Menikah*). Village administrators feel very strongly that there should be employment opportunities for local people, thus they are prepared to provide information to that effect, even when the woman in question is actually married.

Hours of work are usually from 8.00 to 16.00 for non-shift work; 6.00 to 14.00, or 14.00 to 22.00, or 22.00 to 6.00 for shift work. Wages vary according to seniority and tasks, but informants claim that the Minimum Wage Rate (*Upah Minimum Rara-rata*, UMP) for West Java of Rp 4600 a day is always paid.[3] This means that average wages for both male and female workers are between Rp 100,000 and 200,000 monthly, which compare well with some but not all the earnings of other categories of workers, for corresponding hours of work. According to interview data, agricultural workers can earn Rp 3000 (female) or Rp 4000 (male) per day, while a construction worker (always male) may earn more: between 10,000 and 15,000 per day.

Factories provide facilities such as cash meal bonuses, uniforms (twice a year), face masks (which few of those interviewed wear), insurance (*Asuransi Tenaga Kerja ASTEK*) and social security work funds (*Jaminan Sosial Tenaga Kerja* JAMSOSTEK). None the less, many workers felt that conditions of work are less than ideal. Workers are allowed little rest during their shift; their movements when at work are rigidly controlled. Sexual harassment of female workers was also reported as a common occurrence. Though relationships between workers of different sexes are considered normal, those between foremen and young girls under their supervision are said to give the latter some status for a while, but also to lead to a bad reputation.

All the factories offer migrants accommodation: married quarters for managers and their families and barracks for the workers. Because of the basic nature of such accommodation and the control exercised on the (mostly female) workers who use them, many opt for renting shared rooms in the nearby villages, including Cintamulya. Rooms are occasionally rented in the homes of local residents and, with increased frequency, in purpose-built hostels erected using the profits from land sales.

The research shows that in Cintamulya nearly 10 per cent of the total population (12.3 per cent of the total labour force) are employed in factories. Of the total number engaged in industrial work a majority (61 per cent) are in the factories within the research location. Table 7.1 summarizes the employment pattern found in the sample of the population used for the survey, and shows clearly that the factories represent an important source of employment for local people, especially women. Separate survey data reveal that for women factory work is the most remunerative source of earnings, while for men it is fairly similar to that for other occupations.

Table 7.1 Main Occupations in Cintamulya

Occupation	Number	Respondents (%)	Women as % total	No. of women
Farmer	14	9.0	29	4
Agricultural worker	3	1.9	33	1
Teacher	1	0.6	100	1
Food stall owner	1	0.6	100	1
Factory worker	53	34.0	62	33
Civil servant	1	0.6	100	1
Unemployed	65	42.0	54	35
Other	10	6.4	10	1
Total (numbers)	148	—	—	77

Table 7.1 shows other interesting characteristics. One is that agriculture is not an important sector for the local population, for reasons already discussed. The second is that unemployment remains high, especially among women. It is interesting to speculate whether a few years ago people, and women in particular, would have considered themselves 'unemployed', or whether this is a result of the diffusion of new self-definitions prioritizing their role as workers. Others have studied the way rural women 'shift back and forward' (Saptari 1995) between the role of industrial worker and the more conventional one in the household and the community. The disappearance of agricultural

work may contribute to the identification of people as workers, employed or unemployed.

Industrialization and Natural Resources

While the main impact of industrialization has been on land use, equally important are the consequences it has had on other natural resources. In this section, these are described together with the adaptations that households have made to compensate for them. These descriptions reveal that the impact of rapid industrialization on natural resources use is direct and indirect – *direct* in the competitive use factories make of certain resources (such as water), or in the damage they cause to them; *indirect* in the transformation of land use, and in the fact that individuals are engaged in forms of employment (waged work in factories) which cannot be easily combined with tasks and responsibilities connected to such resources.

Water

Textiles and yarn production takes place in several phases, and industries may engage in either some or all of them. Raw materials are successively spun, woven, dyed and then finished before the product emerges. Most stages of the work necessitate abundant water, in particular for dyeing and finishing. Factories draw their water from artesian wells, which are much deeper than the domestic wells of the local inhabitants. Thus, the second major impact of rapid and widespread industrialization has been a considerable decrease in the water available to the community, which lacks the technological advantages enjoyed by the factories. Most wells are now dry, and are often used to dispose of rubbish.

A by-product of the dyeing and finishing processes is industrial waste water. Although some of the factories have treatment plants, the majority discharge raw waste water into the surrounding channels. The open ditches in the village are visibly polluted, and many people comment on the unpleasant odours they emit.

Local officials and the population are extremely vocal in expressing their anger at the water problems they experience as a direct consequence of the presence of the factories. Villagers have tried to compensate for them in various ways. One is to dig deeper and more wells; but despite these attempts less than 26 per cent of the households surveyed have access to a well, while previously this was as high as 65 per cent. Many people make use of public facilities. One is a pond with a portion screened off by a bamboo fence, which provides washing, bathing and toilet facilities. The water is extremely dirty and cannot be used for drinking. Depending on distance, time and type of transport available, some people collect their drinking water from a spring located on the hills about 4 km way. Two of the factories in Cintamulya have made connections which bring water to tanks just outside the factory walls, to which separate houses can be linked up. Less than 50 per cent of the households surveyed – all of them in immediate proximity to the factories – rely on this type of water which, in addition, is only sufficient for drinking and cooking.

Fodder

The disappearance of land has clearly changed the work structure of the community, putting an end to most agricultural activities. It has had other impacts too. When many households had rice fields, however small, several owned water buffalos for ploughing. With the generalized sale of land, this practice has disappeared. Sheep and goats could graze on recently harvested fields – one's own or those belonging to other farmers – or could be fed with the parts of dry crops unfit for human consumption. The research found that no goats are kept now, and only one household has sheep. Women's practice of collecting fodder when returning from the fields has also meant that they are discouraged from undertaking such an activity when – with the disappearance of agricultural responsibilities – it necessitates trips for the purpose. The only livestock still reared are chickens, while ducks have followed the fate of larger animals.

It is not only the disappearance of rice fields (and home-yards) that has influenced this aspect of village life. Employment in the factories is clearly an important source of income. But the long and regulated working hours limit the time (and energy) people have to devote to agricultural and related tasks. As the survey showed, people spend much less time collecting fodder than they did before: 70 per cent of those involved take less than one hour, while in the past this was so for only 25 per cent, and the rest took a much longer time.

Wood fuel

As stated earlier, Cintamulya was already involved in processes of urbanization, thus the recent changes represent a deepening of existing tendencies. This is the case for the shift from wood fuel to kerosene for cooking. Among the households surveyed, 79 per cent use kerosene, 19 per cent wood and 3 per cent gas. In the majority of cases (79 per cent) the fuel is delivered to the house. When collected, wood is obtained from sources fairly close to home. In the past 53 per cent of the households used wood, while all the rest used kerosene. It was usually collected rather than delivered. The time now spent on this task is clearly less: for 67 per cent of the household it is less than one hour per day, while in the past only 28 per cent of the households could complete the task in such a short time.

There are several reasons why women – as the main direct users of domestic fuel – have switched even more from wood fuel to kerosene. These have little to do with women's 'closeness' to nature, and more with a set of interrelated circumstances. The shift in land uses is one reason. Another is that kerosene is more practical to use and, since it does not need constant supervision, it allows women to reduce the time spent on housework. Finally, in the past supply was irregular and the cash necessary to buy it less readily available. Both have improved as a consequence of industrialization; the first because of improved roads and transports, the second thanks to the wages from factory work.

RESOURCES AVAILABILITY AND WOMEN'S WORK LOAD

In the previous sections information have been given on the gendered practices through which water, fuel and fodder are used in Java, on the characteristics of industrial penetration, and on the effects of industrialization on the environment and on the socio-economic life of the community. It is now possible to see how the presence of industries changes the responsibilities that women – and to a lesser degree men – have as they employ such resources for the satisfaction of daily domestic needs.

Shifts in relevant tasks between household members don't 'just happen'. They are the outcome of conflicts and bargaining between them, as well as of consensual decisions. It is beyond the scope of this chapter to document the processes through which such outcomes are determined. However, it is important to say that positions and responsibilities, especially between husbands and wives, are being constantly and privately renegotiated, not without occasional open conflict. Publicly, men often voiced resentment at the easier access women have to factory work, which they saw as a reversal of 'natural' roles. They expressed strong indignation at the employers' preference for migrants, which is perceived as an injustice in the light of the price paid by their community in terms of environmental and social disruption. However, the connivance of local administrators in disguising women's marital status and thus deceiving the employers also indicates, among other things, that there is social acceptance of their new status as industrial workers.

Water

From Table 7.2, an idea can be gleaned of the degree to which different members of the households surveyed are responsible for collecting water, and how this compares with the situation a few years ago. This shows that water collection is principally the responsibility of wives. In longitudinal terms, women's work in water collection has stayed the same, that carried out jointly by the couple has increased, while that of the husband has decreased. This could be explained by the fact that, because of the problem associated with scarcity of water, women are adopting strategies which result in the partial withdrawal of men. For example, women who now have to rely on a public well will combine washing dishes and clothes, and bathing small children – all activities rarely undertaken by men in public. The help of men may be enlisted in this case only to carry water for cooking and drinking. Water collection is one of the tasks which women stated that men contribute to more now, as a consequence of their own engagement in factory work.

Table 7.2 Changes in Water-related Tasks in Cintamulya, as % of Total

Person responsible	Cintamulya in the past ($n=38$)	Cintamulya in the present ($n=19$)
Wife	37	37
Husband	24	16
Husband and Wife	18	26
Son	—	5

Table 7.3 Changes in Fodder-related Tasks in Cintamulya as % of Total

Person responsible	Cintamulya in the past ($n=12$)	Cintamulya in the present ($n=10$)
Wife	17	20
Husband	67	40
Husband and Wife	17	—
Son	—	40

Similar shifts can be seen in tasks related to the collection of animal fodder, as Table 7.3 shows. For work related to the collection of fodder, wives are now involved more than they were in the past, while the reverse is true for husbands. It is possible to speculate that the shift is due to the fact that since in Java men are more often responsible for tending larger animals, the disappearance of cattle means that the work of husbands is not needed, while that of wives remains important because they are traditionally in charge of tending small livestock such as chickens. Sons help more now than in the past. Unfortunately the data do not allow us to differentiate between sons of different ages, and thus to detect a meaningful relation between this and unemployment among young men. Informants believe that unemployment is particularly acute among males between 14 and 19 years of age; it is possible that the help of unemployed sons in this age range is enlisted in the collection of fodder, because they have time on their hands.

Table 7.4 shows tasks distribution for wood fuel collection. The information contained in the table should be placed in the context of the longer-term shift discussed earlier.

Fuel collection reflects broadly similar patterns to those of other resources. The decrease in the labour contribution from husbands is easily explained by the decline in the use of wood as domestic fuel, for which they were traditionally responsible. The weakening of their engagement with agriculture is also an explanation in part. However, the fact remains that women's share of this work has increased, as has that of their sons and daughters. The assistance given by daughters and sons can be explained by the fact that the collection of the relatively small amounts of wood still needed can be entrusted to children, especially when parents are engaged in factory work, which has little time flexibility.

Table 7.4   Changes in Fuel-related Tasks in Cintamulya as % of Total

Person responsible	Cintamulya in the past ($n=37$)	Cintamulya in the present ($n=36$)
Wife	38	44
Husband	46	14
Son	—	11
Daughter	—	11

Since the tasks related to natural resources use are intimately connected to housework and other household-based responsibilities, and often difficult to distinguish from them, it is important to look at other shifts in the domestic arena more broadly. Open-ended questions included in the survey concerned recent changes in the contribution of husbands to housework. A large majority of respondents stated that their husbands were helping much more in the home since they had started working in the factory. In some cases husbands were said to help with cleaning, but less with washing and cooking. Childcare is an area where men are willing to help, for example by adapting their own work schedule to substitute for their wives when the latter are at work. However, women find support for childcare more often from their mothers, other female relatives and neighbours. More generally, there was sufficient evidence to show that husbands are more willing to contribute to all domestic tasks when at least some of the wives' time is spent in waged labour.

An interesting counterpoint was provided by several respondents who considered their husbands' assistance to have declined: because they had taken up more intensive paid work, because their help in collecting water was no longer needed since the connection with the factory supply, or because their support in looking after cattle or collecting fuel was made unnecessary by the disappearance of either or both. One woman stated: 'In the past my husband helped in looking for wood, but now it is difficult to find it, so we use kerosene.' Another said: 'Before my husband used to bring water from the well, now that there is water from the factory, he does not need to bring water from the well.'

CONCLUSIONS

The research has shown that the forces of globalization have reached deep into this peri-urban community. Its effects have been widespread, but contradictory. Despite improvements in the infrastructure and in employment generation, the gains of industrialization are not unmitigated. Industrialization is bringing serious environmental harm.[4] The exclusionary nature of social benefits is evident in the consequences of the changes on land use and its impact on social differentiation. Even the gains of new employment, especially for women, must be counterbalanced by a labour regime which is often extremely repressive (Hadiz 1993).

The changes brought by industrialization to natural resources availability has necessitated certain adaptations in tasks distribution within households. The type of labour demand has brought large numbers of local women into the labour force. As a consequence of both these transformations, tasks within the household have had to be renegotiated. Those directly related to the use of the three natural resources have seen a decrease in the contribution of men, and a sustained and even increased contribution of that of women, often helped by their children. This would seem to confirm the conclusions of those who believe environmental deterioration to have an especially hard impact on women. While this is true, other circumstances have to be considered:

- the work related to collecting and using each of the resources has become less onerous and time-consuming. The exception to this is water, where this is true for some households (those connected to the factories, for example) but not for many others;
- other members of the household, especially sons, help carrying out such tasks;
- when wives are visibly engaged in making use of the opportunities offered by industrialization (i.e. they are employed as factory workers or in earnings through renting rooms to migrants), husbands are more ready to give support in domestic tasks.

Thus, contrary to the view that deterioration in environmental conditions always has more severe effects on women than on any other social group, in Java environmental deterioration results in a more complex picture. Furthermore, the adoption of certain strategies is not a function of an innate bond of women with 'nature', but rather of the combination of very specific conditions, as the example of the decline in the use of kerosene demonstrates.

Finally, in Java gender norms are not inflexible. Within the households this flexibility is shown by the fact that it has been relatively easy for women to step out[5] of the household domain to make maximum use of earning opportunities in the industrial sector. The only resistance they encounter here is, ironically, from employers, who insist in privileging younger, unmarried women. All the same, individual women have taken a progressive stance in relation to the new, contradictory conditions created by industrialization. In their daily lives they perform a difficult balancing act between earning a living on one side, and finding creative solutions to the new environmental challenges on the other. In this, they make active choices which do not render them saviours of Mother Earth (Mies and Shiva 1993: 17) or inert victims of global transformations which are always and necessarily deleterious to them.

The women of the Chipko movement, as reported by Shiva and Mies (1993: 303), 'know that their survival (their bread) as well as their freedom and dignity ... can be maintained only as long as they have control over these [natural] resources ... They do not need the money offered by the government or the industrialists to survive.' In Java, women need the survival opportunities offered by industrialization. Using the opportunities offered by industrialization to make a more comfortable present and secure future for their families and for themselves must surely be a source of dignity.

NOTES

1. Primary research was carried out in four villages: two in West Java and two in Central Java. The information contained in this chapter is limited to one of the villages, in West Java. Findings from all communities varied because of the differences in extent and duration of the process of industrialization. However, the main trends and characteristics presented in the paper apply to all four villages.
2. This section relies mostly on secondary data, while the later ones are based on information gathered through field research.
3. Rp 3,500 = £1 (1995).
4. Environmental protection legislation in Indonesia, like labour legislation, is comprehensive and far-reaching. But like labour legislation, its implementation is very poor and leaves entire communities with severely damaged and depleted natural resources.
5. Neither this or other research has found noticeable resistance from men to their daughters or wives working in factories. However, this chapter does not address the question of what happens in case of such a resistance, nor the issue of the consequences of women's wage work on their autonomy and social status.

REFERENCES

Agarwal, B. (1989) 'Rural Women, Poverty and Natural Resources: Sustenance, Sustainability and Struggle for Change', *Economic and Political Weekly* 28 (October), 46–65.
Agarwal, B. (1997) 'Environmental Action, Gender Equity and Women's Participation', *Development and Change* 28, 1–44.
Aripurnami, S. (n.d.) 'Clean Water Supply Technology: a Means to Ease the Burden of Women' Mimeo, Perpustakaan Kalyanamitra.
Bappeda, Jawa Barat and Kaskoning-Lindesco, the Netherlands 1988 (LTA47). West Java Regional Development Programme, Bandung.
Berninghausen, J. and Kerstan, B. (1992) *Forging New Paths: Feminist Social Methodology and Rural Women in Java*, London: Zed Books.
Biro Pusat Statistik (1992) *Statistik Lingkungan Hidup Indonesia 1992*, Jakarta.
Dankelmann, I. and Davidson, J. (1993) *Women and Environment in the Third World: Alliance for the Future*, London: Earthscan.
Dwyer, D. and Bruce, J. (eds) (1988) *A Home Divided. Women and Income in the Third World*, Stanford, CA: Stanford University Press.

Folbre, N. (1994) *Who Pays for the Kids?* London: Routledge.
Hadiz, V. (1993) 'Workers and Working Class Politics in the 1990s' in C. Manning and H. Hardjono (eds) *Indonesia Assessment 1993*, Canberra: Australian National University.
Hill, H. (1989) 'Indonesia: Export Promotion in the Post-OPEC Era'. Working Paper no. 89/8. Canberra: National Centre for Development Studies.
Jackson, C. (1993) 'Women/nature or Gender/history: a Critique of Ecofeminist "Development"', *Journal of Peasant Studies* 20, 398–419.
Jiggins, J. (1994) *Changing the Boundaries: Women-Centred Perspectives on Population and the Environment*, Wahington D.C.: Island Press.
Joekes, S., Leach, M. and Green, C. (1995) 'Special Issue: Gender Relations and Environmental Change', *IDS Bulletin* 26(1), 1–92.
Locher-Scholten, E. and Niehof, A. (eds) (1987) *Indonesian Women in Focus*, Dordrecht: Fortis Publications.
Manning, C. (1992) 'Rural Problems and Urban Opportunities' in J. Dirkse, F. Husken and M. Rutten (eds) *Indonesia's Experiences under the New Order*, Leiden: KITLV. 87–95.
Martin, J. (1994) 'Interbeing and the "I" Habit: an Experiment in Environmental Literacy', pp. 156–76 in W. Harcourt (ed.) *Feminist Perspectives on Sustainable Development*, London and Rome: Zed Books in association with SID.
Mather, C. (1985) 'Rather than Make Trouble, it's Better Just to Leave', in H. Afshar (ed.) *Women, Work and Ideology in the Third World*, New York: Tavistock. 153–83.
Mies, M. and Shiva, V. (1993) *Ecofeminism*, London: Zed Books.
Palte, G.L.J. (1989) *Upland Farming on Java, Indonesia a Socio-economic Study of Upland Agriculture and Subsistence under Population Pressure*, Amsterdam: Geographical Institute.
Peluso, N. (1992) *Rich Forests, Poor People; Resource Control and Resistance in Java*, Berkeley: University of California Press.
Plumwood, V. (1993) *Feminisms and the Mastery of Human Nature*, London: Routledge.
Saptari R, (1995) *Rural Women to the Factories: Continuity and Change in East Java Kretek Cigarette Industry*, PhD Dissertation, University of Amsterdam.
Sayogyo, P. and Wahyuni, S. (1994) 'An Introduction to the Economy and People of West Java' pp. 31–41 in M. Grijns, I. Smyth, A. van Velzen, S. Machfud and P. Sayogyo, *Different Women, Different Work: Gender and Industrialization in Indonesia*, Aldershot: Avebury.
Shiva, V. (1988) *Staying Alive; Women, Ecology and Development*, London: Zed Books.
Smyth, I. (1986) *The Weaving of Women's Lives: a Case Study of Non-Agricultural Activities in a Sundanese Village (West Java, Indonesia)*. PhD thesis, University College London.
Smyth, I. (1992) *Report of the International Consultant on Gender Issues in Irrigation On Farm Use and Management Training and Development Project*, Jakarta: FAO.
Soegijoko, B.T. and Wahyni (1992) 'Urban Growth, Industrial Development and Migration', pp. 95–105 in J. Dirkse, F. Husken and M. Rutten (eds) *Indonesia's Experiences Under the New Order*, Leiden: KITLV.

van den Hombergh, H. (1993) *Gender, Environment and Development: A Guide to the Literature*, Utrecht: International Books.
van Dok, I. (1991) *Gender Division of Tasks in Water Management and Rice Cultivation: Changes as a Consequence of Industrialisation*, Working Paper. Jakarta: Cidurian Upgrading and Water Management Project B130, DHV.
Wolf, D. (1992) 'Industrialisation and the Family: Women Workers as Mediators of Family and Economic Change in Java'. pp. 89–109 in van S. Bemmelen, M. Djajadiningrat-Nieuwenhuis, E. Locher-Scholten and E. Touwen-Bouswma, *Women and Mediation in Indonesia*, Leiden: KITLV.
Wolf, D. (1993) 'Women and Industrialization in Indonesia' pp. 135–59 in J. Dirkse, F. Husken and M. Rutten (eds) *Indonesia's Experiences Under the New Order*, Leiden: KITLV.
World Bank (1990) *Indonesia: Sustainable Development of Forests, Land and Water*, Washington: World Bank.
World Bank (1994) *Indonesia Environment and Development: Challenges for the Future*, Washington: Washington.

8 Gender and the Global Food Chain: a Comparative Study of Chile and the UK

Stephanie Barrientos and Diane Perrons

INTRODUCTION

The global food chain is an example of a sector that has been transformed through the process of globalization, and as a consequence has had a direct impact on women. A wide range of globally sourced, processed food and fresh produce is now available throughout the year, independent of season or location. Consumers almost everywhere, given sufficient income, are spoilt for choice, and as part of this consumer group some women have clearly been beneficiaries. Global food production and retailing in many countries has also involved a significant proportion of female employment. In many countries women have traditionally been associated with agricultural work, often as unpaid peasant labour or seasonal workers, and women everywhere have long been associated with the preparation and presentation of food within the household. With the extension of transnational capital along the food chain, these activities have become increasingly commercialized at the global level. Paid employment within production and retailing has expanded, and women have been drawn into this work as a logical extension of their socially defined roles. However, much of this female employment is low paid and flexible, which in this study usually takes the form of temporary and/or part-time work. They are a marginalized and fragmented workforce, whose integration has depended upon and reinforced their dual role in the household. For them, the benefits of globalization have been partial and contradictory.

The aim of this chapter is to explore the comparative effects on women of integration into the global fruit chain linking Chile and the UK. In Chile women form a significant proportion of seasonal temporary workers (*temporeras*) drawn upon by fruit exporters, and in the UK women part-time workers form a significant proportion of employment in

Gender and the Global Food Chain 151

supermarkets, through which some of this fruit is sold as part of a wide range of globally sourced products. Women therefore participate in contrasting nodes of the global food chain. Our focus is to explore the comparative effect of this type of flexible employment on gender relations in the household. We examine how, despite the differences in their national and social contexts, women in contrasting situations juggle their dual roles according to the specific form of their employment and that of partners or other household members. In both cases, the flexibility of women's employment is built upon their domestic role and an assumed dependency on alternative sources of income. In reality though, women's earnings are often an essential element in household survival strategies in both locations, and many households have had to adapt to facilitate women's paid employment. We then explore three theoretical approaches – co-operative conflict, gender contracts and arrangements and patriarchy – in order to assess the comparative effect on gender relations of this type of work. The discussion raises issues in relation to the analysis of contemporary gender relations in the context of globalization in developed and developing countries which this case study cannot resolve, but which we hope will contribute to further research.

WOMEN'S POSITION IN THE GLOBAL FOOD CHAIN

The development of agribusiness is linked to a more general process of globalization in which large, profit-seeking firms seek to control production and expand markets on a global scale. The growth of agribusiness has been facilitated by technological transformation in the processes of production, transportation and communication, but also owes its development to the concentration of retailing operations in the developed world, which have contributed to and depend upon changing consumption patterns in food (Bonanno et al. 1994; Friedland et al. 1991; McMichael 1994; Wrigley and Lowe 1996). Increasingly food is bought in a highly processed or packaged form and a wide range of basic and exotic global produce is provided throughout the year at prices which are accessible to an expanding range of income groups (Bell and Valentine 1997). The supply chains facilitating this have increased and tightened the links between localities in developing and developed countries (Gereffi and Korzeniewicz 1994). There has long been North–South agricultural trade. But new consumer-driven chains supplying non-traditional exports have expanded in the contemporary global environment. In many developing countries pockets of local (and sometimes even peasant) producers have been integrated into high-tech supply chains, transforming production through integration into northern export markets during the latter's winter (Friedland 1994). Chilean fruit exports to the UK are a very specific example of a thread running through the global food chain linking developing and developed countries.

This global supply chain has become increasingly dominated by large multiples (supermarkets), which are able to exercise control from one end of the chain to the other (Wrigley and Lowe 1996). The growth of multiples has been linked to changing patterns of shopping which they have only in part helped to create. Increasingly, for many households (especially dual income) the 'main grocery shop' takes the form of a once-weekly trip based on 'one-stop shopping', often outside 'normal working hours' or at the weekend when the 'family' car is more likely to be available. This pattern is associated with increased participation of women in the paid labour force, rises in household income and consumption standards, including the purchase of consumer durables that makes the home storage of food possible, together with increased car ownership and transport policies favouring the private car (Fine 1995; Wrigley 1996).

Fresh fruit sales have also increased as a consequence of the changes in the pattern of food consumption. Social scientists have never counted how often people eat with their families so there is insufficient evidence to know whether, in fact, family meals have declined. Much of the evidence that is available comes from mass marketing magazines and so there is bias in the sampling frame (Murcott 1997). However, what is certain is that separate eating, 'eating on the hoof' and snacking form a significant part of contemporary patterns of food consumption (Bell and Valentine 1997). Fruit, which is perceived to provide health and vitality, is easily prepared and can form part of a meal, packed lunch or snack, and so permits the potentially conflicting demands of quick preparation and food value to be reconciled. The appearance of the fruit and its quality and hygiene are thus very important (Jackson and Holbrook 1995) and the close monitoring of their produce through the chain enables supermarkets to meet these expectations.

The food chain is linked to a global consumer market, including many developing countries where high-income groups have also been integrated into changing consumption patterns (Sklair 1994; Hoogvelt 1997). The process of moving towards increased domination by large supermarket chains, paradoxically, is a trend that is being replicated in Chile and other parts of the developing world. Chile has become a highly urbanized society, and the urban centres have also experienced the effects of globalization, with the growth of a credit-driven middle-class consumer elite and rising inequality of incomes (Silva 1995). There has been a significant expansion of supermarkets within larger towns and cities, especially in affluent locations. Certain chains of multiples are also establishing a dominant presence in some areas. These form part of the consumer boom, which has gripped Chile during the 1990s. These supermarkets are staffed from the urban poor and provide low-paid, flexible employment, much of it female. In a refracted way this replicates developed country trends in global consumerism, and increasingly supermarkets are becoming an outlet for fruit supplied to the internal market.

A common feature of non-traditional horticultural production and supermarket retailing is the significant employment of female labour, often on a flexible basis. In many developing countries, pockets of nontraditional agricultural production have generated large amounts of insecure, low paid seasonal work for the export market based on the use of a female labour force (Arizpe and Aranda 1981; Barrientos 1996; Macintosh 1989; Sachs 1996). In developed and developing countries, as multiples become an increasingly dominant outlet for the retailing of food, women form a significant proportion of the staff employed, again on a flexible or part-time basis (Neathey and Hurstfield 1995; Scott 1994). This global use of female labour is partly linked to trends found in other industries throughout the developed and developing world. Female employment has increased as a result partly of structural adjustment, labour market liberalization, and a preference by transnationals and subcontractors for socially perceived 'feminine' skills and a more 'docile' female labour force (Afshar and Dennis 1992; Elson and Pearson 1981; Mitter 1986).

In the case of food production and retailing, this also reflects a social stereotyping of women's roles. In most countries women have traditionally been associated in different ways with the production, preparation and handling of food within the household. As these activities have become increasingly commercialized, some of these socially defined female functions have shifted from unpaid to paid work drawing women into the labour force. This social modernization has given rise to women's increased engagement with the market economy in both production and consumption. As women become more involved in paid work, their time is more limited and they become more dependent on commercially produced and processed food (Goodman and Redclift 1991). Correspondingly, their income from paid work generates the purchasing power necessary to finance the purchase of goods previously prepared in the household. In the food sector, this process has not fundamentally altered the gender division of labour in that women continue to be associated with food production and preparation, but it clearly impacts on gender relations within the household as part of women's labour is relocated into external employment. In non-traditional agricultural exports and supermarkets, much of this employment is flexible, seasonal and part-time, hence the shift is often partial. Women thus combine and juggle their roles in complex ways, with household adaptation depending on personal and social circumstance as well as the specific forms of employment. Gendered roles have been transformed yet reinforced within the context of a more globalized food chain.

COMPARATIVE HOUSEHOLD STRATEGIES AND GENDER RELATIONS

Our case study is a comparison of two very specific nodes linked within the complex network of global food supply. This chapter is part of a broader study of the comparative effects of women's integration into the food chain in Chile and the UK. Elsewhere we have examined in detail how the supply chain itself links the two countries through an analysis of the production, distribution and retailing links by which Chilean fruit enters UK supermarkets for a period of 3–4 months each year, and examined the importance of flexible female labour at each end of the chain in facilitating this. (For more detail of this aspect of the study, see Barrientos and Perrons 1996.[1]) In this chapter, we are focusing not on the employment itself (which we shall only briefly summarize), but its impact on gender relations in the household, how women juggle their dual roles as they become employed in the more commercialized food sector, and how households have had to adapt to sustain flexible employment, often of both partners and other household members.

The impact on gender roles and relations within households in the two locations is mediated by the different national contexts and the specific employment requirements of fruit production or supermarket retailing. Employment is flexible in both cases, but the form of flexibility differs. Fruit production in Chile takes place in concentrated areas of monocultivation and the vast majority (80 per cent) of workers are employed on a temporary basis for approximately four months each year for harvesting and packing. There is little alternative employment for either women or men in these areas (Barrientos 1996). During the season, the rhythm of work is extremely intense. Hours are long and work takes place on most days of the week in order to match the output and sustain export volumes, that is, to ensure that the fruit produced is harvested and packed in good condition for export. In contrast, although increasingly flexible, employment contracts in the UK supermarkets are extremely varied and tailored to meet the daily, weekly and seasonal variations in sales. Supermarkets are widespread throughout the country and in most areas many other forms of employment can be found. However by offering a variety of different, although predominantly permanent, contracts the supermarkets are able to draw upon a labour force, not so much trapped by geographical location and the lack of alternatives, as in Chile, but by the prevailing gender order and limited childcare facilities which create a pool of female labour willing to work short hours for relatively low pay at times of the day and night either when children are in school or when partners or other relative are at home. These two forms of flexible employment (temporary and part-time) both help to sustain the highly profitable, just-in-time production and distribution systems across the food chain (Barrientos and Perrons 1996). Despite the different forms of flexible employment and the diversity of household compositions within and between the two locations it is nevertheless possible to identify some similarities and common tendencies in the coping strategies that have evolved as households juggle their multiple commitments in different ways to sustain their livelihood.

Chile

The overall impact of global integration has been more visible on households in Chile. Over the past 20 years the rural sector in the central regions has been dramatically transformed by the commercialization of agriculture largely associated with the production of fruit for global markets. Much of the rural labour force is now landless and depends solely on wage labour. Fruit production, however, generates mainly temporary employment and each year a large army (approximately a quarter of a million) of temporary fruit workers are mobilized. Women make up 52 per cent of this army, which is significantly higher than their representation in the labour force as a whole (31 per cent). There is little migration, and most of the temporary workers live in or within access of the fruit growing regions (Barrientos and Perrons 1996).

Fruit workers constitute a heterogeneous labour force drawn from households with different degrees of attachment to the land and their own production and from areas with different levels of urbanisation. These backgrounds affect the experiences of women. Three broad categories can be defined: (1) rural peasant households which still retain some access to land and generate some of their own production; (2) households with no access to land, except possibly a small garden plot, living in rural towns and settlements; and finally (3) households living in large towns and cities, from which fruit workers travel out on a daily basis (Gómez and Echeñique 1988; Venegas 1992). In the more traditional rural households, which still retain access to some land, women juggle their roles between domestic labour and childcare, traditional peasant production usually for the domestic market and commercial paid employment in the export market. The flexibility of fruit employment can facilitate this, and women move between household crop production and fruit employment depending on the specific crop cycles (Bee 1996; Barrientos et al. forthcoming). These households illustrate the mediation of the traditional and modern through globalization. However, the majority of temporary workers no longer have access to the land and we will concentrate on this group.

The size, age and gender profile of households drawn into fruit work varies, affecting how many work and how many remain at home. Rodriguez and Venegas (1991) have undertaken the largest published survey of fruit workers across all categories of household. They estimate the average age of women temporary workers is 30 years, and women tend to be older than men, with a much larger percentage of women (47 per cent) partnered or married. They found that the average household size of temporary fruit workers was 5.6 members with an average of 2.9 members economically active and 2.8 children (Rodriguez and Venegas 1991). Nineteen per cent of *temporeras* are female heads of household, which is slightly above the national average in Chile (Venegas 1992), and reflects an increasing trend in Latin America and elsewhere (Chant 1997 and this volume). At the height of the season in areas dominated by fruit production all adults able to do so will work in fruit, if they have no other employment, in order to maximize household income.

In many households, therefore, all adults are working long hours during the season and there is little possibility of juggling paid work with childcare. As a result, in the daytime, many rural communities are populated only by children, the sick and the elderly. Most women temporary workers see childcare as by far their main problem. Since the return to democracy a state childcare programme for temporary workers has been initiated, but only a very small minority of the children of temporary workers have access to state childcare facilities, and they cannot afford private childcare (Matear 1997; Barrientos et al. forthcoming). Many women use older resident family members or relatives in close proximity to care for younger children, but reduction of the extended family and displacement of families through past rural/urban migration have reduced these options. In the absence of any alternative, care of younger children is often left in the hands of older children, especially girls. Given that the fruit season falls during the school vacations, there is a major problem of older children of temporary workers hanging around the streets with little to occupy them. The length of time in the day during which children are left unattended is tempered by the different shift patterns women and men tend to occupy. Men tend to be concentrated in field work, starting early in the morning and finishing in the early evening. Women are more concentrated in packing, starting later in the morning and often working late into the night (except in some larger packing houses which have introduced shift systems). Thus when men return from work they are in a position to look after children. The extent to which they actually do this varies between households, but childcare is one area where male partners are more likely to participate (Vogel 1997).

Despite often working longer hours than men in the season, most women temporary workers continue to take primary responsibility for domestic work within the household. Although the distribution of domestic work is clearly gendered, the composition of the household can affect the extent to which it falls on an individual woman, with girls and female relatives more likely to help out. We found considerable differences between households as to whether the husband or male partner contributed, with some women saying they did absolutely nothing, and some saying that they would help a lot. Overall we found that most men gave some (if limited) help when woman were actually at work, but this was likely to fall away once seasonal employment for the woman had finished. Venegas (1992) found in her survey that women were least likely to get help with washing of clothes and cleaning, but more likely to get help with cooking. Shopping was the activity which male partners were most likely to help with, and in more urban areas where there are supermarkets, some temporary workers have recounted the weekly family shopping trip to the supermarket as in the UK (Vogel 1997). On average, Venegas (1992) calculated that women temporary workers spent three hours a day on domestic work during the fruit season, in addition to a working day of 8–16 hours, despite some participation by male partners and children. Therefore the dual burden carried by these women remains very onerous, with an intense concentration of work for approximately four months each year.

Poverty amongst temporary fruit workers households is high (Barrientos 1996; Venegas 1992). During the season when all able adult members are working, household income can reach reasonable levels, but these incomes are often the major source of household earnings, as there is little work during the rest of the year.[2] Women are less likely to be able to find other work during the winter months than men are, but the problem of unemployment is significant for both. Most women report that their fruit earnings are essential to household income and survival, and Díaz (1991) found that 88 per cent of women said their earnings were indispensable. An anomaly in Chile is that the most productive women packers are able to earn more at the height of the season than male field workers (Barrientos 1996), therefore in some households it is possible that the woman may contribute more to household income than the man, but only for a short period of time. This belies the perception by employers that women work for 'pin money' (PREALC 1990).

Women's earnings in particular tend to go towards two areas of expenditure. The first is children's school clothes, books and any other educational expenditure. Given that the fruit season falls during the summer holiday, women's earnings coincide with the need to equip children for the forthcoming school year. The other area of expenditure is on household items that cannot otherwise be purchased, and making provision for the winter months. These range from essential items such as household equipment or maintenance, and more luxury items such as radios or televisions. Many of these latter items are often bought on credit, and some women recount a cycle of purchasing a television on credit at the beginning of the season, and losing it during the winter months when they are unable to maintain the payments. Thus women's earnings can facilitate partial access to the global consumer market. Poorer rural households are unlikely to be able to get access to credit or these types of consumer items.

It is very difficult to generalize regarding the effect of fruit work on personal relations between men and women, and during the course of our research we encountered very different situations. Generally women and men work at the same time. Macho male attitudes are still very persistent in Chile (Fisher 1993), particularly in the rural sector where social traditions are more prevalent. Given the high level of poverty and dependence on women's earnings, men have little choice but to accept women working. Men often preferred their wives to work in the packing plants than in the fields, as there was greater supervision and the workforce there was predominantly female (Bee 1996). Vogel (1997) found that some men accepted their wives working because it was only temporary, and they would return to their 'normal' role once the season was over. Some men appeared to be more accepting and supportive than others, and wide differences were voiced by individual women about the attitude of their male partners in our study. Overall, the message coming through from most research including our own is that most women fruit workers, despite all their problems, like working in fruit. As one put it, 'We have always worked and now we are being paid for it.' It is important to remember that the options for rural women are very limited – given monocultivation and export specialization there is little alternative employment except in domestic service, which is considered far worse. Women say that fruit work gives them a greater sense of independence, enables them to socialize with other women, breaks the drudgery and isolation of domestic work within the household, and allows them to earn their own money (Barrientos 1998). Traditional rural households have to adapt to women taking paid employment during the season if the household is to survive, but there is a tendency to return to more 'traditional' gender roles within the household during the winter months.

UK

Supermarkets have increased their share of the UK consumer market.[3] Part of their success derives from their ability to supply a stable and wide range of produce throughout the year, independently of season. This produce is sourced from all over the world and includes fruit from Chile during the winter months. Competitive prices are also important and arise from just-in-time delivery systems, which minimize working capital and storage costs, and from the employment of low-cost labour, tailored on a flexible basis to match fluctuations in sales. Both of these savings have been facilitated by electronic information systems. Increased opening hours, including evenings and weekends which have stimulated and responded to changing shopping patterns, have also contributed to their increase in market share. As a consequence many stores now operate 24 hours a day seven days a week as deliveries and shelf-filling take place more efficiently at night. Consequently labour needs cannot be met from a 'standard' workforce.

Supermarkets meet their labour needs by using a complex variety of shift systems and almost individualized contracts. The majority of labour is female and increasingly part-time, although young people, particularly students (women and men), make up approximately 25 per cent of the workforce.[4] Excluding students, men generally occupy the higher positions in specific crafts or in management. The women in our study work on average 20 hours a week over five sessions but there are many deviations from this trend. Some work two nights a week, others four evenings which may stretch into the night. There is, in fact, a whole variety of different patterns which in principle should enable women to match their paid employment with other activities including family responsibilities. However, in practice, work patterns are determined by the requirements of the store – to match the flow of clients, maximize work intensity and minimize costs (Barrientos and Perrons 1996; Neathey and Hurstfield 1995; Perrons and Hurstfield 1998; USDAW 1996) although greater flexibility is given to longer-serving employees.

Many of our informants valued the short hours and the ability to work at nights and weekends as they could work while their partners or other relatives cared for their children. This picture is matched by larger scale surveys which report on the prevalence of part-time work amongst mothers with pre-school children (EC 1997; Glover and Arber 1995; Marsh and Mackay 1993), the numbers of mothers working unsocial hours (Ferri and Smith 1996), the comparatively low level of publicly provided childcare especially for young children (in relation to other EU countries) (EC 1997) and the way in which childcare is provided by relatives (70 per cent of all care irrespective of the age of the child) (Ferri and Smith 1996).

For the evening and night workers in our study the hours were chosen specifically to fit in with the partner's pattern of working (Barrientos and Perrons 1996). One common pattern was to work two nights a week from 8 pm to 7 am and another to work between 4 and 5 'twilight' shifts originally 6 pm until 10 pm but extended as the stores opened later. Thus working unsociable hours is a common response of mothers' need to work but in the absence of socially provided childcare. Private provision and even the payment of childminders would not be feasible from the wages women receive (Marsh and Mackay 1993; Ward et al. 1994). There were only two cases in a wider study where any payment for childcare was made (Perrons and Hurstfield 1998). In one case a mother, seeking to become a student herself, paid for her child to go to nursery school one day a week for pedagogical reasons and another full-time employee (male) paid for his child to attend the subsidized crèche run by the local authority where his wife worked full-time, but the fees took between 60 and 70 per cent of his earnings. The lack of publicly provided childcare meant that life was particularly difficult for single parents, especially if they were required to work at the weekend and they reported that on occasions they reluctantly and 'guiltily' left their children on their own.

The low pay provided by supermarkets (basic hourly payments are around £4 per hour) are roughly equivalent to half the average hourly male earnings (NES 1997) which together with the low level of public childcare provision clearly limits choice. However, many of our respondents stated that they preferred either to look after their children themselves or for another member of the family to do so. With few exceptions it was considered desirable and natural that their paid work should take second place to both their childcare responsibilities and their husband's career. One supermarket worker had given up work as a ballet teacher when her child started school as the timing of the ballet classes meant that she would not 'be there' for her child. She would not wish things to be different as her husband's career was 'progressing so well at present'. Thus in the UK, while much less overt than in Chile, patriarchal gender relations are nevertheless pervasive. Some of the workers indicated that they would seek better employment in 'social hours' as soon as the children were older but for the time being both the hours and the lack of responsibility at work were considered attractive. Many found that their present jobs were sufficiently demanding and neither considered themselves nor were considered for higher posts – though in principle promotion was said to be possible.

Working patterns with serial childcare often require a great deal of cooperation and co-ordination between partners in a household. While our respondents, again in conformity with larger scale national surveys (for example, Ferri and Smith 1996), reported that it was they, the women, who played the major role and had responsibility for managing childcare and domestic work, partners had to carry out these functions when they were absent. When women worked short hours during the day there was virtually no reallocation of household duties and while twilight and nightworkers generally prepared their children for bed before leaving for work men nevertheless had to take responsibility when they had gone and similarly during the daytime at weekends. One effect of this type of arrangement was that the family as a whole had little time together. The pattern of one parent leaving the house as the other returned was quite frequent and the co-ordination problems were intensified when both partners had flexible work. In general male partners were said to be happy with these arrangements because they recognized that the income was essential. Night work, however, caused more consternation and one twilight/night worker (working 8.30 pm until 1 or 2 in the morning, sometimes later, five nights a week) indicated that she was under considerable pressure from her husband to switch to daytime hours now that the children were at school. She preferred working nights because it meant that she would 'be there' in the holidays for the children without having to change her working pattern. This respondent also said that night work placed a lot of stress on marriages.

Despite the problems of juggling household arrangements most of the respondents had a positive attitude towards going out to work, if not the work itself, which was physically demanding and on occasions stressful. The income was viewed as essential, but also provided them with some independence; the companionship of colleagues was valued and many including a store manager (also a mother with a young child) found coming to work 'a rest' from home and childcare responsibilities and somewhere where they could 'be themselves' (Perrons and Hurstfield 1998).

At one level, then, there is harmony between the needs of the supermarkets for flexible workers who are available for varied periods during the day and night, during the week and at weekends. However, these jobs provide little more than short-term income. This form of employment may be useful for those seeking work on a part-time basis for a limited period, but many of the women interviewed had been in this form of employment, if not this job, for some time. Because this work replicates their domestic role within the commercial sphere it is socially undervalued. The supermarkets are in effect benefiting from the unequal division of labour between women and men which creates this pool of labour willing to accept these employment patterns, and from the sex-typing and social undervaluation of the jobs women do, which enables them to pay partial wages. Even though male workers tend to colonize the higher-paid jobs they also experience comparatively low wages associated with this feminized sector of employment.

THEORIZING GENDER RELATIONS IN THE HOUSHOLD

Women in very different countries are linked by their involvement in a specific commodity chain. The form of their involvement differs according to their location and position within the chain and the type of employment available. Nevertheless they share some similar experiences in combining flexible work with primary domestic and childcare responsibility, which we will now explore at a more analytical level. Our focus is very specific in that we are examining an aspect of the increased global commercialization of food production and distribution. Although women have now been drawn into paid employment in the commercial food sector, as a temporary or part-time workforce it has been a partial integration. They have thus had to negotiate partial change in the gender division of labour both within the household and within paid employment in complex ways, within a social and economic context which has both transformed and reinforced their stereotypical role. In this section we explore this complexity from the standpoint of three approaches to the analysis of gender relations: co-operative conflict, gender contracts/arrangements, and patriarchy. Although gender relations are subject to far broader influences than we have been able to consider in our small case study, we nevertheless aim to throw light on some of the comparative effects of this global chain on gender and household relations within two diverse but interconnected contexts, and raise questions for further research.

Co-operative-Conflict Model

Recent studies of female employment have pointed to the potentially empowering effects paid employment can have for women at a personal, household and social levels (Afshar 1998; Kabeer 1995). Our interviewees mainly supported this perspective, despite their low pay and difficult working conditions. An important aspect of the empowerment of women comes through their improved bargaining position within the household as a result of their independent earnings. From the perspective of 'co-operative-conflict', involvement in paid work can be a contradictory process as: 'the members of the household face two different types of problem simultaneously, one involving *co-operation* (adding to total availabilities) and the other *conflict* (dividing the total availabilities among the members of the household)' (Sen 1990: 129). Women's paid employment enhances household income and therefore its ability to purchase or command goods (its entitlements) and often requires co-operation within the household as unpaid duties have to be reallocated. However, the extent to which women themselves benefit from new arrangements depends on the division of resources within the household that is the degree of 'co-operative conflict'. Overall, taking up paid employment should enhance the relative bargaining position of women. 'Outside earnings can give the woman in question (1) a better breakdown position [e.g. fall back position if they separate from their partner], (2) a possibly a clearer perception of her individuality and well-being, and (3) a higher perceived contribution to the family's economic position' (Sen 1990: 144).

Our case study suggests that the nature of employment affects women's relative position differently. In Chile, poverty has stimulated women's entry into the agro-export sector as their earnings are often crucial to household survival. Male partners consequently have little choice but to co-operate with this arrangement. However, the fact that much of this employment is temporary and that they return to a more traditional role out of season means that their contribution to household income, the strength of their bargaining and fall back positions are constrained and dislocated. By contrast in part-time supermarket work, household relations generally have to adapt on a more consistent basis throughout the year. Women's paid work is often less visible as it is squeezed into the interstices of the day or night, but nevertheless requires the 'co-operation' of their partners at least to juggle working hours so that children are looked after when at home. Thus although weak, the strength of women's bargaining position is more consistent.

The co-operative-conflict model provides some interesting insights into the effects of female employment on the complexity of gender relations within the household. There are also broader social and cultural influences on the type of work available, the socially appropriate scale and nature of women's employment and the gender division of labour within the household. Labour market liberalization in both countries has increased the flexibility and insecurity of male employment, which had traditionally been more stable, so more households are dependent on multiple incomes. In Chile traditional agricultural work for men has declined with commercialization and monocultivation, while in the UK the earnings capacity of low-skilled men has been reduced by both job insecurity and income polarization through which the earnings of the lowest decile have remained stable while those on average and higher earnings have increased (Gosling et al. 1997). In this situation the bargaining position of men relative to women in poorer households is correspondingly weakened and the household becomes more dependent on co-operation as a survival strategy, as the breakdown position of all members is undermined.

There are also societal influences or boundaries (albeit flexible) on the socially legitimate scale and nature of women's paid work and it is within these boundaries that bargaining at the household level takes place. These constraints or boundaries vary between different societies and over time within any society depending on the kinds of jobs available and the need for household income. These wider social influences are addressed more directly in the gender arrangement and differentiated patriarchy approaches to gender relations and are discussed below (see also Perrons and Gonas 1998).

Gender Contracts and Gender Arrangements

The gender contracts or gender arrangements approach to gender relations derives from the work of the Swedish social historian Yvonne

Hirdmann (1990) and has been extended and modified by Birgit Pfau-Effinger (1995) (for a review see Duncan 1996). They refer to the development of a sociocultural consensus about the desirable social division of labour between women and men. Although founded on a basic asymmetry of power between men and women, women nevertheless are said to play an active role in the development and renegotiation of the contract in the course of social modernization (Duncan, 1994; Pfau-Effinger, 1995). In the case of Sweden, Hirdmann (1990) defines different phases in the modernization of the gender contract: the housewife contract (1930s–1960s), with male breadwinner and female homemaker; a transitional phase (1950s–1960s) in which women were entering paid employment but were essentially faced with a double burden of paid and domestic work; an equality contract, in which all adults were expected to engage in paid work and caring (1960s–1980s); an equal status contract 1980s–present, with women seeking to obtain a more equal status in paid work and in the political sphere. These different phases have not evolved in a simple linear way but have been the outcome of struggle by women for improvement especially through the women's groups in the Social Democratic Party in the context of economic restructuring and more general social change. Thus the actual bargaining, arrangements or contracts formed at the household level would be influenced by the prevailing social consensus.

In our case study, the socio-economic contexts in which gender contracts are formed clearly differ. However, the process of globalization, bringing with it new forms of economic activity, working practices and forms of integration, appears to cut across any singularly national determination. The forms of female employment mirror the requirements of the production and distribution process independently of social context. In rural Chile, this increase in women's paid work, in the context of intense poverty, has forced the pace of change, and gender contracts have had to adapt rapidly, often in conflict with social and cultural norms where notions of *machismo* continue. A dramatic transformation has clearly taken place over the past two decades, and the *temporeras* face numerous tensions in mediating their traditional and modern roles. This tension is reinforced by the temporary nature of employment and highlights the contradictory nature of global integration. In the UK, part-time female employment has been more consistent with existing social perceptions of gender roles, and given rise to less overt change in the gender contract. The net result is a reduction in the divergence in gender relations between countries. However the gender division of labour and sex-typing of women's association with food persists along with the asymmetry of power relations between women and men in work and the household. Nevertheless the position of women as active agents in the negotiation of the gender contract at the household level would appear to have been strengthened by their paid employment in both countries, perhaps providing the basis for further change at the societal level.

The gender contract/arrangement perspective facilitates analysis of the forms of gender inequality and tries to identify mechanisms of change in relation to the political economy, cultural norms and gender relations. The modernization of the contract, however, is linked with women's paid employment and yet in our case studies although there have been changes in both the nature of productive and reproductive work by women and men, women still continue to be subordinate in both spheres. This persistent power asymmetry between women and men in which the activities that women do, in our particular case food-related nurturing and provisioning, whether in the home or in the workplace, continue to be of low social status and reward. It is for this reason that we turn to explanations based on patriarchy, which place gender inequality at the centre of the analysis even though the concept of patriarchy has been criticized in recent years.

Patriarchy

Patriarchy has been defined as 'a system of social structures and practices in which men dominate, oppress and exploit women' (Walby 1990: 20). Recently it has been criticized for being universal, trans-historical and trans-cultural, for tending towards biological essentialism and reductionism and for being a grand narrative or meta-theory of little value (Acker 1989; Charles 1993; Pollert 1996). Because it implies an unchanging structure it appears to overlook the diversity between women and to foreclose the possibility of women effecting change. However Sylvia Walby (1994) has developed the concept of differentiated patriarchy which allows diversity between women's situations to be recognized while not abandoning male domination as a central organizing concept. Different forms (public and private) and different elements (in paid work, the household, the state, male violence, sexuality and culture) of patriarchy are identified which are continua along which the degree of patriarchy can vary. Differentiated patriarchy therefore allows a wide variety of different forms and degrees of oppression (Walby 1994) and so permits determination, i.e. the structuring of past events without determinism (Duncan 1994). In other words, this approach allows for both diversity of experience and the possibility of change, but these possibilities are set within a structure which emphasizes the continuing importance of social constraints – in this case male power – which shape individual life chances (Perrons 1995).

Anna Pollert (1996) argues, however, that even this conceptualization of patriarchy provides only description and not explanation. She draws a contrast with the concept of the wage relation and argues that while the capital–wage relation has a clear internal dynamic which can explain why certain actions have to be taken to maintain the social order, there is no equivalent dynamic to patriarchal relations and neither is the maintenance of patriarchal relations crucial to social reproduction. Rather in many situations women and men have more to gain from acting in harmony or in co-operation (Pollert 1996). As we have seen, while women and men often co-operate, as for example in the negotiation and renegotiation of the domestic division of labour, the power difference is still evident – women continue to have primary responsibility for domestic work and childcare which constrains their time and energy for paid work. Similarly, as the history of women's employment demonstrates, while the form of patriarchy or nature of sex-typing in employment may change, hierarchical divisions between women and men tend to reappear. Moreover, persistent gender inequalities are not singular to capitalist societies and so it is not sufficient to argue that 'gendering takes place inside capitalist relations' (Pollert 1996: 640). Thus the process of gendering and recurring gender inequalities and power imbalances need to be in the foreground of analyses and explained even if so far we do not have very sophisticated analytical tools to do so. A feminist historical materialism needs to identify theoretical concepts and categories that help to make sense of the chaotic common-sense world and for the time being the concept of patriarchy seems to be all we have to account for the way in which social inequalities are structured by gender as well as social class. A comparative focus on women's specific coping strategies and 'patriarchal bargains' (Kandiyoti 1988) within different contexts also provides the basis for analysing the process of transformation, which is prevalent under globalization.

Our case study provides a very concrete example of the way global accumulation in the fruit sector has intermeshed and interacted with women's lives in different countries but also shows how globalization has been shaped and reinforced by an existing gender division of labour based on an asymmetry of power relations. An understanding of the capitalist production process is essential to analysing the development of global food chains, but this analysis alone cannot explain the gendered form it has taken. In both cases, flexible female labour has been employed which has transmuted older and patriarchal relations in complex and contradictory ways. Agribusiness and multiples depend on women returning to their traditional gender roles to sustain them as a reliable flexible female labour force. Hierarchical relations based on a gender division of labour, have been recast rather than removed, recreating new forms of subordination. Thus patriarchy should not be excluded from the analysis, but be seen as a component in the understanding of the mosaic of diversity and contradiction which makes up women's experiences of employment in different locations at different times in a centralized global food chain dominated at its heart by transnational capital.

CONCLUSION

Waged employment and commercialized consumption patterns have expanded and deepened in Chile and the UK as a consequence of globalization, especially in rural Chile as a specific outcome of the development of the global fruit chain. In both countries women's paid work has expanded and employment in fruit production or supermarkets is deemed to be socially acceptable, extending women's traditional role in the household into the commercial food sector. While the form of work varies between the two countries in both cases it is flexible and low paid.

The impact on household relations varies depending on whether it is concentrated seasonal work or part-time work all year round. The extent of the transformation also varies between Chile and the UK, with the former undergoing a much greater change in the social relations of production through the decline of traditional agriculture, and therefore change in traditional household division of labour. The net result is complex, with varied effects in each location, but there is a greater homogeneity of experience than before. In both, women continue to bear the main burden of domestic work and childcare, and in both women prefer to have paid work given the options. The impact on gender relations varies because of pre-existing differences in the nature of the household relations, and because of the different coping strategies needed to combine domestic roles with seasonal or part-time employment.

Households in both locations have been affected by global economic and political processes and have adapted gender roles as part of their household survival or coping strategies in the modern commercial world. The form of adaptation varies as global integration meshes with historically different gendered social formations, and varies according to differences in the nexus linking the local to the global. The process of adaptation generates tensions and contradictions at both the household and community levels as traditional gender roles are mediated as a consequence of this integration. Yet despite significant differences, there are many similarities in the outcomes faced by women in both locations. This case study has explored the organic links that have been increasingly, if imperceptibly, forged through the process of globalization between women in different countries. The expansion of the global fruit chain is part of a process of combined and uneven development which has had complex and contradictory affects on households in developing and developed countries, but has also drawn together a greater commonality of women's experiences in the context of a global commercial world.

NOTES

1. The overall research was based on a small qualitative study of women fruit workers and supermarket workers in Chile and the UK, along with interviews of professionals, producers, exporters and supermarket retailers in the trade between 1995 and 1996. In Chile we conducted four in-depth interviews and three semi-structured focus group interviews of between 5–8 *temporeras*, as well as ten interviews with professionals from trade unions, women's and community groups, NGOs and government departments working with the *temporeras*. In the UK we carried out 12 in-depth interviews and two small focus group interviews of 3–4 women supermarket workers, plus five in-depth interviews with human resource managers. D. Perrons has since continued to interview supermarket workers as part of a comparative EU project. This research complements larger-scale surveys: in Chile by Venegas (1992), Díaz (1991), Rodriguez and Venegas (1991), and PREALC (1990); in the UK by Neathey and Hurstfield (1995); Dex and McCulloch (1995) and Casey et al. (1997). We found consistency between our findings and these larger scale studies which our qualitative study helps to illuminate (Maynard 1994).
2. It is difficult to estimate precise earnings, especially of women as they are mainly paid piece rate, and can be very variable. Bee and Vogel (1997) estimated that in the Norte Chico in 1993/4 a woman packer can earn 2.7 pence per 8.2 kg box of grapes, and earn between £5.36 and £8.07 per day for a 12-hour day.
3. At the end of 1996 the big four supermarkets had 63 per cent of all grocery sales (Verdict Research, cited by *The Guardian*, 30 September 1997, p. 19).
4. In the retail sector as a whole, which accounts for 2.4 million workers (10.4 per cent of national employment), 62 per cent of employees are female. Of these 22 per cent work full time and 40 per cent part-time (NRTC 1995). Thus about 80 per cent of the part-time workers are female. In the supermarket sector the proportion of females and part-timers is estimated

to be higher. Students make up 10 per cent of the retail workforce as a whole and again their representation is greater in supermarkets.

REFERENCES

Acker, J. (1989) 'The problem with patriarchy', *Sociology* 23, pp. 235–40.
Afshar, H. and Dennis, C. (1992) *Women and Adjustment Policies in the Third World*, Basingstoke: Macmillan.
Afshar, H. (ed.) (1998) *Empowering Women: Illustrations from the Third World*, Basingstoke: Macmillan.
Arizpe, L. and J. Aranda (1981) 'The "Comparative Advantages" of Women's Disadvantages: Women Workers in the Strawberry Export Agribusiness in Mexico', *Signs* 7(2), pp. 453–73.
Barrientos, S. (1996) 'Flexible Work and Female Labour: The Global Integration of Chilean Fruit Production', in R. Auty and J. Toye (eds) *Challenging the Orthodoxies*, Basingstoke: Macmillan.
Barrientos, S. (1998) 'Fruits of Burden – the Organisation of Women Temporary Workers in Chilean Agribusiness', in H. Afshar (ed.) *Empowering Women: Illustrations from the Third World*, Basingstoke: Macmillan.
Barrientos, S. and D. Perrons (1996) 'Fruit of the Vine – Linkages between Flexible Women Workers in the Production and Retailing of Winter Fruit'. Paper presented to the Globalization of Production Conference, University of Warwick, September.
Barrientos, S., A. Bee, A. Matear and I. Vogel (forthcoming) *Women in Agribusiness. Working Miracles in the Chilean Fruit Export Sector*, Basingstoke: Macmillan.
Bee, A. (1996) *Regional Change and Non-Traditional Exports: Land, Labour and Gender in the Norte-Chico, Chile*, unpublished PhD Thesis, University of Birmingham.
Bee, A. and I. Vogel (1997) '*Temporeras* and Household Relations: Seasonal Employment in Chile's Agro-export Sector', *Bulletin of Latin American Research* 16:1 pp. 83–96.
Bell, D. and Valentine, G. (1997) *Consuming Geographies: We Are Where We Eat*, London: Routledge.
Bonanno, A., L. Busch, W. Friedland, L. Gouveia and E. Mingione (eds) (1994) *From Columbus to ConAgra, The Globalization of Agriculture and Food*, Kansas, University of Kansas Press.
Casey, B., Metcalf, H. and Millward, N. (1997) *Employers' Use of Flexible Labour*, London, Policy Studies Institute.
Chant, S. (1997) *Women-headed Households: Diversity and Dynamics in the Developing World*. Basingstoke: Macmillan.
Charles, N. (1993) *Gender Divisions and Social Change*, Hemel Hempstead: Harvester Wheatsheaf.
Charles, N. and Kerr, M. (1988) *Women, Food and Families*, Manchester: Manchester University Press.
Dex, S. and McCulloch, A. (1995) *Flexible Employment in Britain: a Statistical Analysis*, Equal Opportunities Commission Research Discussion Series 15, Manchester, EOC.

Díaz, E. (1991) *Investigacíon Participativa Acerca de las Trabajadoras Temporeras de la Fruta, San Bernando*, Santiago: Centro EL Canelo de Nos.
Duncan, S. (1994) 'Theorising Differences in Patriarchy', *Environment and Planning* 26:8, pp. 1177–94.
Duncan, S. (1996) 'The Diverse Worlds of European Patriarchy', in M.D. Dolors García-Ramon and J. Monk (eds) *Women of the European Union: the Politics of Work and Daily Life*, London: Routledge.
EC (1997) *Equal Opportunities for Women and Men in the European Union*, Annual Report 1996, Luxembourg: European Commission.
Elson, D. and Pearson R. (1981) 'Nimble Fingers Make Cheap Workers, an Analysis of Women's Employment in Third World Export Manufacturing', *Feminist Review*, (Spring), pp. 87–107.
Ferri, E. and Smith, K. (1996) *Parenting in the 1990s London: Family Studies Centre*, London: Joseph Rowntree Foundation.
Fine, B. (1995) 'From Political Economy to Consumption' in D. Miller (ed.) *Acknowledging consumption*, London: Routledge.
Fisher, J. (1993) *Out of the Shadows, Women, Resistance and Politics in South America*, London: Latin American Bureau.
Friedland, W. (1994) 'The New Globalization, The Case of Fresh Produce' in A. Bonanno, L. Busch, W. Friedland, L. Gouveia and E. Mingione, *From Columbus to ConAgra. The Globalization of Agriculture and Food*, Kansas: University Press of Kansas.
Friedland, W., Busch, L. Buttel and F. Rudy (1991) *Towards a New Political Economy of Agriculture*, Boulder: Westview Press.
Gereffi, G. and M. Korzeniewicz (eds) (1994) *Commodity Chains and Global Capitalism*, Westport, Conn.: Greenwood Press.
Glover, J. and Arber, S. (1995) 'Polarisation in Mother's Employment', *Gender, Work and Organisation* 2(4): 165–79.
Gómez, S. and Echeñique, J. (1988) *La Agricultura Chilena, Las Dos Caras de la Modernización*, Santiago, FLACSO.
Goodman, D. and Redclift, M. (1991) *Refashioning Nature, Food, Ecology and Culture*, London: Routledge.
Gosling, A., Johnson, P., McCrae, J. and Paull, G. (1997) *The Dynamics of Low Pay and Unemployment in early 1990s Britain*. London: Institute for Fiscal Studies.
Hirdmann, Y. (1990) 'Women – from Possibility to Problem? Gender Conflict in the Welfare State – the Swedish model' Research Report Series No. 3, Arbetsliuscentrum/The Swedish Centre for Working Life, Stockholm.
Hoogvelt, A. (1997) *Globalization and the Postcolonial World, The New Political Economy of Development*, Basingstoke: Macmillan.
Jarvis, S. and Jenkins, S. (1997) 'Marital Splits and Income Changes: Evidence for Britain', Working Paper 97–4 University of Essex: ESRC Research Centre on Micro-Social Change.
Jackson, P. and Holbrook, B. (1995) 'Multiple Meanings: Shopping and the Cultural Politics of Identity', *Environment and Planning* 27, pp. 1913–32.
Kabeer, N. (1995) 'Necessary, Sufficient or Relevant? Women's Wages and Intra-household Power Relations in Urban Bangladesh', IDS Working Paper 25, Institute of Development Studies, Sussex.
Kandiyoti, D. (1988) 'Bargaining with Patriarchy', *Gender and Society* 2(3), pp. 274–90.

Macintosh, M. (1989) *Gender, Class and Rural Transition, Agribusiness and the Food Crisis in Senegal*, London: Zed Books.
Marsden, T. and Wrigley, N. (1996) 'Retailing, the Food System and the Regulatory State', pp. 33–47 in N. Wrigley and M. Lowe (eds.) *Retailing, Consumption and Capital: Towards the New Retail Geography*, London: Longman.
Marsh, A. and McKay, S. (1993) 'Families, Work and the use of Childcare', *Employment Gazaette*, 3 August, pp. 61–70.
Matear, A. (1997) 'Gender and the State in Rural Chile', *Bulletin of Latin American Research*, 6(1), pp. 97–106.
Maynard, M. (1994) 'Methods, Practice and Epistemology: the Debate about Feminism and Research', in M. Maynard and J. Purvis (eds) *Researching Women's Lives from a Feminist Perspective*. London: Taylor and Francis.
McMichael, P. (ed.) (1994) *The Global Restructuring of Agro-food Systems*, New York: Cornell University Press
Meulders, D., Plasman, R. and Vander Stricht, V. (1993) *Position of Women in the Labour Market in the EU*. Aldershot.
Mitter, S. (1986) *Common Fate, Common Bond, Women in the Global Economy*, London: Pluto Press.
Murcott, A. (1997) 'The lost supper', *The Times Higher*, 31 January p. 15 and published as 'Family Meals – A Thing of the Past?' in P. Caplan (ed.) *Food, Health and Identity*, London: Routledge.
Neathey, F. and Hurstfield, J. (1995) 'Flexibility in Practice: Women's Employment and Pay in Retail and Finance', EOC/IRS Discussions Series no. 16, Manchester, EOC.
NES (1997) *New Earnings Survey 1996*. London: The Stationery Office.
Perrons, D. (1995) 'Gender Inequalities in Regional Development', *Regional Studies* 25(5), pp. 465–76.
Perrons, D. and Gonas, L. (1998) 'Perspectives on Gender Inequality in European Employment', *European Urban and Regional Studies* 5(1).
Perrons, D. and Hurstfield (1998) 'Flexible Working and the Reconciliation of Work and Family Life – or a New Form of Precariousness'. Employment and Social Affairs, V/768/98 CE-V/2-98-003-EN-C. Brussels: European Commission.
Pfau-Effinger, B. (1995) 'Social Change in the Gendered Division of Labour in Cross-national Perspective.' Second European Conference of Sociology Working Group, 'Gender Relations and the Labour Market in Europe'. Budapest. September.
Pollert, A. (1996) 'Gender and Class Revisited; or the Poverty of Patriarchy', *Sociology* 38(4): 639–59.
PREALC (1990) Programa Regional del Empleo para Americana Latina y el Caribe, *Ciclos Ocupacionales y Disponibilidad de Mano de Obra Temporal en Dos Communas de Valle de Aconcagua*, no. 344, Santiago.
Rodriguez, D. and S. Venegas (1991) *Las Trabajadores de La Fruta en Cifras*, Santiago: GEA.
Sachs, C. (1996) *Gendered Fields, Rural Women, Agriculture and Environment*, Boulder, Col.: Westview Press.
Scott, A.M. (1994) 'Gender Segregation in the Retail Industry', in A.M. Scott (ed.) *Gender Segregation and Social Change: Men and Women in Changing Labour Markets*. Oxford: Oxford University Press.

Sen, A. (1990) 'Gender and Co-operative Conflicts' in I. Tinker (ed.) *Persistent Inequalities, Women and World Development*, Oxford: Oxford University Press.

Silva, P. (1995) 'Modernization, Consumerism and Politics in Chile' in D. Hojman (ed.) *Neo-liberalism with a Human Face? The Politics and Economics of the Chilean Model*, Institute of Latin American Studies, Liverpool, Monograph Series No. 20.

Sklair, L. (1994) *Sociology of the Global System*. London: Harvester Wheatsheaf.

USDAW (1996) 'Women in Usdaw – an Integral Role: The Agenda for 1996'. Manchester: USDAW.

Venegas, S. (1992) *Una gota al día, un chorro al año, El Impacto Social de la Expansión Frutícola*, Santiago: GEA.

Vogel, I. (1997) *The Labour Market, Gender and Rapid Social Change in Chile: Working Women's Experiences*, unpublished PhD, University of Liverpool.

Walby, S (1990) *Theorising Patriarchy*, Oxford: Blackwell.

Walby, S. (1994) 'Methodological and Theoretical Issues in the Comparative Analysis of Gender Relations in Western Europe', *Environment and Planning* 26(9), pp. 1339–54.

Ward, C., Dale, A. and Joshi, H. (1994) 'Combining Employment with Childcare: an Escape from Dependence?', NCDS User Support Group Working Paper 38, SSRU, London: City University.

Wrigley, N. (1996) 'Sunk Costs and Corporate Restructuring: British Food Retailing and the Property Crisis' in N. Wrigley and M. Lowe (eds) *Retailing, Consumption and Capital: Towards the New Retail Geography*, London: Longman.

Wrigley N. and M. Lowe (eds) (1996) *Retailing, Consumption and Capital: Towards the New Retail Geography*, London: Longman.

9 Women's Work in Changing Labour Markets: the Case of Thailand in the 1980s[1]

Rachel Kurian

INTRODUCTION

The distinctive characteristic of globalization in its relation to contemporary capitalism is, according to Scholte, the 'rise of supraterritoriality', or the trend for territorial frameworks to hold limited significance for markets, production, commodities, business organizations and finance. An important dimension of this process is the speed of the growth and spread of the corporate organizations involved in transborder operations in recent decades (Scholte 1997).[2] These global companies represent significant loci of power as they control an estimated 70 per cent of the products in international trade and an equivalent proportion of foreign direct investment.[3] This increase in foreign direct investment has been accompanied by different corporate strategies, including the siting of production itself in countries which suited an array of corporate objectives such as market-seeking, (natural) resource-seeking, efficiency-seeking and strategic asset-seeking (Dunning 1993). The host governments themselves have also in many cases enacted policies which were intended to make their country a more favourable environment for foreign direct investment. These factors have had their effect on local labour markets, and in turn, on women's work and lives.

This chapter examines the impact of foreign direct investment on women's work in Thailand in the 1980s. It argues that it resulted in the greater feminization of the labour market and increased fragmentation of women's work and lives. Both horizontal and vertical segmentation of local labour markets were accentuated in this process while the non-market labour segment continued to remain primarily women's responsibilities.[4] An important consequence was that women were often simultaneously working in different labour segments, which gave rise to increasing fragmentation of their identities and responsibilities.

Women in Changing Labour Markets

A special dimension of this process in Thailand was the relatively high degree of temporary migration undertaken by women from the agricultural sector for urban based export oriented manufacturing.

In the first section I examine some of the relevant theoretical discussions on gender and labour market segmentation and their impact on fragmentation of women's lives in the context of trade liberalization, market-oriented economic reform and increased investment foreign direct investment. Second, I consider the case of Thailand in the 1980s, a period during which the economy experienced considerable success with regard to export-oriented industrialization and growth. This section examines the influence exerted by foreign direct investment in generating a particular type of demand in the labour market. In the third section I examine the dynamics in the rural sector, the main source of labour, and see how it has been affected by trade liberalization and economic reform. This indicates that there was little potential for increasing productive employment and adequate income in this sector, so creating possibilities for labour to be released from agriculture to move into industry. In the fourth section the focus is the process of migration – something that historically has been important in Thailand's history, but which took on a special significance in the light of the problems in the rural sector and the demands for labour by foreign direct investment. Here it will be seen that women formed a dominant part of the rural–urban temporary migration stream in the 1980s in response to demands of the pattern of industrialization in the 1980s. In the fifth section I analyse how the combined pressures on the labour market resulted in more women joining the waged labour market and being employed (sometimes simultaneously) in the more vulnerable labour 'segments', a process reinforced by their relatively high degree of participation in the temporary rural–urban migration stream. At the same time, whether they were in the rural or urban sector, women continued to contribute financially and with their labour-time to taking care of the household and family needs. As a result of these multiple and yet separate spheres of work and responsibilities, women's lives became more fragmented. I conclude with some observations on the future prospects for the women workers.

GENDER AND LABOUR MARKETS

Labour segmentation, or the existence of separate sub-labour markets, can take place along horizontal and vertical lines.[5] Horizontal segmentation occurs when the production process is separated into different 'segments' according to the labour process. Vertical segmentation can occur by personal characteristics: sex, age, experience, education, personal connections or race. Rodgers (1986) introduced a certain dynamism into the analysis of labour market segmentation by postulating segmentation as an intrinsic part of labour market functioning. The patterns of segmentation would reflect, within this perspective, the strategies and relative power of the labour market actors in terms of capacity to organize, to exercise monopoly or monopsony, to exert political influence and control resources (1986: 243). Such a perspective is particularly relevant to and influences the analysis adopted in this chapter. It underscores the historical and political nature of labour market segmentation and provides a framework to analyse gender segmentation in different contexts.

Segmentation along gender lines has characterized labour markets in most industrialized and developing countries, where women have been disproportionately represented in certain labour-intensive and repetitive segments of production and services, their work usually associated with lower pay than men (even for equivalent work). Women have also tended to be at the lowest rungs of the industrial hierarchy. The economic argument that these differences reflect the lower skills and productivity of women workers (the basis of the human capital school) has been contested by empirical evidence. In fact, Phillips and Taylor (1986) suggest that skill definitions are, as they see it, 'saturated with sexual bias', resulting in a situation in which the work that women do is viewed as inferior because it is women who do it. Clearly gender in itself appears to have been the cause of segmentation, although this is also mediated by segmentation along other lines, such as age, ethnicity, colour and race. For the purposes of this chapter, it is important to see how gender segmentation has been articulated in the context of trade liberalization and market-oriented economic reform in the 1980s, particularly in the South East Asian context.

Trade liberalization and market-oriented economic reform were part and parcel of neo-liberal philosophy, which gained dominance in the 1980s. Promoted in many developing countries by the IMF, the World Bank as well as several regional development banks and institutions, these included the devaluation of the local currency, the reduction or removal of tariffs and duties, an easing of restrictive practices on foreign companies gaining access to local resources and markets, and the switching of resources from non-tradables to tradables. Within this framework, restructuring of the local economy along competitive lines required access to modern capital, technology and management practices, an important source for these inputs being multinational corporations. Thus, implicitly and explicitly, this policy framework gave high priority to foreign direct investment to stimulate growth.

But, as has been witnessed in the 1980s, the implementation of many of these policy instruments did not result in any significant increase in foreign direct investment, the latter continuing to be concentrated in the industrialized countries.[6] In reality, the vast majority of the developing countries that undertook monetary and fiscal reforms essentially operated at the margin in terms of receipts of foreign direct investment, with ten countries accounting for some 84 per cent of average annual flows of foreign direct investment in 1985–9.[7]

The governments of some developing countries attempted to adopt what were termed 'flexible labour policies' as an extra incentive for multinationals to invest in their economies. These incentives were in line with the broader policy framework of limiting government intervention in order to promote efficiency and profitability of production. Specific labour market policy measures included the easing or removal of wage policies, social security policies, access to jobs and incomes, and to collective bargaining and unionization on the grounds that they served as unnecessary interventions which could lead to misallocations. These policy measures resulted in greater vertical segmentation of the labour market, with some workers being more privileged in terms of wages and conditions of work, while others – and these constituted often the majority – had to be eased out of employment through rationalization and/or to be employed in relatively vulnerable categories of work.

Increased horizontal and vertical segmentation of the labour market was also related to the emphasis by multinationals – particularly those of Japanese origin in the 1980s in the East Asian region – to the development of competitive advantage through overseas manufacturing and international subcontracting.[8] Management practices in the large Japanese firms emphasized flexibility, efficiency and quality in a demand-driven market and minimized costs of stock maintenance by the use of extensive systems of subcontracting by smaller firms which could provide quality products at short notice: the so-called just-in-time system.[9] Within an economy, this essentially represented a degree of horizontal segmentation of the labour market with a clear demarcation between workers who worked in the subcontracted firms and those who worked for the larger companies. There were, however, distinctly different types of privileges associated with work in the two 'segments', with those working for the large companies enjoying substantially better conditions of work and pay than those employed in the subcontracting firms. Thus vertical segmentation of the labour market was implicitly promoted by these types of subcontracting arrangements.

There was a spread of Japanese foreign direct investment in East Asia in the 1980s driven by the need to reduce costs, promote domestic restructuring (in Japan), protect against the vagaries of other countries' market-access policies, deal with fluctuating exchange rates and hedge against the possible consequences of regionalist tendencies elsewhere. Japanese multinational corporations also had the support of key ministries and agencies of the Japanese government in promoting their corporate interests in the East Asian region (Machado 1995). They jointly promoted 'complex international work sharing' to 'optimize complementarity within specific transnational industries' (Machado 1995: 54). The principle of 'work sharing' was to 'segment' the labour process horizontally according to cost efficiency and was intended to result in an integrated process based on agreed specialization. (Machado 1995: 54).

While at the international/regional level 'work sharing' implied increased outsourcing or procurement from overseas affiliates to cut production costs, often the affiliates in turn used the same principles and systems of subcontracting within the local economy. The problem of quality control in these small subcontracting firms – a major risk – was hedged to some extent by having a wide network of competitive suppliers. In effect, therefore, such a cost effective sourcing policy relied on the downloading of risk and costs to producers and workers at each lower layer of the subcontracting relationship.

This trend for horizontal segmentation of the labour market via subcontracting was accompanied by increasing vertical segmentation. This, as we saw previously, was related to some extent to the flexible labour market policies which increased hierarchization in the workforce. But vertical segmentation was also linked to the system of 'work sharing' and cost-effective sourcing promoted by the Japanese multinationals where, as unlike those employed on a full-time basis directly by the company with high wages and good working conditions, those employed further down the line by the subcontracting firms worked in the more vulnerable segments of the labour market. Thus, in these different ways, the pressures of economic reform, trade liberalization and foreign direct investment accentuated horizontal and vertical segmentation in the local labour market creating in this process high vulnerable categories of workers at the lower levels of the industrial hierarchy.

Women's labour took on special significance in this context. The plentiful supply of low-skilled and cheap female labour was highlighted as an important comparative advantage by many developing countries, something that was particularly important with the liberalization of trade and economic reform in the 1980s.[10] Additionally, female workers could play an important role at the lower levels of the industrial and work hierarchy in the context of flexible labour markets and the 'cost-effective sourcing policies' of multinationals. As we saw previously, flexibility and lower fixed costs could be realized by employing female workers on a temporary basis and/or by subcontracting low-skilled labour-intensive work to firms (affiliates or locally owned) which had to supply products at short notice and which usually then hired women to do the work. Finally, the scale of production at the lower levels of subcontracting was smaller and it was assumed that workers/women here were less likely to be involved in labour organization or trade unions, something that was often considered to be anti-management.[11]

While market reform and multinational corporate involvement tended to generate demand for certain types of labour in host economies, the specific response of the workers to these demands reflected the dynamics of the local economies. Important influences on the supply of labour included the options and pressures in agriculture and the rural sector in general (the main source of the labour supply in most developing countries) and their ability to provide productive employment and adequate income.

As far as the majority of women were concerned, one important pressure lay in the accepted societal sexual division of labour and the accompanying ideology which held the caring tasks in the household to be the responsibility of women. The increased use of subcontracting interfaced well with these duties, as some of this work could be done within the household, allowing women to combine paid work with their household tasks. At the same time, the flexibility of the demand for labour allowed the release of some women from the household sector for this work on a temporary basis. Often, but not always, this meant migration from the rural areas to the cities for waged employment.

These different pressures led, in some circumstances, to increased feminization of the labour force with increased fragmentation of women's lives. Feminization occurred via worsening income distribution (normal in the first stages of trade liberalization and market-oriented economic reform) where low-income families are forced to seek temporary/permanent/waged or other employment. Feminization happened through the demand for cheap labour as women's relatively lower wages could provide a comparative advantage in export-oriented industrialization.[12] But feminization in the context of increased vertical and horizontal segmentation of the labour markets can and has resulted in many cases in women being associated with the more vulnerable segments of the labour force and the category of workers on which the risks of production are downloaded. At the same time, their work in the non-market labour segment continued as part of the accepted division of work in society. The pressures for adequate income often forced them to work simultaneously in two or more of these segments, each segment associated with different identities and responsibilities. In this process, the majority of women tended to operate and survive in increasingly fragmented existences with increasingly separate and multiple spheres of production and reproduction.

THE CASE OF THAILAND

For most of the twentieth century Thailand was essentially an agricultural-based economy with over 80 per cent of the population living in the rural areas. The major changes in terms of trade liberalization and market-oriented economic reforms were undertaken in the 1980s and were linked to the conditions under which the World Bank provided loans to Thailand[13] The main adjustment programmes were taken only around the mid-1980s and included increased prices and rates on public services and utilities, strict controls on government spending and foreign borrowing. Additionally, there were several devaluations in the 1980s which were important in lowering the costs of local labour and thus making it attractive for foreign direct investment to investment in the manufacturing and services sectors of the country.[14]

In response to these different incentives, foreign direct investment (FDI) increased dramatically in the second half of the 1980s. It grew from 9259 million baht in 1980 at a rate of 4.7 per cent per annum between 1980 and 1987, but from 1988 this figure expanded until it reached the order of 74,858 million baht in 1990. The major sources of FDI in Thailand were Japan, the United States, the European Community (EC) and the Asian newly industrializing economies (NIEs). Japan took the lead from the United States in 1988, the latter's share being over 50 per cent in 1988 but down to 44.5 per cent in 1990. (Thailand's share of Japanese FDI worldwide was about 2 per cent in 1990.)

This increased influence of multinationals was, to a large extent, linked to greater emphasis on export-oriented industrialization. Export-oriented FDI projects increased from 10 per cent of total promoted FDI projects in 1984 to more than 80 per cent in 1988 (69 per cent in 1990). The manufacturing sector was particularly significant in terms of exports and between 1985 and 1991 Thailand's total exports quadrupled in value and manufactured exports grew sixfold. Control by foreign capital can be gauged from the fact that the proportion of wholly foreign-owned projects increased from 4.6 per cent in 1980 to 36.8 per cent in 1987, and majority foreign-owned projects from 6.8 per cent in 1980 to 22.1 per cent and 25.2 per cent in 1988 and 1990, while minority foreign projects declined.

This export-led pattern of industrialization was also highly urban oriented, with the highest concentration of industry (state and public enterprises, multinational manufacturing and trading corporations and domestic capitalist enterprises) in the Bangkok Metropolitan area. This region accounted for nearly 75 per cent of value added in manufacturing between 1981 and 1988 (Rimmer 1995: 197).[15] The urban orientation of these firms accentuated the tendency for rural–urban migration, a significant proportion of which were women.

This pattern of export-led industrialization with trade liberalization and a high input of foreign direct investment resulted in multinationals being able to exercise considerable influence on the local labour market. In line with the principles of outsourcing and subcontracting, there was an increase of FDI going to medium and small companies, mainly Japanese, who were on a subcontracting basis for large Japanese multinationals (Phongpaichit 1988).[16] Essentially the latter attempted to minimize costs through subcontracting low-skilled labour-intensive segments of production to local firms. This type of horizontal labour segmentation was evident in the manufacturing sector, where manufactured exports had risen sharply since 1986 in a number of industries which used low to semi-skilled labour. The labour-intensive segments of relatively high-tech industries (such as semiconductors) also rose in importance. Important exports included processed food, textiles, shoes, gems and jewellery, artificial flowers, integrated circuits, toys and steel pipes (Sussangkarn 1990: 3).

The production structure of manufacturing in Thailand came to be heavily based on small enterprises, which generated 50 per cent of total employment and accounted for a little less than 50 per cent of value-added.[17] A study done in 1989 covering 300 small and informal activities in 19 districts in Metropolitan Bangkok showed how self-employment and employment in micro- and small firms are linked through complicated subcontracting chains with the world market. Their emergence was directly linked to the macroeconomic strategy of export-oriented industrialization, which emphasized Thailand's comparative advantage in terms of cheap, labour-intensive manufacturing (Romijn and Mongkornratana 1991).

The vertical segmentation of the labour market was most evident in the increasing significance of hierarchization or informalization of the labour market. It was estimated that, during 1984, some 45 per cent of people in employment in Metropolitan Bangkok were in the informal sector, the figure being somewhat higher (49 per cent) in the five adjoining provinces (NESDB, May 1986, quoted in Pitayanon 1990: 12). This figure has since increased. Workers with a low education level were also concentrated in the informal sector. This is partly in response to the type of employment utilized in the informal sector, where the returns to education above the primary level were zero, or almost zero. Furthermore, the use of small subcontracting firms often sanctioned the used of small and illegal factories and workshops in unfavourable working conditions. The workers were typically associated with low wages and long working hours. Work in textile firms and frozen food and chemical factories are also exposed to health hazards (Phongpaichit 1992: 87). We shall see in the subsequent sections how gender segmentation resulted in women being concentrated in the more vulnerable segments of work. But before we analyse the nature of their involvement, it is important to consider the impact that trade liberalization and economic reform had on the agricultural/rural sector, and how this affected the process of migration and segmentation.

THE DECLINING OPPORTUNITIES FOR LABOUR IN THE AGRICULTURAL SECTOR

The promotion of export-led growth was accompanied by declining opportunities for labour in the agricultural sector. There were three processes that directly contributed to declining employment opportunities in the agricultural sector. The first was the growing scarcity of land; the second related to the impact of trade policy and export prices on incomes in agriculture; and the third was the limited potential for employment through rural industrialization. All these factors contributed to increasing numbers of people moving away from employment in agriculture, either on a temporary basis or a semi-permanent basis. Each of these issues will be dealt with briefly in this section.

Agricultural expansion in Thailand historically relied almost entirely on extensive methods, resulting in substantial deforestation and increasing scarcity of land, and even landlessness by the early 1980s (Keyes 1987).[18] This problem was exacerbated by the negative environmental consequences of trade liberalization and export-led growth through the intensification of renewable-intensive production (forest produce, some food and cash crops, some polluting industries).[19] The booming tourist industry also impacted the environment and the availability land for agriculture. Cases have been recorded of prime agricultural land taken over by housing projects, resorts and golf courses (for details see Phongpaichit and Baker 1996: 141–66; Ross and Thadaniti 1995). All these factors contributed to the scarcity of land for peasant/local agriculture in the 1980s.

The early 1980s also witnessed some structural changes in the rural sector brought about by government policy as well as by movements in the world prices of its products and which resulted in increased differentiation and poverty in the rural areas. Between 1980 and 1986 there was a fall in the export price of rice (by 7 per cent per annum), rubber (by 5.1 per cent per annum) and sugar (by 9.1 per cent per annum). This resulted in a decline in absolute terms of per capita GDP in agriculture over this period (from 900.1 baht per month to 856.8 baht per month) and a fall in nominal per capita income of agricultural households (Sussangkarn 1990: 4–6). However, these average figures disguise to some extent the differential effect within the sector. The devaluations in the 1981 and 1984 at the first instance increased the incomes of export producers, and the country remained competitive and an important exporter of agricultural products.[20] However, there was an increase in absolute poverty, with more people living below the poverty line: an increase from 23 per cent in 1981 to 29.5 per cent in 1986. Income distribution worsened within the sector as well as between the rural and urban sector. By 1986 the ratio of per capita income of non-agricultural households to agricultural households was 2.7, reflected in turn in urban and rural disparities in household incomes (Sussangkarn 1990).

Thirdly, rural industrialization, and thereby the employment prospects of rural industrialization, were limited. Rural industry was concentrated in those sectors that could employ workers in the dry season and had low capital:labour ratios (to allow for capital lying idle in the wet season). They consisted of small shops, transport services, handicraft production, silk production, fishing nets, carpets, mats, baskets, cloth, etc., usually made in households or small factories and often using female or child labour on a seasonal basis. The slow growth of rural industry was linked to rural poverty, small market size in the rural areas, inadequate and poor infrastructure facilities and negative government policies against rural and small-scale industries. In the north-east and the north were rice mills, which had no impact on technological transfer, employed some five persons at most (small-scale) and did not improve the distribution of income in the rural areas (Jesdapipat 1990).

These three processes had the effect of limiting productive employment and adequate income in the agricultural sector. At the same time the agricultural workforce constituted nearly 71 per cent of the workforce in 1980. And while open unemployment and underemployment were relatively moderate (some 5 per cent unemployment in the beginning of the 1980s), women were worse off than men in both these categories. Seasonal unemployment was, however, significant for both men and women (Pitayanon 1990: 31). By the mid-1980s rural household members spent nearly 55 per cent of their working time on off-farm activities, with women doing more such men than men (Onchan 1984: 19). Over the decade there was a shift away from employment in agriculture, particularly for women. In order to analyse this process it is necessary to consider the seasonal nature of agricultural employment, a factor that was important in the fragmentation of their work and lives.

Aggregate figures of agricultural employment tend to disguise the high degree of seasonal employment in Thai agricultural, with substantially more people employed in the wet season and a fairly significant drop in the dry season. This drop was sharper for women than for men. In 1974, 63.4 per cent of men (6,015,300) and 68.0 per cent of women (5,210,900) were employed in agriculture in the wet season, the corresponding figures for the dry season being 53.5 per cent (4,411,800) and 49.0 per cent (2,643,800). This figure increased both absolutely and proportionately by 1983 when some 67 per cent of men (9,055,400) and 71 per cent of the women (8,345,900) were employed in agriculture in the wet season with the corresponding figures being 56.1 per cent (6,730,700) and 55.5 per cent (4,797,800) in the dry season.

There was a shift in the pattern from the mid-1980s, with a drop in the absolute level of employment for women even in the peak (wet) season. By 1987 only some 8,249,900 were employed in agriculture and they constituted only 64.8 per cent of female employment in the wet season. On the other hand, the number of men in employed in agriculture in the wet season increased in absolute terms (to 9,539,200) although this number represented a proportional fall in men employed in agriculture (64.0 per cent) in 1987. It was estimated that by the early 1990s some 4 million people dropped out of the agricultural workforce in the off-season (Phongpaichat and Baker 1995: 198). The combined effect of the dry and wet season employment patterns reflected a trend to move away from seasonal labour in agriculture. However, in aggregate terms agriculture still accounted for some 60 per cent of the workforce by the end of the 1980s.

MIGRANT LABOUR FOR URBAN INDUSTRIALIZATION

Migration on a seasonal basis was not new in Thailand. However, the dominant pattern of migration in Thailand in the last three decades had been rural-to-rural migration on a seasonal basis. From the 1980s, however, the rural–urban stream gained in importance, increasing from 10.5 per cent of the migration in 1965–70 (348,000) to 14.3 per cent (420,600) in 1975–80, and 18.4 per cent (738,400) in 1985–90 (National Statistical Office 1993). Temporary migration was an important phenomenon for both men and women in the rural areas. In fact, the figures provided by the National Migration Survey (1992) suggest that at least one third of the migrants in Thailand were temporary migrants (Pejaranonda et al. 1995: 187).[21] Most of this is a flow from the north and the north-east to Bangkok and the central region in the dry season and a return in the wet season.[22] Some industries, such as wood products, shoes and toys, used a factory environment but accepted a high turnover in the workforce and major fluctuations between agricultural seasons (Phongpaichat and Baker 1995: 199)

The migrant flow accelerated in the 1980s and the early 1990s with Bangkok continuing to be an important destination.[23] While men dominated the streams for rural destinations, women outnumbered men in certain urban destinations. The sex ratios of the rural–urban migration streams in 1980 and 1990 were 120.8 and 127.7 respectively. At the same time, there have been little changes in the sex ratios in other migration streams, reflecting the significance of female migration from rural to urban areas.

A recent study by Pejaranonda, Santipaporn and Guest, based on 1990 census samples from the National Statistical Office, indicates that part of the increased demand for labour in export-led growth in the 1980s, particularly in Bangkok, was met by female migrants. Between 1985 and 1990 there were 87 male migrants for every 100 female migrants to Bangkok. In 1970, the proportion of female migrants in production, transport and services was 65.4 per cent. This rose in 1980 to 81 per cent, then dropped marginally in 1990 to 76.2 per cent (Pejaranonda et al. 1995: 212–13).[24] While the most common occupation for rural–urban young (below 25 years) female migrants was in the transport and production sector, there were more males than females overall in these sectors. However, there was a majority of females in the clerical and sales sector and services sector, the latter being the second largest source of employment for female rural–urban migrants, usually in retailing, construction, food services and tourism-related work (Phongpaichit 1992:

83). Other studies have also highlighted the high concentration of migrant women in the services sector (Leenothai 1991; United Nations 1987). Large numbers of young female migrants also entered the sex industry in urban areas (Archavanitkul and Guest 1993) to supply the demands of the growing tourist trade. Additionally, the rural–urban migration streams have sex ratios that reflect the growing significance of young women (aged 15–25) in the occupational categories of private employees, unpaid family workers and those not in the labour force. They suggest, on the basis of their study, that as women become older they tend to be excluded from formal occupations and are concentrated in sales and service occupations working as self-employed or as unpaid family workers (Pejaranonda et al. 1995: 207).

Temporary migration has played an important role in terms of fragmentation of women's lives. While they might stay for longer periods in the urban regions because of income and employment opportunities, they tend to remain closely linked to their rural base and return to their families at least once a year for religious festivals. If their families own farmland, they may even be called upon to help during the planting and harvesting seasons, making the returns home more frequent. It has been shown that some employers are reluctant to take on workers who admit that their families own farmland because of the likelihood that these workers will leave during the peak labour needs of agriculture (Tonguthai and Pattaravanich 1991: 126).

FEMALE EMPLOYMENT IN COMMERCE, MANUFACTURING AND SERVICES

The pressures to find productive and gainful employment in the agricultural sector in the context of trade liberalization and market-oriented reform, as well as the demands of foreign direct investment, resulted in more men and women being employed in other sectors. Women were concentrated in manufacturing, commerce and services. Some of these jobs were in the rural sector and could, as we saw previously, be undertaken in the dry season. Others involved migration to the cities, either on a temporary or semi-permanent basis.

The fact that increasing numbers of young adult women were seeking waged work can be seen in the data on classification of employment by work status, gender and age group. Between 1980 and 1989 the non-municipal areas saw a fall in the proportion of women classified under the category 'unpaid family worker' and a corresponding increase in the category 'private employee'. In 1980, 71 per cent of the women were classified as 'unpaid family workers', while this proportion dropped to 51 per cent in 1989 (the highest fall being between the ages 15 and 44). In 1980 only 10 per cent of the women were classified as private employees but this had doubled to over 22 per cent by 1989 (again the most significant increases being in the age range 15–44).

Data on female labour-intensive industries (where the proportion of female labour is higher than the proportion of female labour in total employment) in 1980 and 1989 reflect the increasing importance of women in those manufacturing and service industries that were linked directly or indirectly via subcontracting to foreign direct investment. While agriculture was the highest female employer in 1980 and in 1989, the numbers had dropped from 7,988,817 to 7,113,205 over this period. However, we see that a significant proportion of female labour was absorbed into the expanding manufacturing and services industries. Women constituted 78.8 per cent of the workforce in footwear handicrafts, wearing apparel and other wearing apparel and finished textile industries (325,308), 76.3 per cent of the workforce in textile handicrafts (229,136) and 66.3 per cent of the workforce in personal services. (Phannaniramai 1993: 9 and Table 2.2.2). The garments sector, one of the highest growth sectors, also relied heavily on subcontracting, which was done either in the home or in small subcontracting firms. Putting out systems which used the same principle of work were used in gem cutting and some food industries (Phongpaichat and Baker 1995: 199).

In 1980 women constituted 47.5 per cent of the total workforce, the figure for 1989 being 44.1 per cent. In 1980, the female-intensive industries were agriculture, textiles, footwear, Wearing apparel and finished textiles, paper handicrafts and paper products, wholesale and retail trade as well as personal services. The numbers of female-intensive industries increased in 1989 to include non-metallic mining and precious stones, food manufacturing (except beverage industries), tobacco manufactures and snuff, wood handicrafts (excluding furniture) and bottle caps, rubber handicrafts and rubber products, general handicrafts, public services, leisure services and specified other activities. These industries represented 93 per cent of total female employment and generated 47.7 per cent of GDP (Phananiramai 1993: 9 and Table 2.2.2). Many of these were important export industries. By 1992, 80 per cent of the workers in seven of the ten leading export industries were female (Phongpaichat and Baker 1995: 199). Women were also employed in the growing services sector, particularly the tourism sector.[25] Private agencies were also responsible for luring poor women into prostitution.

The fragmentation in women's work and lives can be gauged from the data on employment, which suggest that there was a substantial increase in the numbers of women employed temporarily in commerce and manufacturing. In fact, the latter two categories represented over 75 per cent of the incremental jobs in which women were employed in the wet seasons in 1983–7, while they were only 3.8 per cent of the incremental jobs for women in the period 1974–9. Just 40.5 per cent of these jobs were in the rural areas, with 59.8 per cent in the urban areas. Women also took a larger proportion of the incremental jobs than men in manufacturing (366,100 women and 259,300 men), commerce (418,900 women and 383,100 men) and services (294,900 women and 115,300 men) during the wet seasons between 1983 and 1987. While men had a higher proportion of the incremental jobs than women in commerce in the dry season in the same period (338,800 women and 411,900 men), women were substantially more involved in the incremental jobs in manufacturing (177,800 women and 47,000 men) and in services (405,900 women and 47,700 men).

The demand for women in export-oriented manufacturing was closely linked to their relatively low wage costs. Child labour was also used in a large number of establishments. It has been argued with justification that this fairly elastic supply of labour had the effect of maintaining low wage rates in spite of increased labour demand, something that was also influenced by the suppression of labour organization and the poor policing by the government of the implementation of the minimum wage (Phongpaichat and Baker 1995: 153). It has been argued by some that women were preferred by employers as they were more 'controllable' than men and had lower levels of job turnover (Pejaranonda et al. 1995: 200). However, this notion of female docility has been contested by empirical studies which indicate that female Thai workers were more militant than their male counterparts and formed the backbone of the union movement (Porpora, Lim and Prommas 1989; Kurian, Aurland and Kamalam 1994).

Studies have shown that the labour segments where women's employment is concentrated are typically those associated with low wages, few opportunities for skill improvement and training, inadequate welfare facilities and are generally at the lowest rungs of the labour force (Tonguthai and Pattaravanich 1993). At the same time, studies have shown that much of this employment has no long-term prospects. A recent study by Boonsue on the status of women in Thailand showed that both skilled and unskilled women were paid less and have lower prospects of upward job mobility than unskilled men.[26] In her interviews with NGOs and trade union leaders it was suggested that skilled women were most efficiently used in their first five years of employment, after which they begin to have eye deficiencies (in electronics, garments, and lace textile firms) resulting in less efficient hand–eye co-ordination. Additionally, women had less access to paid sick leave and annual leave. Most of them appear to have an employment cycle of 2–5 years (Boonsue 1996).

At the same time, women continued to play an important role in the non-market labour segment providing substantial labour input in the domestic chores, such as cooking and cleaning. Studies have also shown that most female migrants also supported their family members in the rural economy and sent a substantial part of their wages as remittances to their households. The task of childcare during the working day was assumed in some cases by domestic (female) help, or by the child's grandparents. For migrant women this often meant separation from their children with visits a few times a year only (Tonguthai and Pattaravanich 1993; ESCAP 1992: 15; Porpora et al. 1989). Their high involvement in the non-waged labour segment at the same time as their waged activities forced them to take on a range of identities and responsibilities. This aspect of their lives constitutes yet another facet of fragmentation.

PROSPECTS FOR THE FUTURE

The pattern of industrialization based on trade liberalization in the 1980s tended in many cases to accentuate imbalances with regard to location and distribution of production and employment. The high control exerted by multinationals over production (particularly with regard to capital, technology and management practices) influenced the quantity, quality and length of this employment. In Thailand, this process was also linked to the nature of migration from the rural to the urban areas, particularly of women to Bangkok, who supplied most of the cheap, lowskilled labour for the manufacturing and service industries, and the informal sector. There were few facilities and opportunities for upgrading human skills and technological capabilities. The vast majority of these workers intended to stay only on a temporary basis and were part of a short-term circulatory form of migration. However, the continued decline of the agricultural sector means that agriculture will not be able to absorb the labour surplus. This labour, being relatively low skilled and poorly educated, will not be able to cope with the demands for more educated skilled labour necessary at the next stage of industrialization. At the same time, the continued decline in agriculture, the increasing exploitation of the land for the hotel and other tourist industries, capitalization of land, speculation and sale of land, together with serious environmental problems have closed many options for these workers even if they decide to return to the rural areas.

NOTES

1. My thanks to Jan Aarte Scholte for his comments on an earlier draft of this chapter.
2. Making a clear distinction between 'internationalization', 'liberalization' and 'globalization', Scholte has argued that the particular significance of globalization is not the fact that borders are crossed or opened but rather 'transcended'. Thus, he sees globalization has 'a fundamental transformation of human geography' where territorial distance and territorial borders have limited significance. The shifts in foreign direct investment, in this sense, fit well within this perspective (Scholte 1997).
3. Recent estimates suggest that some 40 per cent of world trade is controlled by 350 firms, while some 37,000 MNEs with over 170,000 foreign affiliates who control about 70 per cent of products in international trade (UNCTAD, World Investment Report 1994/95). Estimates also indicate that some 300 companies control 70 per cent of foreign direct investment (Scholte 1997).
4. The term 'non-market labour segment' is used in the sense developed by Makgetla (1995), which essentially constitutes unpaid household and other production. While her analysis indicated that the unpaid labour segment was mainly done by women in the rural areas in the South African economy, there is every evidence that in other contexts this is women's responsibility in the urban and rural settings.
5. While labour market segmentation theories have been derived to a large extent from work on the United States, this has also been developed to discuss labour markets in developing countries (Rodgers 1986).
6. In 1992, the total figure for all countries was US$1940 billion (from a figure of US$104 billion in 1960–79) out of which industrialized countries accounted for US$1520 billion (from US$71 billion in 1960–70).
7. These countries were China (16 per cent), Singapore (16 per cent), Mexico (13 per cent), Brazil (9 per cent), Egypt (7 per cent), Malaysia (5 per cent), Thailand (5 per cent), Chile (5 per cent), Nigeria (5 per cent) and Korea (4 per cent), accounting for the total of the 84 per cent of direct foreign investment flows to the developing countries (Hanmer et al. 1977: Table 1.7)
8. According to Machado the second half of the 1980s witnessed the third 'wave' of Japanese foreign direct investment, driven by the pressures of the convergence of rising value of the yen, surplus savings and pressure to reduce the trade surplus (Machado 1995).

9. While the literature on this subject is wide, the central features of these forms of industrial organization is found in a recent article by John Humphrey (1995).
10. This chapter does not explicitly deal with, but assumes knowledge of, the discussions on patriarchal ideology and the sexual division of labour, which justified the women's involvement in labour-intensive, time-consuming repetitive tasks and which is reflected in the division of tasks within the household and generally in society.
11. Women had already been employed from the mid-1970s in several Export Processing Zones onwards, although the numbers involved were fairly insignificant in relation to the overall female workers (Elson and Pearson 1981; Lim 1990).
12. It has been shown that increased openness of an economy (as measured by the increase in the ratio of exports to GNP) has tended to make the export-oriented sector particularly feminized in the process (Cagatay and Ozler 1995).
13. In 1979–80, Thailand borrowed US$542 million from the World Bank to tide over the balance of payments problem and ranked the fifth in terms of World Bank loans. It also lent money to Thailand under its structural adjustment programme, the loans being dependent in principle on the reorientation of the economy towards exports through institutional and policy reforms (Phongpaichit 1995: 147–8).
14. There was a devaluation in 1981 (when the baht was devalued from about 20.5/dollar to 23/dollar) and another major devaluation of the baht in November 1984 by 14.7 per cent making it about 27/dollar. The baht was delinked from the dollar and linked to a basket of currencies of its major trading partners. But while it maintained more or less a parity with the dollar, the dollar declined against the yen and other major European currencies. Between 1985 and 1987, the baht experienced an effective devaluation of 20 per cent (Phongpaichat and Baker 195: 150) and between 1985 and 1992 it experienced a deviation of roughly 100 per cent against the yen, Swiss franc and the Deutschmark, and 50 per cent against the pound sterling (Falkus 1995: 27).
15. Decentralization which had been emphasized since the Fourth National Economic Development Plan (1977–81) resulted in channelling economic and urban growth away from Bangkok to some extent in the second half of the 1980s. Thus, the high growth period from 1987 onwards witnessed the establishment of manufacturing enterprises in the inner and outer rings of Bangkok as well as the north-east (Nakhon Ratchasima and Khon Kaen) and the north (Chaiang Mai, Phitsanulok and Nakhon Sawan) and in the south (Songkhla and Surat Thani). By 1991, Bangkok accounted for 36.5 per cent of the manufacturing establishments (20,248), while the second and third nodal points were the north-east region with 15.05 per cent (8581) of the manufacturing establishments and the inner ring with 13.68 per cent (7801) (Division of Factory Control, Department of Industrial Works quoted in Poapongsakorn 1995: Table 6.1). However, it is worthwhile to note that except in the inner ring area, manufacturing activities in the regions outside Bangkok were concentrated in a few resource-based industries, the most important of these being food, beverage and

16. machinery industries although there was a tendency for a broader base in these regions as well (Poapongsakorn 1995).
17. In time, and particularly after 1987, domestic capital was to also play a significant role in this boom in the forestry, property, telecommunications, finance and assorted manufacturing and even moved into foreign markets (Phongpaichat and Baker 1995: 164f).
18. Large enterprises with over 200 employees (mainly in resource-intensive sectors such as petroleum derivatives and tobacco, or scale-intensive sectors such as glass products and basic metal industries) account for 40 per cent of the employment
19. Forest areas has shrunk from 26.9 million hectares in 1960 to 13.6 million hectares by 1993. The population increased over this same period from 27 million to 58 million.
20. The commercial value of the teak and other valuable wood were important exports. Several export-oriented Taiwanese, Japanese and European firms (along with large local companies) bought up land cheaply and grew eucalyptus trees – which siphoned off much needed water – to service the needs of the paper and pulp industry. There were cases recorded of fish poisoning caused by the release of waste from pulp factories into the rivers. Dams (in order to supply the electricity needs of urban development) flooded forests and displaced people. The extensive shrimp culture farms also resulted in the deterioration of mangrove forests. Around 80 factories pollute the Chin river which runs through an industrial and population area.
21. It was the largest exporter of rice and cassava in the world and ranking among the top 5–10 in exports of rubber, sugar-cane, maize and fisheries (Sussangkarn 1990: 3).
22. If individuals had moved only once in the previous two years they were classified as 'single movers'. If they had moved two or three times in that period and at least one of them was for seasonal employment reasons they were classified as seasonal migrants. A person who had moved two or three times with no move being associated with seasonal employment reasons was considered to be a 'repeat' migrant. The latter two categories can be seen as 'temporary migrants'.
23. These moves are also more common with those who have completed only primary school education (compulsory). However, it would appear that men are more important in this category than women. Men who were in this category were largely associated with employment in agriculture, labour/production and unclassified (mainly daily wage employees). Women in this category were high only among agriculture and unclassified workers.
24. Estimates indicating that only 39.6 per cent of the urban growth was due to natural increases in the period 1980–5, while 60.4 per cent was due to migration and reclassification. The corresponding figures for 1985–90 were 31.4 per cent and 68.6 per cent (quoted in Perera 1993: Table 7.2.2).
25. This migration is also associated with higher ages of marriage although it is likely that the type of employment opportunities available has a preference for single young women.
26. The receipts from tourism increasing from about 300 million baht in 1985 to 110 billion baht in 1990 (Phongpaichat and Baker 1995: 152–3).

26. In this study the notions of skill were related to the requirements of the job and the level of training required for the job. Unskilled labour relied primarily on manual capacity with minimal formal education and short on-the-job training. Skilled labour involved advanced technology and required a higher level of education usually required longer-term on-the-job training.

REFERENCES

Archavanitkul, Kritaya and Quest, Philip (1993) 'Migration and the Commercial Sex Sector in Thailand'. Paper prepared for the seminar 'AIDS Impact and Prevention in the Developing World: The Contribution of Demography and Social Science', Annécy, France, 5–9 December.
Boonsue, Kornvipa (1996) 'Women's Status and Industrialization in Thailand', part of a doctoral dissertation in progress on the same subject at the Asian Institute of Technology, Bangkok, made available by the author.
Cagatay, N. and Ozler, S. (1995) 'Feminization of the Labour Force: The Effects of Long-Term Development and Structural Adjustment', *World Development* 23(11), pp. 1883–94.
Chirativat, Suthiphand (1994) 'Transnational Corporations in Thailand's International Trade in Sugar, Fish, Shrimps and Prawns' pp. 203–33 in *Transnational Corporations and the International Trade in Primary Commodities*, New York: United Nations.
Dunning, John (1993) *Multinational Enterprises and the Global Economy*, Wokingham: Addison-Wesley.
Elson, Diane and Pearson, Ruth (1981) 'Nimble Fingers Make Cheap Workers: an Analysis of Women's Employment in third World Export Manufacturing', *Feminist Review* (Spring), pp. 87–107.
ESCAP (1991) *Industrial Restructuring in Asia and the Pacific in Particular with a view to Strengthening Regional Cooperation*, March, United Nations: Bangkok.
ESCAP (1992) *Migration and Urbanization in Asia and the Pacific: Interrelationships with Socio-economic Development and Evolving Policy Issues*, Selected Papers of the Pre-Conference Seminar Fourth Asian and Pacific Population Conference, Seoul, 21–25 January 1992, New York: United Nations.
Falkus, Malcolm (1995) 'Thai Industrialization: an Overview' in Medhi Krongkaew (ed.) *Thailand's Industrialization and its Consequences*, New York: St. Martin's Press.
FAO (1993) 'Women, Population and Rural Development' pp. 105–9 in *The Fourth Asian and Pacific Population Conference, 19–27 August 1992, Bali, Indonesia, Selected Papers, Asian Population Studies Series*, No. 124, New York: United Nations.
Hanmer, Lucia, de Jong, Niek, Kurian, Rachel and Mooij, Jos (1997) *Social Development: Past Trends and Future Scenarios*, Stockholm: Sida.
Humphrey, John (1995) 'Industrial Reorganization in Developing Countries: From Models to Trajectories', *World Development* 23(1), pp. 149–62.
International Labour Office (1995) *World Employment 1995: an ILO Report*, Geneva: International Labour Office.

Jansen, Karel (1995) 'The Macroeconomic Effects of Direct Foreign Investment: The Case of Thailand', *World Development* 23(2), pp. 193–210.

Keyes, C. (1987) *Thailand: Buddhist Kingdom as Modern Nation-State*, Boulder, Co.: Westview Press.

Kurian, Rachel, Aurland, Eva and P. Kamalam (1994) *Evaluation Report of the ICFTU/LO-NI Training Programme for Women Trade Unionists South East Asia: Integration of Women into Trade Union Organisation*, April, Brussels: International Confederation of Free Trade Unions.

Leeontha, Sunee (1991) 'The Role of Growth Centres in Migration of Women. Destination Choices of Female Migrants', in *Proceedings of the 1991 Thai National Symposium on Population Studies*, Bangkok.

Lim, Linda Y.C. (1990) 'Women's Work in Export Factories: the Politics of a Cause' in Irene Tinker (ed.) *Persistent Inequalities: Women and World Development*, New York and Oxford: Oxford University Press.

Machado, Kit G. (1995) 'Japanese Foreign Direct Investment in East Asia: the Expanding Division of Labour and the Future of Regionalism' pp. 39–66 in Steve Chan (ed.) *Foreign Direct Investment in a Changing Global Political Economy*, London: Macmillan.

Makgetla, N.S. (1995) 'Women and the Economy: Slow Pace of Change', *Agenda*, 24, 7–20.

National Statistical Office (1993) *Migration*, 1990 Population and Housing Census, Subject Report No. 1, Bangkok.

Onchan, T. (1984) 'Rural Off-farm Employment and Rural Development in Thailand', paper presented at IFPRI Board Meeting, Bangkok, 9 February.

Pejaranonda, Chintana, Sureerat Santipaporn and Philip Guest (1995) 'Rural–Urban Migration in Thailand' pp. 171–243 in *Trends, Patterns and Implications of Rural–Urban Migration in India, Nepal and Thailand*, Economic and Social Commission for Asia and the Pacific, *Asian Population Studies Series*, No. 138, New York: United Nations.

Perera, P.D.A. (1993) 'Migration and its Implications for Socio-Economic Development Policies' pp. 126–33 in *The Fourth Asian and Pacific Population Conference, 19–27 August 1992, Bali, Indonesia, Selected Papers*, *Asian Population Studies Series*, No. 124, New York: United Nations.

Phananiramai, Mathana (1993) 'Women's Economic Roles in Thailand'. Paper presented at 'Women and Industrialization in Asia', Seoul National University, 9–10 September.

Phillips, Anne and Taylor, Barbara (1986) 'Sex and Skill' in Feminist Review (ed.) *Waged Work: A Reader*, London: Virago Press.

Phongpaichit, Pasuk (1982) *From Peasant Girls to Bangkok Masseuses*, Geneva: International Labour Office.

Phongpaichit, Pasuk (1988) 'The New Waves of Japanese Direct Investment and Thailand' pp. 179–97 in Juangai Ajanant and Jittapatr Kuravan (eds) *External Capital and the Role of Japan*, Bangkok: Chulalongkom Printing House.

Phongpaichit, Pasuk (1992) 'Female Internal Migration and The Labour Market' pp. 81–90 in ESCAP, *Migration and Urbanization in Asia and the Pacific: Interrelationships with Socio-economic Development and Evolving Policy Issues*, New York: United Nations.

Phongpaichit, Pasuk and Chris Baker (1995) *Thailand: Economy and Politics*, Kuala Lumpur: Oxford University Press.

Pitayanon, Sumalee (1990) 'Labour Market Information in the Rural and Urban Informal Sectors of Thailand' in *Strategic Approaches Towards Employment Promotion, Discussion Paper* THA/4, June, Bangkok: ARTEP/Department of Labour, Ministry of Interior.

Porpora, Douglas, Lim Mah Hui and Prommas, Usanee (1989) 'The Role of Women in the International Division of Labour: The Case of Thailand', *Development and Change* 20(2), April, pp. 269–94.

Rimmer, Peter J. (1995) 'Urbanization Problems in Thailand's Rapidly Industrializing Economy' pp. 183–217 in Medhi Kronghkaew (ed.) *Thailand's Industrialization and its Consequences*, New York: St. Martin's Press.

Rodgers, Gerny (1986) 'Labour Markets, Labour Processes and Economic Development', *Labour and Society*, 11 (2), May, pp. 23–8.

Romijn, Henny and Mongkornratana, Kwanta (1991) *Growth and Employment in the Informal Sector of Bangkok: A Study of Six Sectors*, The Hague: Institute of Social Studies Advisory Service.

Ross, Helen and Suwattana Thadaniti (1995) 'The Environmental Costs of Industrialization' pp. 267–88 in Medhi Kronghkaew (ed.) *Thailand's Industrialization and its Consequences*, New York: St. Martin's Press.

Scholte, Jan Aart (1977) 'Global Capitalism and the State', *International Affairs* 73(3), 427–52.

Supapol, Atipol Bhanich (1995) 'Thailand' in *Transnational Corporations and Backward Linkages in Asian Electronics Industries*, New York: United Nations.

Sussangkarn, Chalongphob (1990) 'Labour Market in an Era of Adjustment: a Study of Thailand'. Paper prepared for the Workshop on *Labour Market in an Era of Adjustment*, Warwick University, 22–25 May, Bangkok: Thailand Development Research Institute.

Tonguthai, Pawadee (1995) 'Asian Women in Manufacturing: New Challenges, Old Problems' in Mihaly Simai (ed.) with Valentine Moghadam and Arvo Kuddo, *Global Employment: an International Investigation in The Future of Work: Volume One*, London and New Jersey: Zed Books.

Tonguthai, Pawadee and Pattaravanich, Umaporn (1993) 'Employment and Mobility in the Bangkok Labour Market with Special Reference to Women in the Manufacturing Sector' in *Promoting Diversified Skill Development for Women in Industry: Volume II*, New York: United Nations, Economic and Social Commission for Asia and the Pacific, United Nations Development Program and International Labour Office.

10 Health Education for Women as a Liberatory Process? An Example from Tajikistan[1]

Colette Harris

INTRODUCTION

A significant aspect of the process of globalization has been the opening up of the former Soviet states to free market reform and integration into the global political economy. In September 1991, with the dissolution of the Soviet Union, Tajikistan laid itself open in one fell swoop to global penetration. This had major consequences for a country that for centuries had been almost totally isolated from the outside world. Already poor, its economy virtually collapsed after independence. The situation has not been improved by Tajikistan's subjection to the general principles of the transition to a free market espoused by the international monetary bodies, in compliance with which in January 1992 it liberalized the prices on 80 per cent of all goods (Kaser 1997: 10). The hyperinflation and poverty that followed were partly responsible for the tremendous social upheavals of that year, which ended in civil war. Although the main fighting lasted only a few months, the violence continues and the country will take a long time to recover from the effects on its economy and its social fabric.

The war and its aftermath have greatly slowed Tajikistan's economic transition. Foreign investment has remained minimal. Privatization has been carried out only on the smallest enterprises. Agriculture has yet to undergo this process, with collective and state farms remaining intact and land still the property of the state, available to individuals only on lease (Kaser 1997). Although the IMF, the World Bank and a number of UN agencies have a significant presence in the country, the full extent of their influence has yet to be seen.

In common with the countries discussed in this volume, the move to a market economy in Tajikistan is also producing fragmentation on a number of levels. This process has been exacerbated by the civil war, as a result of which the country has become split along regional lines. The war separated families through the death and exile of their members, as the transitional economy has done by forcing migration in search of labour markets. In response to the dual forces of war and market the level of daily violence (in particular the incidence of robbery and murder, but also, albeit to a lesser extent, the rape and abduction of girls and young women) is escalating rapidly, in part as a result of increased poverty.

The delay the war has caused in reconstructing the shattered economy has made the financial and social costs of transition even higher than they might otherwise have been and fiscal problems have seriously affected the functioning of the social services. Education has been the most adversely affected. The low level of remuneration has forced most male teachers and many female ones to abandon their profession for more lucrative work. The better urban schools now demand parental contributions in order to retain staff. The rest make do as best they can, but rarely manage to provide more than a couple of lessons a day. Large numbers of rural schools no longer function at all. Under these circumstances the current literacy rate of nearly 100 per cent for those between the ages of 20 and 60 will be severely eroded within a generation. In any case, many young people today have little interest in education as this no longer appears to be a path to a well-paid job.

In the current economic situation few families can afford to live on the earnings of only one of their members. For this reason, as well as because of a big increase in female-headed households, far more Tajik women than previously are forced into paid work. These women generally do not enter the formal labour force but most commonly work informally, for instance as market traders. At the same time Tajikistan is also being affected by the global trend of religious conservatism. Although changes are due in part to the resumption of openness in the practice of rituals that had been forced underground during the decades of Soviet repression, they also stem from the Islamic Opposition's desire to introduce much stronger religious control, especially over women, in line with that existing in Tajikistan's southern neighbours (Iran, Pakistan, Afghanistan), a tendency strongly opposed by large segments of the population.

For most Tajiks any advantages that have accompanied the transition period are of lesser value than the concomitant economic and social disadvantages. The Soviet Union was far from an ideal system. However, globalization and the emergence of a market economy are bringing few obvious gains to Tajikistan. On the contrary, the fragmentation of the country, the social services, the labour market and the family that has followed on global penetration has brought in its wake insecurity, poverty, violence, poor health and fear for the future for members of both sexes.

Even though Tajikistan still retains some of the characteristics of a second world country, these are fast vanishing. If real, constructive shoring up of the material and social infrastructure is not carried out soon, globalization may end up pushing the country over the thin line that now separates it from developing countries. Meanwhile, most of those women who at the end of the Soviet era were living in seeming stability with most of their basic needs met directly by the state now find themselves virtually without any state support, in respect to income, social services or help with acquiring mechanisms for coping with the new situation. It has become clear that the Soviet strategies for keeping its citizens in a state of dependence by denying them access to knowledge and information have left them particularly ill-equipped to fend for themselves.

This chapter examines the direct consequences of this process by focusing on women's health education. It uses the specific example of a health education project being carried out in two villages in southern Tajikistan to explore some of the problems faced by women in the era of transition and context of upheaval as a result of war. The next section presents a discussion of women's position in Soviet Tajikistan and the effect of transition. It is followed by an examination of health education during and since Soviet domination. I then discuss the methodology we are using in our health project to try to counter the current situation by providing the women with mechanisms to deal with it, and explore the gender issues raised by the extension of health education through our project. I conclude by examining the broader problems faced by Tajik women in the context of rapid transformation.

WOMEN IN SOVIET TAJIKISTAN

The Central Asian Republic of Tajikistan is a Muslim country with much in common culturally with its southern neighbours. It has remained a poor rural state, despite the decades of Soviet rule. Russo-Soviet cultural penetration was far less in Tajikistan than in most other Union republics and its values made less impact. Little was done to transform its basic material circumstances, with the result that gender relations and the society as a whole experienced surprisingly little change (Harris n.d.). Today Tajikistan hovers somewhere between a second and a third world country.

The gains that women made under the Soviet system were contradictory. Women achieved a large degree of mobility and a basic education. However, the latter was explicitly part of the campaign to implant Soviet ideology and was anything but liberatory. It did little, therefore, to change the fundamental outlook of Tajik society, where women continued to live according to the old traditions. The educational levels of Tajik women and their waged employment outside the agricultural sector remained well below those of men. One of the reasons for this was that they tended to have very large families. Five children was usually a minimum, with 10–14 not uncommon in rural areas. In the 1980s over 25 per cent of Tajiks had seven or more children (Djanko 1990: 477). Even when women did work outside the home the Soviet regime did its best to ensure that any small reduction in their dependence on their families was compensated for by their dependence on a paternalistic state. The education system, together with the media, formed part of the state disinformation process. In this situation, neither education nor waged labour provided women with a path to emancipation.[2] On the contrary, despite the superficial changes described above and relatively liberal laws, Tajik women are more conservative and far less open to concepts of social struggle than those in many other Muslim societies. This is hardly surprising since the essence of Soviet politics was the repression of all power struggles except those headed by the state.

However, the Soviet state did provide a job for most of those who wanted one, monthly allowances to mothers of large families, wages to the great majority of rural Tajik women who worked on the collective and state farms, and free education and health services. Everyone had a basic income and some sort of roof over their heads. There were virtually no beggars or street people, no shanty towns or prostitution. In short, Soviet society was able to provide at least the basics of life for virtually all its citizens.

The Soviet state very explicitly used education and health care as weapons in the struggle for total control over its citizens. The government saw political domination as requiring the exercise of direct power in every aspect of life within the Union, the centre of state strategy being the planned economy. In the end this proved ruinous and its remains have left the governments of the newly independent states in the very difficult position of bearing sole responsibility for all aspects of their economies, without the resources to manage them. The subsequent drive towards a market economy has dramatically worsened the situation. The imposition of a market system on a people accustomed to almost total dependence on the state has brought extraordinary hardship as they grapple with the need for self-reliance and individual initiative totally foreign to Soviet ideology. This has been especially hard on the women, who to a large extent have been left bewildered and uncertain of how to proceed. They are coping as best they can in the absence of any real support, but inevitably they have not been able to develop long-term strategies, and instead merely react to each event as it occurs. It is clear that the loss of free medical care has been one of the most deleterious results of the change. This is especially problematic since knowledge of traditional healing has been largely destroyed by the Soviet regime as part of their drive to eradicate local cultures. The resultant medicalization of all aspects of health has left the population dependent on health professionals and their drugs. Soviet doctors, like their colleagues elsewhere, tended to exercise their position of authority in the interests of maintaining public order. This was especially notable in their approach to women's reproductive functions, both in the way that the reproductive processes were dealt with medically, as well as in the information provided to the women themselves. This had a big impact on women's lives, given the fundamental relationship between reproduction and social control.

I was first confronted with these issues in Tajikistan when I went into the villages to discuss their situation with the women. They made it very clear that their major concern was control over their fertility. Further research uncovered an additional need for health education. It was decided, therefore, to set up a project to meet both these necessities, with the intention of helping women deal with the wider (health) problems they face during this period of social and economic upheaval.

However, we wished the project to go far beyond these narrow goals. We wanted to use health education as Freire used literacy teaching[3] – as a liberatory process to help women reformulate positions on reproduction and sexuality as well as to take back responsibility for their own health care from the medical profession. This is particularly important as health care is one place where the women have no real strategies for coping (other than relying on the doctor, the religious leader[4] or leaving it to nature) and where their current lack of financial resources produces great hardship. In addition, the importance of reproduction in women's lives makes health education an ideal prism through which to examine and eventually perhaps challenge existing (gendered) power relations from the level of the state down to internal family structures. In the following sections I examine the achievements of the first stages of the project. Before I do so, I set the scene with a brief outline of health education before and since Soviet rule.

HEALTH EDUCATION IN TAJIKISTAN

The Soviet Period

By the mid-1960s the state had built up a considerable network of health providers so that most people had access to some form of official health care (Ministry of Health of the USSR 1967). Even though this was administered in the authoritarian manner typical of Soviet ideology it did at least contribute to a significant improvement in the population's health status. However, there was a strong emphasis on curative medicine and the use of hi-tech machinery and drugs, rather than on prevention and self-help. Diagnosis skills were poor and doctors tended to prescribe a cocktail of drugs, including multiple antibiotics, in the hope that one of them would work.

The population at large received little formal health education. The state preferred to leave this in the hands of professionals. Such health education as there was concentrated largely on attempts to introduce the population to 'modern' health practices, especially hygiene, one of the very few aspects of preventative medicine emphasized. The media was used to impart the government point of view on health as on other aspects of life. Here the popular magazine *Zdorov'e* (Health) espoused the official Communist Party line. Nothing could be published without the approval of the state publishing commission (Pipes 1994: 296), so that alternative approaches were not presented. In any case, the majority of Tajiks had little access to literature on health.

Sexuality and reproduction were rarely if ever mentioned in public and scarcely discussed even in private. Sex education for young people was considered morally harmful (Bridger 1992: 181). The only formal instruction on the subject of reproductive health consisted of courses for pregnant women to teach them how to behave at childbirth and how to look after their babies in the approved (that is, the Russian) manner. Hardly surprisingly, therefore, few Tajik women attended these courses. In fact, many women, especially in rural areas, avoided consulting doctors at all during their pregnancy and gave birth at home, rather than subject themselves to the ministrations of often highly incompetent state medical personnel.

The state provided little in the way of contraceptives because of the expense of production coupled with its pro-natalist policies. This meant that abortion was women's chief means for regulating their fertility. The attempt in 1936 to raise the birth rate by banning abortion failed and in 1955 it was legalized once more. Russian women might have 25–40 abortions over their fertile lifetimes in a bid to keep their families small. Moslem women considered abortion a sin and large families a means to prosperity. This was enhanced by the benefits the state offered to heroine mothers – those with eight or more children.

By the end of the Soviet period, therefore, most Tajik women had learned very little about health from official sources, in part due to state policies and in part due to resistance to interference in their culture. At the same time this lack of understanding made them dependent on health professionals educated in the very culture they were resisting.

The Post-Soviet period

In its current approach to health care, the Ministry of Health (MoH) retains many Soviet practices but is also heavily influenced by global trends. In the last few years there has been significant entry into Tajikistan of international organizations working in the field of health. These include the World Health Organization, UNICEF, the International Federation of the Red Cross and Red Crescent, and a number of NGOs. Although the primary mandate of these organizations is not to educate, they do provide information on public health matters, particularly in connection with epidemics such as typhoid. Although attempts are made to make this culturally relevant, the content is naturally based on international health practices, many of which differ significantly from those in force in Soviet times.

One of the main areas in which globalization is making itself felt in health policies is that of family planning. In line with its policies elsewhere, the United Nations openly supports population reduction. The United Nations Population Fund (UNFPA) supplies large quantities of contraceptives to Tajikistan as well as funding family planning clinics. Tajik health professionals have been given courses on modern methods of birth control. However, there has as yet been little attempt at educating the population in the use of contraception. There is a certain resistance to this, especially from gynaecologists, who can ask for much higher payments for carrying out abortions than for supplying birth control.

There is no official policy of population limitation, but there are discussions at government level on the advisability of trying to reduce growth which has tended to be very high – in 1990 the annual increase was around 3.26 per cent (Human Development Report 1995: 2). The popular perception is that large families are no longer acceptable and that there is now pressure to have smaller ones. This perception is not without foundation, although as yet this has not been explicitly stated.

However, the MoH is already beginning to work on developing programmes to educate the populace on the advantages of small families. Such programmes are, of course, designed to produce compliance, the very opposite of what our project is trying to do.

THE WOMEN'S HEALTH PROJECT

As stated above, the project combines the provision of contraceptives with health education. As far as the latter goes, the project aims at drawing out knowledge and developing ideas rather than cramming in facts or reinforcing ideology, using the women's own experience as a starting point. It is hoped that such a methodology will open up a psychological space in which women may be able to start examining the existing structure of their social relationships and perhaps even eventually start working towards change.

The project takes a holistic approach to health and health education. It tries to get women questioning their current assumptions in as many areas as possible. By linking nutrition, hygiene, common illnesses and general, as well as reproductive, health matters it aims to provide the tools for women to be able to take control over some of the most important aspects of their lives, including the provision of free contraceptives to give them control over their fertility. From a long-term perspective the most important thing about the project is to see whether it can indeed prove Freire's contention that, given the right approach, <u>education can</u> lead to <u>social transformation under these specific and most difficult socio-economic circumstances</u>. This is the real question to be answered here.

The Participants

The project is being carried out in the southern Tajik region of Bokhtar in two villages, Schmidt and Lakhuti, inhabited by people originally from Gharm. Before the war, they were noted for being a hard-working and therefore relatively affluent group, many households owning several cars as well as television sets and refrigerators. They were also among the most religious of all Tajiks, even managing to keep their women in semi-seclusion throughout the Soviet era.

During the civil war the Gharmis were on the losing side and the villagers were forced into exile. On repatriation they found their homes had been sacked and burned. Since then most homes have been reconstructed and some people have even managed to furnish them with a few electrical goods. Before the war, around 40 per cent of the villages' adult men had completed further education and held skilled or semi-skilled jobs. Most women had completed 8–10 years of schooling but none of their parents had allowed them to leave the village to continue their studies. The village schools provided little of use beyond literacy and numeracy, so that even those men who completed further education have very limited general knowledge.

Women were married by their parents on leaving school and most of them then went to live in the homes of their husbands' families where their function was to serve their mothers-in-law and produce children. They left their courtyards only in the company of a family member and had to cover most of their faces with their headscarves when they did so.[5] They were rarely allowed to go shopping and were not permitted even to visit the doctor without the permission, and usually also the presence, of their mothers-in-law or husbands.

The main reason for these women leaving their homes was to go to work, generally as labourers in the cotton fields of the collective farm. Although they earned income for their families in this way, this did little, if anything, to increase their status with their in-laws. The work was considered as an extension of their household duties and the collective farm automatically paid their wages to their parents-in-law or husbands so that they remained financially dependent. Those women who later lived neo-locally gained a small amount of freedom but remained economically dependent.

The impact of the war and the free market has made radical changes in these women's lives and has given them more independence than ever before. Now none of them cover their faces, nor are they secluded. Instead they take an active part in economic life. They go to market, sell the produce from their private plots and make decisions about family purchases. Many of them have become actual or *de facto* heads of household since their husbands were killed in the war, or have lost their jobs and migrated to Russia or the Tajik capital in search of work, while the women still live permanently in the village and continue to work on the collective farm. However, they now do this for a share of cotton stalks to use as fuel for the winter and a small cash payment at harvest time, rather than for a regular wage as in the past, and the work itself has become considerably more arduous in the absence of the machinery, such as tractors and harvesters, that were available in Soviet times. This makes the women complain bitterly about working as virtual slaves.

They also complain about the difficulty of coping with large numbers of children. They no longer consider it ideal to have big families, and would prefer to have no more than four children. Not only do they have to feed and clothe them out of a steadily diminishing budget, but they also have severe time restraints. Besides their farm work they have to do the housework and cooking, and cultivate their private plots which serve as an important source of income as well as of food. As a result, they have virtually no time for childcare – a task made more difficult by the absence of the former crèches and even of schools.[6] Where possible they get their daughters to help, so that children as young as 10 are left in sole charge of the home and younger siblings, while their older sisters and sisters-in-law labour in the cotton fields.

In the last few years health status in the villages has deteriorated markedly. This is partly due to increased poverty and the renewed spread of diseases such as malaria, but also to post-traumatic stress disorder – a direct consequence of the civil war, coupled with the feeling that life in the transition period has lost its former predictability and is out of control.

It is small wonder that these women, in common with most Tajiks, regret and deeply mourn the passing of the Soviet Union and of socialism. They have no doubt that their lives were infinitely preferable in the days when they all had assured incomes, free social services and bread sold for 20 kopecks a loaf. They share the general desire for the restoration of the old system and see no reason why this should not happen, because they do not understand the implications of the collapse of socialism and the market economy that has come in its wake. The transition period so far has given them little they prefer to their previous way of life. Even their new independence is not without its negative aspects and might vanish with changes in material circumstances, including either the possibility of increased income generation for their menfolk or forced Islamization. In any case, they do not prize independence since their former dependency brought them greater benefits.

This is not a good basis for the sort of conscious restructuring of lifestyles that will be needed to cope successfully with the new free market conditions. It is also not an attitude that welcomes an educational programme rather than a project to help restore the material advantages of socialism. Some women have stated openly that unless the project provides free medicine and/or a combine harvester it is useless. However, the majority have come to see that the strategies discussed may be of help as they come to terms with the idea that their former way of life has gone for ever.

The Project Strategies

The project was set up in April 1997 with a local staff consisting of a woman teacher, midwife and paramedic, a male paediatrician who served as educator for the men, and myself as consultant. Its methodology is based on that of Freire and of grassroots-style health education programmes in developing countries,[7] both trying to validate the women's own experiences and to use the educational process for emancipatory purposes.

The narrowness of Soviet education, coupled with its authoritarian approach and its total isolation from other viewpoints, means that the local staff need guidance and exposure to other systems in order for them not simply to reproduce Soviet methodology. This is where I came in. My function has been to provide new ideas and the strategies to accompany them, and then, after an initial period of training and supervision, gradually withdraw, leaving the local workers to continue on their own. In the longer term we should like the staff to make way for the villagers to run the project themselves.

We work in a woman-centred way, opening up to dialogue areas that had previously been left unspoken, in order for women to be able to make them their own. We hope to be able to demedicalize many aspects of health such as menstruation, pregnancy, childbirth and the menopause which medical professionals treat as if they were diseases rather than normal parts of women's lives which they are quite capable of managing for themselves, albeit at times with some assistance.[8] These strategies are especially important for reproductive health. That is, for everything connected with women's reproductive organs and the well-being of women during all phases of the reproductive process.

As I stated at the beginning of this chapter, the regulation of all aspects of reproduction – sexuality, marriage, fertility, etc. – is fundamental to the social control of women. Such control is very strong in Tajikistan. Therefore, providing women with the tools necessary to take back any part of reproduction into their own hands may make a significant contribution to the liberatory process. We also work with the women on the prevention of illness and on alternative therapies to redress the strongly curative and drug-centred approach of the Soviet medical system. Armed with sufficient knowledge they should be able to make changes in their lifestyles as well as informed judgements on when to consult a doctor, and be able to evaluate the cures on offer. Using such strategies women should find it easier to deal with their current situation and be less dependent on professionals and drugs. This should release some of their scarce resources to be spent on nutritious food rather than medicine, which on its own would already greatly improve the general level of health. Finally, the project aims at encouraging critical awareness and questioning the status quo, not only on matters of health but on all aspects of life.

The Project in Practice

Translating our approach into practical terms means that we do not draw up a preconceived lesson plan, nor use textbooks or a formal classroom setting. At their own request, the women are divided into groups according to age, since the younger women do not feel comfortable talking in front of the older generation. We try to keep an informal atmosphere, working in collaboration with the women rather than setting ourselves up as experts. Together, we devise work plans and specify the subjects for discussion. Our approach is to draw out the women's own knowledge and, supplementing this with added information where needed, help them to organize it all into coherent narratives, which should then serve to explain not only the workings of the process of maintaining health, but also those of the new world they have been thrust into, and ultimately the structure of the social relations in which they are bound up.

We start, therefore, by asking each group of women to write down a list of those problems which particularly concern them, not necessarily limiting these to health matters. A composite version of this list has been reproduced in Table 10.1. Then, little by little, we begin to explore the issues related to these problems and develop new approaches to enable the women to cope with them as far as possible without outside aid or expensive drugs. Table 10.1 groups the problems according to categories. The first section is devoted to services that used to be supplied by the Soviet state but are either no longer provided or provided only inadequately. Obviously we cannot organize such services in the way the state used to. The idea is to offer alternatives, including reducing dependence on the services. For instance, the two most common reasons why ambulances are used are for acute childhood illness and complications in childbirth. By learning to recognize the symptoms of serious illness so that this can be caught early, and by pregnant women understanding better when they are likely to be at risk, it should be possible significantly to reduce the number of medical emergencies.

208   Colette Harris

Table 10.1 Composite List of Problems Given by All the Women's Groups in Two Villages in Bokhtar Region, Khatlon Oblast, Tajikistan, April–May 1997

	Problem	Schmidt	Lakhuti
1	lack of drinking water	x	x
2	insufficient fuel for cooking	x	x
3	absence of crèche/kindergarten	x	x
4	absence of schools	x	x
5	absence of medical centre	x	
6	absence of trained midwife	x	x
7	absence of rubbish dump	x	
8	absence of ambulance services	x	
9	lack of humanitarian aid	x	
10	lack of wages and pensions	x	
11	difficulties in housework	x	
12	rats and mice in the house	x	
13	problems of getting sufficient food	x	x
14	infertility	x	x
15	infant and child mortality	x	
16	need for contraception	x	x
17	gynaecological problems	x	x
18	problems in childbirth	x	x
19	problems of child development		x
20	anaemia	x	x
21	stomach problems/diarrhoea in children	x	x
22	goitre	x	x
23	malaria	x	x
24	scabies	x	x
25	typhoid	x	
26	hepatitis	x	x
27	diphtheria	x	
28	measles	x	
29	flu and respiratory diseases	x	x
30	throat problems	x	
31	toothache	x	x
32	eye problems	x	
33	rheumatism/arthritis	x	
34	heart disease	x	
35	kidney problems		x
36	earache		x

The second section is devoted to problems that have arisen in connection with the housing conditions and the difficulties in procuring sufficient food in the new economic circumstances. Once again, we cannot provide building materials, replace subsidies or provide food. We can, however, discuss nutrition from the point of view of how to get the best value for money. This is particularly important in view of the recent introduction of junk food and soft drinks, which are rapidly becoming fashionable.

The third section deals with reproductive health; this is discussed in greater detail below. In the fourth section, on illnesses common in the village, we concentrate on causes and prevention rather than on cure, for instance, discussing the use of iodine to prevent goitre and how not to pass on scabies. Too frequent resorting to antibiotics, especially in injectable form, has had many negative consequences, including the spread of serious disease through dirty needles. We, therefore, emphasize shunning their use unless absolutely necessary, recommending herbs and other natural remedies instead.

During the educational sessions we vary our approach according to the subject, largely depending on the level of women's own knowledge and interest. We always start by eliciting their ideas before we present our own, and use dialogue rather than lectures. The best sessions are those to which the women themselves make the largest contribution. We almost always find that they listen and retain much more when it is one of their own number talking. However, when it comes to reproductive health it is much more difficult to do this. This is partly because the women know much less about this than most other health issues, a clear reflection of the silence imposed by the extremely prudish policies of the Soviet Union, but also because discussing such subjects in public is clearly very embarrassing even for married women with children. It was also very difficult for our staff, as they too were unaccustomed to talking about these matters.[9] However, once they got used to discussing the subjects openly and in non-repressive surroundings, their embarrassment gradually vanished and they were able to start contributing to the discussion. We particularly concentrate here on explanations of the internal reproductive organs, menstruation, the process of conception, birth control, sexually transmitted diseases (STDs) including HIV/AIDS, and sex education for girls.

Interest in the subject of family planning varies according to age group. The younger women are more likely to be worried about producing children than preventing their conception and to feel that birth control is purely for limitation of family size and, therefore, of no immediate concern for them. These women are under such pressure from their husbands and families that most give no thought to the possibility of planned birth spacing, even when they get pregnant almost every year. On the other hand, older women who are worried about their capacity to feed another child and would prefer not to have any more, feel that access to contraception is of paramount importance. The project workers put no pressure on women to limit family size, but rather stress the use of contraception as a means for enabling them to make their own decisions regarding their fertility.

The women are greatly concerned about infertility, of which the incidence is relatively high. They clearly regard this as a major calamity especially when threatened with divorce by their husbands and in-laws. Many of these women already have one or more children, but their husbands want still more. The women are desperate for any help that might enable them to conceive. This situation would seem to be tailor-made for introducing the subject of (gendered) power relations. However, the women are concentrating so hard on trying to avoid the consequences of their infertility[10] that they have no energy to spare for considering the wider implications. This is certainly understandable in view of the difficulty in finding another husband and the severe economic and social problems they would face without a husband.

Another place where power relations between spouses come into contact with reproductive health is in the matter of STDs and AIDS. Although they did not put these on their lists, the women are most anxious to learn about them. They have heard just enough to be worried, without knowing what to do and want to know how much their husbands' infidelity[11] exposes them to risk. After our first informational session on this topic some of the women responded by telling their husbands they now knew the dangers of unprotected sex and refused to continue with this. They asked us for condoms, insisting they did not want to run the risk of contracting a disease. At the same time their husbands insisted that the other women they were sleeping with during their absences from the village were clean-living and therefore could not be diseased.

It was at this point that the men started to feel at a disadvantage because their wives understood these topics better than they did and began to lobby for educational sessions for themselves. This was obviously in part because of their own concern about STDs, but they also appeared to resent the idea of their wives having more knowledge than they did, seeming to feel this lessened their power over them. It was interesting to see that women's knowledge really is perceived as empowering, by their menfolk at least. We now provide the men with educational sessions, as had been our intention all along, since we consider it essential to bring them into the process of taking responsibility for their families' health. However, at the same time, this raises the question of whether it is always helpful to the women to bring men in. It may give the women higher status with their menfolk if such knowledge remains in their hands only, but conversely it may prove harmful.

It was never clear at what point the men might have considered it threatening for the women to have sole access to such information. The problem is that if power resides in knowledge, then the converse is also true. Had we not included the men they might very well have come to the point of feeling themselves losing so much power in relation to their womenfolk that the situation might have ended in serious conflict, which would have been detrimental both to internal village relations and the project.[12]

The question of power relations also arises in connection with teaching unmarried girls. In Tajik culture it is considered preferable for girls to be uneducated as this is supposed to make them more submissive and therefore more compliant as daughters-in-law and wives.[13] It is also preferred that unmarried girls be completely ignorant of sexual matters. We believe that this is short-sighted and that the girls should at least have a right to learn about the processes of sex and reproduction. For this reason our project includes a sex education component. At first when we started to teach this we feared a strongly negative response from the parents. However, to our great surprise and relief, they were actively in favour. One woman told us that her elder two daughters had experienced great problems in dealing with the sexual side of their marriages, problems that they attributed to their mother's failure to provide them with any information on this. She was, therefore, extremely glad that we were giving sex education to her two younger daughters since she said she neither knew enough about it, nor could overcome her embarrassment sufficiently to be able to discuss sex with her children.

In addition to questions of reproductive health we discuss all the subjects listed in Table 10.1, as well as others that the women bring up themselves, or that we feel would be useful to them to know about. Although these may not all be crucial to power relations, they are still part of helping women to improve their health, often simply through understanding the relation of lifestyle to well-being. Knowledge about all these issues is important to banish the women's fear of the unknown and goes some way towards enabling them to construct a coherent picture of the world around them. This should aid them in taking control of their own lives and hopefully in the end will act as an impetus to challenge existing social relations.

CONCLUSION

At the time of writing, the health project had been running for only three months. So far it has raised as many questions as it has answered and shows the needs of the village women to be far more varied than had appeared from my superficial preliminary research. Some positive results can already be seen, but these remain very much on the mechanical level. It is far from clear if the project will succeed even in its modest aim of helping women to adjust to the new circumstances of a free market.

The central question – whether the project can lead to real changes in the various dimensions of power relations – remains completely open. It will clearly need much longer than three months for such radical change to become visible. The small amount of struggle around issues raised by the project that has taken place so far revolves around sexuality, most specifically around husbands' infidelity and the resulting health problems this can cause their wives. There, it is true, the project was able to provide women with knowledge of STDs/AIDS with which to confront their husbands. Whether this might presage far-reaching power changes is difficult to say – who knows from what small beginnings a movement towards change can develop?

However, it must be realized that our project does not exist in a sociopolitical vacuum, nor within a static environment. On the contrary, Tajikistan is experiencing a particularly fast rate of change at present as a result of opening up to a global political economy. Major contributors to this are the transition to market, the return of the opposition forces (especially problematic because of their attempts to introduce a more strongly Islamic culture), the forthcoming general elections and the incipient global penetration. All these factors will impact on gender relations.

Such a situation will make it difficult to judge the effects of one particular factor in any transformation that does take place. The parameters within which our project might influence women's lives will depend on the type of society that will emerge in Tajikistan. However, the chance that this will be one favourable to the concept of including women as actors on an equal level with men is remote in the extreme. In the circumstances, any tools that women can acquire that might enable them to challenge and subvert the dominant power structures cannot but be a good preparation for the future. We can only hope that in the long run our project will prove capable of providing real assistance towards this end. Should it prove to be an aid in positive transformation, such a project could serve as a model for future undertakings in both Tajikistan itself and in its culturally related neighbours.

NOTES

1. This chapter is based on fieldwork I carried out in three trips to Tajikistan, between December 1994 and July 1997, as well as on the work I did in connection with the Bokhtar women's health project. I should like to thank Christian Aid of London for providing the funding for this project. I also wish to thank all those who kindly allowed me to interview them during the course of my fieldwork as well as those who have been involved in this project, especially the members of the project staff and the villagers of Schmidt and Lakhuti, without whom the project would not exist. My further thanks to Stephanie Barrientos for her comments on earlier versions of this paper.
2. Contrary to the claims of the Soviet state. See Raskreposhchenie (1971).
3. See Raskrepashchenie 1967, for instance.
4. In Tajikistan traditionally people turn to such leaders for healing purposes.
5. Unlike most Tajik women whose scarves cover only their heads.
6. The village schools have practically stopped functioning as their teachers are no longer paid a living wage. Most girls under 16 know little more than their letters and cannot count much further than 10, thus producing the extraordinary situation of a generation of literate grandmothers and illiterate granddaughters. The educational gulf between girls and boys is greatly on the increase as fathers send their sons to school where possible but will not allow their daughters to go to school out of the village partly for fear of their abduction and rape, and partly because they think there is no point if all the girls are going to do is to work as farm labourers. Mothers prefer to keep their daughters at home to help them. They are too preoccupied to be able to spare much thought to the effect this might have on their daughters' future lives.
7. See Werner and Bower (1982) who place an emphasis on using health projects for empowering disadvantaged communities.
8. See Martin (1987) for a fuller account of the way the medical profession continues increasingly to encroach on women's autonomy in all aspects of women's health and of the way they mechanize the birth process and ignore women's agency in regard to it.
9. However, even western school teachers often find it embarrassing to teach sex education.
10. Although the women believe that their husbands should also be tested to see if the problem lies with them, until this is proven everyone assumes it must be the women's fault.
11. Practically all the women are convinced that their husbands are unfaithful to them. Perhaps they had been faithful formerly when they lived full-time in the village and worked in or near it. However, now that the men spend so much time away from home, the women believe that most have taken a second wife and/or visit prostitutes.
12. Consider the backlash that the women's liberation movement has produced in the West.
13. The order reflects the fact that it is most often the mother who chooses her son's wife according to what suits her best. The son himself and his requirements are rarely taken into account, nor of course the girl's.

REFERENCES

Bridger, S. (1992) 'Young Women and Perestroika' p. 178 in Linda Edmondson, *Women and Society in Russia and the Soviet Union*, Cambridge: Cambridge University Press.
Djanko, T.A. (1990) 'Sem'ya i byt narodov Sredney Azii i Kazakhstana' pp. 440–512 in K.D. Basaeva, N. Bikbulatov and V.N. Birin et al. (eds) *Semeyny byt narodov SSSR* [Family and lifestyles of the peoples of Central Asia and Kazakhstan, in *Family Lifestyles of the Peoples of the USSR*], Moscow: Nauka.
Freire, P. (1967) *Educação como Práctica da Liberdade*, Brazil.
Freire, P. (1990) *Pedagogy of the Oppressed*, New York: Continuum.
Gray, Francine du Plessix (1991) *Soviet Women walking the Tightrope*, London: Virago.
Harris, C. (n.d.) 'Traditionalism versus the Soviet system: Social Change in Tajikistan (1866–1996), a Marxian viewpoint'. Unpublished paper.
Human Development Report (1995) *Republic of Tajikistan: Human Development Report*, Dushanbe: UNDP/Government of Tajikistan.
Islamov, B. (1994) 'Post-Soviet Central Asia and the Commonwealth of Independent States: the Economic Background of Interdependence', in Beatrice Forbes Manz (ed.) *Central Asian Survey* 16(1): 5–26.
Kaser, M. (1997) 'Economic Transition in six Central Asian Economies', *Central Asian Survey* 16(1), pp. 5–26.
Martin, E. (1987) *The Woman in the Body: a Cultural Analysis of Reproduction*, Boston: Beacon Press.
Ministry of Health of the USSR (1967) *The System of Public-Health Services in the USSR*, Moscow.
Pipes, R. (1994) *Russia under the Bolshevik Regime, 1919–1924*, London: Harper.
Raskreposhchenie (1971) *Velikiy Oktyabr i Raskreposhchenie zhenshchin Sredney Azii i Kazakhstana (1917–1936 gg): sbornik dokumentov*. [Great October and the Emancipation of Women of Central Asia and Kazakhstan (1917–1936): collection of documents], Moscow: Mysl.
Werner, D. and Bower, B. (1982) *Helping Health Workers Learn*, Palo Alto: Hesperian Foundation.

11 Why Rural Technologies Fail to Meet the Needs of Nigerian Women: Evidence from Hausa Women's Groups in Kano State

Sintiki Tarfa

INTRODUCTION

The global emphasis on modernization of agriculture often takes an ungendered perspective and remains unaware of the specificities of technologies in terms of their impact on the lives of farming women (Agarwal 1984). The effect of modernization can be seen in terms of the expansion of female employment in large-scale agribusiness and export-oriented farming (see Barrientos and Perrons this volume), but also affects the resources given to deal with the needs of women working on small, arid plots on the margins of the agricultural sector. The latter is particularly problematic for women in the African subcontinent who are the providers of basic food for much of the population. This chapter is concerned with the policy initiated by the Nigerian government, entitled the Better Life Programme (BLP), in response to greater World Bank focus on women farmers, who remain the backbone of the livelihood of the poorest section of people in Nigeria. This policy was formulated in the context of the global vision of relocating responsibility to the non-governmental and local agencies that are expected to replace and/or enhance governmental policies in the rural context. Although Nigeria is at the forefront of the liberalizing economies, what is of interest in this case is that the state itself funded and created the BLP and facilitated its activities, which mirror those of other NGOs to help develop a support network.[1]

This chapter discusses the trajectory of the Better Life Programme as it affected the lives of a Hausa women's group in Kano State.[2] The BLP was launched in 1987, with the important aim of providing technological support for small-scale women farmers. Technology development has traditionally been biased towards men's productive activities, neglecting the important economic contribution that women make through their work in agricultural production and marketing. The BLP reflected a recognition that technology development must reach women to improve their productivity, which has resulted in various strategies and programmes to ensure that women have access to technology. However, the process involved in technology transfer to women has often not produced the desired results. This chapter explores the contradictions of a top-down policy designed to address the needs of a marginalized and secluded group of women. To address this question, the chapter examines a group of Hausa women who had a small-scale cottage industry established for them through a loan by the Better Life Programme in order to process crops for sale.³ It is a contribution towards the on-going debate to identify the constraints affecting the process of technology transfer and use among women, and why technology support often fails to meet the needs of women.

The chapter is divided into four sections. The first describes the socio-economic characteristics of Hausa women in order to understand the context within which the introduction of improved technology for processing food crops by women took place.

The second section presents the case study of a women's group as users of technology supported by the BLP. The third section describes the reasons for failed attempts to transfer technology to women. The fourth section concludes by drawing out the broader implications of this example.

HAUSA WOMEN: SOCIAL AND OCCUPATIONAL CHARACTERISTICS

Hausa is primarily a linguistic term but has definite social connotations and refers to the Hausa-speaking Muslim populations of northern Nigeria and adjoining French territories which are typically organized in large cities. Such a definition excludes the non-Muslim Hausa, who are called the Maguzawa, but whose native speech is Hausa (Smith 1954:15). Hausa women in purdah⁴ are not involved in direct agricultural production outside the home and early studies among Hausa communities show traditional form of labour organization (*gandu*) did not include women except old women, divorced women and unmarried girls, who often participate in farm wage labour. There are many explanations for the non-involvement of Hausa women in fieldwork. Smith identified the abolition of slavery and the spread of Islam as the main factors. Islam is the strongest social influence among the Hausa and they see seclusion as sanctioned by religious values and teaching; the liberty to wives to go outside the home compound is, by implication, an act of religious ignorance (Smith 1954).

However, the exclusion of Hausa women from direct fieldwork can be explained by other factors, which include the higher economic returns from food processing and the social prestige associated with seclusion. The high returns and low drudgery and risk associated with food processing compared to farm work are important reasons why women may prefer to stay in seclusion to carry out their income-generating activities or may explain why women voluntarily choose to negotiate for seclusion at marriage. Studies by Simmons (1975), Longhurst (1982) and Jackson (1989) have found the returns from processing higher than farm wage employment. Longhurst (1982) found the female wages for cotton picking was 26 Kobo per day, whereas planting was 16 Kobo per day. The daily rates for making *fura* (millet paste ball consumed with yoghurt) was 15 Kobo and for *kulikuli* (groundnut cake) was 94 Kobo. In a study among Hausa women in the Kano River Project, the hourly rate of return for a farm wage earner of low wealth status was 2.7 Naira as compared to 37.50 Naira for a woman of high wealth status involved in the processing and marketing of rice, in addition to other supplementary sources of income from trading (Tarfa, 1997).

The Islamic practice of purdah, the uncertainty and risk associated with agricultural production and high returns from food processing explain the preference and predominance of Hausa women in petty trading and food marketing. It also explains their performing the secondary functions of processing, storage and preservation of food crops for consumption and sale within the confines of the household. In carrying out their activities women are helped by their children to buy and sell. The money Hausa women earn from their various trades is theirs and they do not necessarily have to make contributions to the household, but use it to meet their needs and those of their children (Pittin 1987). Hausa women use their income to make major contributions to the dowry items they buy for their daughters, with the value of items purchased varying considerably with the wealth status of the family. Traditionally, they include basic items like the bed, mattress, enamelware, bowls and foodstuffs. However, the increased monetization of the rural economy, coupled with the effect of trade liberalization and the opening up of rural markets to a wide variety of relatively cheap imported products, have rapidly displaced traditional items. Thus, items such as television, radio, jewellery, upholstered chairs and cupboards have replaced the traditional dowry items, reflecting the increased effects of global consumerism. The pressure on mothers and daughters to save and accumulate for the dowry is responsible for the fact that children are introduced to trading and hawking at a very young age.

The exclusion of Hausa women, the small-scale nature of women's productive activities in the processing and marketing of agriculture and non-agricultural products explains the consistent neglect of Hausa women by agricultural development programmes and projects. It is this seeming neglect that led the Better Life Programme in Nigeria to initiate a programme to introduce labour saving technologies to rural women's groups. The Better Life Programme was initiated by the wife of the then head of state and had as one of its main policy objectives the improvement of the socio-economic status of women through access to and use of technology. The programme has pioneered the creation of groups in rural communities aimed at ensuring that rural women have access to post-harvest technology to improve the productivity of their labour and income. Although the BLP strategy has come under heavy criticism, the innovative idea has created awareness of the important role of women in development.

In 1991, the BLP established about 17 small-scale cottage industries for women's co-operative groups in Kano state. However, the introduction of technology faced many problems, which often led to the discontinuation of most projects. Evidence of the problems, which forms part of the case study detailed below, was also highlighted by the report findings of the Institute for Agricultural Research (IAR), the pioneers of the transfer of proto-type technology to selected women's groups in northern Nigeria. The report revealed that groups have problems with the management and use of technology and suggested further study to understand the dynamics of groups as a crucial factor in the successful adoption of technology among women (Kaul 1993). The concern over failed attempts and evidence from research reports generated the need for a more in-depth, systematic analysis and documentation. The next section presents a case study of one Hausa women's group and explores some of the reasons for failed attempts with technology for processing.

WOMEN'S GROUP COTTAGE MILL – THE KURA RICE PROCESSING GROUP (*KUNGIYAR ZAB-ZABAN SHINKAFA TA KURA*)

Kura is located approximately 30 km southeast of Kano state, and has an estimated population of 227,548 people, 115, 264 of whom are females.

A vast area of land in Kura belongs to the Kano River Irrigation Project. The major occupation is farming. Many farmers have secondary occupations such as trading, tailoring and blacksmithing. Kura is a major agricultural market for local and regional trades, for products such as rice, wheat, tomatoes, onions, maize and other varieties of vegetables. Kura is the most developed district in terms of economy and per capita income in comparison with the other areas studied. Local communications include roads and public transport, and other infrastructural facilities include pipe-borne water, hospitals, primary and secondary schools, electricity, markets, police stations and mosques.

Women in Kura play an important role in agricultural production activities. The majority of women and young girls who are not in strict seclusion actively participate in fieldwork. Tasks such as planting, transplanting, fertilizer application and weeding are undertaken. All the post-harvest operations (picking, threshing, winnowing, parboiling and drying rice) as well as secondary processing for consumption/sale are traditionally performed by women. Women in seclusion perform rice processing at home. Normal household utensils such as drums, pots, calabashes and baskets are used for processing. The husband, children or other male relatives arrange the purchase of raw materials and transport the rice to the mills and market for sale. Women inherit or purchase farmlands that are leased out, or managed on their behalf by husbands, children or relatives.

The formation of a women's rice processing group at Kura was initiated by Hajia Ladi Salisu, the leader of the group and the youngest of the three wives of Alhaji Salisu, a large-scale farmer and a civil servant in Kura. The husband fully supported his wives' participation in the group activities. Hajia Ladi is relatively wealthy and educated to primary school level. She is literate in Arabic only. With the assistance of the village schoolteacher, she persuaded neighbours to form a group, which was established in 1989. The reasons given by the leader for forming the group include the need to acquire machinery for processing rice, to have access to government services and to advance the status of women in Kura.

The group consists of 25 members. An executive committee of eight members was selected to manage the activities of the group. The group initially started by meeting weekly at the residence of the leader to discuss activities. The meetings were later held monthly. In 1989 the group actively participated in an agricultural show organized by the Better Life Programme for Women. The leader claimed their display attracted the attention of the wife of the governor of Kano state. Impressed by the women's efforts, the governor's wife promised to establish a cottage industry for rice processing.

Kura Cottage Industry

The cottage industry is equipped with one large fabricated parboiler with a capacity of 1000 kg purchased from the Badegi Cereal Research Institute, four gas cylinders, two rice hullers, one sealing machine and one polisher purchased from Kano State Supply Company[5] (KASCO). The project became the responsibility of the women's group. A loan of 30,000 Naira, repayable in 3 years with 3 months' moratorium beginning in January 1990 was allocated to the project. The women started with the initial sum of 10,000 Naira as operating capital.[6] The women buy paddy rice to process and sell. The profit generated was divided by three; one-third repays the loan, one-third is utilized as operating capital and the final third is shared among members of the group. To ensure that the women have the necessary skills to operate the technology, three members of the group were selected to attend training sessions at the Badegi Research Institute, Bida for two weeks. The husband of the leader refused to allow her to attend the training session.

The local government contributed a multi-purpose centre to house the machinery. The building was located away from the market within the village and fenced, because the practice of seclusion does not allow women to be seen in public or have direct contact with men. A male security guard was also employed to ensure the safety of the equipment. The wife of the governor of Kano state launched the project, and many government functionaries attended. The project was perceived as a major achievement of the Better Life Programme (BLP). Therefore, an abundance of resources went into the implementation and it has received a lot of publicity. The BLP was promoted and the government's commitment and effort towards raising the status of women illustrated. However, in the rush to establish the project, the women were not consulted on the choice of technology and were inadequately trained in the skills necessary to manage the scale of the project. The first attempt to process rice failed. Only half the rice was parboiled and the women had to resume traditional processing. The women, when asked why they have abandoned the use of the technology, gave a variety of reasons:

1. The parboiler is operated by gas, which is expensive and unavailable in the village. In the town cooking gas is not readily available as the supply is withheld to create an artificial scarcity in order to increase

prices. Women processing rice at home in the traditional way use cheaper sources of fuel, such as wood and rice chaff.
2. To operate the parboiler the tank requires 100 gallons of water. Water is not easily or always available in the village. Women cannot collect water as they are in seclusion. Men sell water in the community. Therefore, to operate the parboiler women have to buy water from men. The technology consequently creates more employment/income for men.
3. The steamer is placed on top of the parboiler. The women have to climb to pour water into the steamer. But the women considered this task to be socially inappropriate, labour, demanding and risky.
4. Women cannot use the rice-milling machine to polish the rice as it broke down. The difficulty of acquiring spare parts and a skilled technician in the village contributed to the frequent breakdowns.

The mills were also expensive and women had more problems maintaining them compared to mills purchased locally. Local dealers proved more reputable in supplying appropriate and less expensive mills than the government-recognized channel of purchase, the KASCO. The local dealers expressed the opinion that they could not afford to take the same level of risk as a government specialized agency, if machinery sold to traders fails to work the suppliers run the risk of losing their business or credibility. Local traders, if effectively assisted and monitored by government, can play a key role in the technology transfer and adoption process. In the case of government, political and economic interests take precedence in the choice of technology.

However, for Hausa women it would be mistaken only to attribute frequent breakdowns to the fact that the technology was imported. Owing to seclusion, the women were unable to organize themselves to supervise and monitor the use of their processing mill. This meant that those who actually operated the mill were expected to work in the best interest of the women, but this was obviously not the case.

The women's group project also faced competition from mills operated by large-scale farmers in the area. At the time of study there were about 44 rice mills in Kura. The majority of these are located along the major highway in close proximity to the regional rice markets. Some of the mills, with parboiler attachments, create work for women not in seclusion in soaking, parboiling and drying activities. The location of the women's project is an additional disadvantage, as most people prefer to take their rice to mills located near the market. Apart from the favourable market location which large-scale farmers enjoy, they have better access to market information and prices, in addition to effective supervision and economies of scale in the use of services. For example, a group of mill owners agreed to share the cost of employing a guard at night. The competition forced the women to reduce processing charges to attract more customers to their mills. However, this proved unsuccessful because the location of the project within the village influenced by the need to limit the appearance of the women in public was not convenient to most of those who needed or wanted to use their services. Thus in this case the socio-cultural practice of seclusion, which was the main determinant of the location of the women's group project, was in effect a major impediment to their integration in the market economy.

For the BLP, locating the project in the centre of the village appears to be a way of conforming to the norm of women's invisibility and their interest not to confront the status quo. The question is, if a Hausa woman owns a mill where is she likely to locate it: in the market or in the community? Obviously, economic rather than social reasons are likely to take precedence. The BLP defines this as 'protection' but it has proved costly, especially in economic terms. The BLP in this case, as in most development projects, is in a conflicting role as the vanguard of socio-economic emancipation of women and the guardian of socio-cultural values. The two factors are difficult to reconcile. We cannot 'integrate' women into the economy without addressing issues based on their gender that subordinate them.

While seclusion was the major factor influencing the choice of location, discussion with the women revealed that their decision to work outside the home was influenced by other factors. First, women can combine working outside the home with their domestic responsibilities of childcare, preparing meals and carrying out their income-generating activities. Home processing enables the women to accomplish a variety of tasks simultaneously; for example, preparing meals, taking care of their children, petty trading and processing food for sale. In particular cases there *may* be no conflict between market work and household activities. Second, women expressed concern about the pressure they face from their husbands to account for their time or to justify their absence while working outside the home. Third, some respondents claimed financial gain was the main incentive for their husbands to allow group participation, because the men saw the opportunity for women to earn an independent income as a means for the men to withdraw from their traditional responsibilities towards women and children. Without any tangible benefits men perceive the group as a means of socializing, which is generally unacceptable. The women themselves did express the fact that economic independence comes with increased responsibility in the household.

CONCLUSION

The discussion in this chapter has centred on why government-supported rural technologies have failed to meet the needs of rural Hausa women. The study identified that a major constraint concerned the question of the appropriateness of the technology and the fact that women have little or no control over the choice of technology. The government through the BLP took responsibility for providing and determining the availability of technology to women and ensuring that the technology was appropriate. In this case it was observed that private entrepreneurs were more efficient providers of the services than the government through their direct involvement via the BLP. The role of the government should be that of facilitating and creating an appropriate environment for technology development and transfer, through research, extension and private entrepreneurs. Whatever the mechanism, the views of the women themselves need to play an instrumental role in determining the form of technology provision to ensure it is appropriate to female agricultural producers. The government needs to monitor and maintain effective control to ensure that the rights of people, including women, who need and depend on the services, are not exploited. As it was, the top-down implementation of the BLP in the short term has proved more beneficial to the government than to the women.

Second, as this case study shows, the problem lies not only with the implementation of the technology, but with the various socio-cultural restrictions women face. Discussion and observation of Hausa women, however, revealed that they are constantly devising ways to work around the problems posed by seclusion or even exploit it, which suggests that there may be room for manoeuvre. On the other hand, it does suggest that extension agents or NGOs must recognize and make an effort to understand the difficulty of reaching this class of women. Once reached, the multiplier effect is enormous and the satisfaction that is gained by seeing that a little effort can bring a change in the lives of people who want and desire change is worthwhile.

The preceding discussion has centred on the factors that served as barriers to technology transfer to rural Hausa women. There are three key factors that are considered important in technology transfer to women. They include the role of government in creating a favourable environment and resources for the development of technology of particular relevance to the needs of rural women. Also important is the need to ensure that women have access to the resources (credit, training and extension service) that will enable them to adopt technology. Finally, strategies that seek to improve the socio-economic status of women through new technologies must contend with the socio-cultural constraints women face. Failure of extension agents to recognize and identify ways to deal with some of the problems highlighted in this chapter will mean women will continue to be marginalized by development. Globalization has affected the lives of all women, and the BLP reflected an increased global awareness of the problems faced by women. However, the BLP also reflected the limitations of implementing a top-down policy, and the contradictions which ensue when the underlying issues of gender inequality are not addressed. Policies of modernization must incorporate the grassroots participation of women, especially in the case of secluded women, whose voices are not normally heard, if they are not to remain marginalized group.

NOTES

1. I would like to thank all those who have made the writing of this chapter possible. I am greatly indebted to Haleh Afshar, Patricia Goldey and Stephanie Barrientos for their comments and in-depth discussions about the content of this chapter.
2. For the purpose of this study the term women's groups refers to a group of women based in the rural community studied who had organized themselves with the objective of meeting the social and economic obligations of themselves, their families and the community as whole. The focus is on small-scale cottage industries equipped with improved technologies that have the potential to save women's time and energy when processing rice and maize.
3. This chapter presents evidence from one village, which was studied as part of a case study conducted among two Hausa women's groups located southeast of Kano state, northern Nigeria. The period of data collection lasted for about seven months, between November 1994 and May 1995. During this period the case studies drew information from three main sources of data, namely interviews were held with members of women's groups and key informants within the community. The key informants were people who had the knowledge of the issues and situations in which the researcher was interested. In the study extension agents, community development officers and community leaders working directly with women's groups were selected as key informants for the study. Information was

also gathered from officials of the Better Life programme working with women's groups on the cottage mill project. For the full study see Tarfa (1997).
4. Purdah is the word used to describe the system of secluding women.
5. The Kano State Supply Company (KASCO) is the marketing company of the World Bank assisted Kano Agricultural and Rural Development Agency (KNARDA) which supplies mainly imported agricultural implements to farmers.
6. The currency conversion was £1 = 32 Naira (official exchange rate until January 1995). The UN official rate was £1 = 120 Naira. 1 Naira = 100 Kobo.

REFERENCES

Agarwal, B. (1984) 'Rural Women and High Yielding Rice Technology', *Economic and Political Weekly* XIX(13), March.
Jackson, C. (1989). *Women's Roles and Gender Differences in Development*. The Kano River Project. Prepared for the Population Council. West Hartford: Kumarian Press.
Kaul, R.N. (1993) 'An Overview of Agricultural Mechanisation in the Context of Women's Participation'. Paper presented at the Regional Workshop on Role of Women in Agriculture with Focus on Farm Tools and Related Technologies in Commonwealth Africa, Held at the Ahmadu Bello University, Zaria, 8–13. November.
Longhurst, R. (1982) 'Resource Allocation and the Sexual Division of Labour: A Case Study of a Moslem Hausa Village in Northern Nigeria', pp. 95–117 in Lourdes Benería (ed.), *Women and Development: The Sexual Division of Labour in Rural Societies*, New York: Praeger.
Pittin, Renee (1987) 'Documentation of Women's Work in Nigeria: Problems and Solutions' pp. 25–44 in C. Oppong (ed.), *Sex Roles, Population and Development in West Africa*, Policy-related Studies on Work and Demographic Issues.
Smith, F. (1954) *Baba of Karo: a Woman of the Muslim Hausa*. London: Faber and Faber.
Simmons, E.B. (1975) 'The Small-scale Food Processing Industry in Northern Nigeria', *Food Research Institute Studies* 14(2), 147–61.
Tarfa, S.B. (1997) 'Technology Transfer and Use among Women: Case Studies from Hausa Women's Groups in Northern Nigeria', PhD Thesis, University of Reading.

Index

abortion, 201–2
activism, political, 7, 44, 45, 47, 86–7
agency, 47
agribusiness, 4, 151
agricultural employment, Thailand, 184
agricultural sector, Thailand, 182–4
authenticity, 49
autonomy, state, 7, 27
Ayodhya, 40

Babri mosque, 40, 41
banjaras, 19–20ff
Beijing Conference, 9
Better Life Programme, 215–16, 218, 222
Bhagwati, Justice, 28
BJP, 41, 43, 46
boundaries/borders, 2, 25–6
bourgeoisie, Indian, 39
breadwinners, women, 8
bureaucracy, Indian, 30

capacity, political, 29–31
capital movement, 1, 77
capital-wage relation, 167
caste, 39, 45
child labour, 188
childcare, 8, 97, 145, 156–7, 160, 161, 189
children and poverty, 102
Chile, chapter 8 passim
Chipko movement, 146
civil society, 31–2
co-operation, 167
collective mobilization, 43
colonialism, 48
communal violence, 40–1
communalism, 44
communication networks, 2
comparative advantage, 3, 178, 181
complementarity, 56, 66
conditionality, 3, 32
consumer elites, 153

consumer society, 2
contraception, 201
co-operative-conflict model, 163–4
coping strategies, 3
corporate organizations, 174
corporate strategies, 174
corruption, 30
Costa Rica, chapter 6 passim
cottage industry (Kura), 218, 220–23
cultural imperialism, 48
culture of poverty, 103

debt, consumer-led, 8
deindustrialization, 5
Delhi, 19
democratization, 77
deregulation, 1, 5
disadvantage, childhood, 112
discourse, Islamist, 70
discourse, masculinist, 26
discourse on women, 81–4
disempowerment, 5
division of domestic labour, 105–6
divorce, effect on children, 103
divorce rate, 93
domesticity, 4, 60, 83, 84
dowry, 217–18
Durga Vahini, 41
duty and entitlement, 71

economic liberalization, 2
education, 104, 199
Egypt, chapter 5 passim
elite men, 2
elite women, India, 32; Iran, 54ff
embeddedness, 28–9, 31–2
empowerment, 5, 163, 210
entitlement and duty, 71
environment, negative effects on, 182–3
environmental issues and gender, 132
environmental change, 135–42
equality, 56
equality and gender, 82–3

Index

ethnic minorities, 2
exclusion, 32, 60
exclusion/inclusion patterns, 138
exoticization, 20
exploitation, 5

family and informal sector, 81
family as productive unit, 81
family, idealization of, 86
family planning, 209
family values, 93
family wage, 96
father absence, 102, 104–5
female employment, 4, 153, 186–9
female-headed households, 6, 96–7, 156, 197, 204
female identity, 88
feminisms, diversity of, 55
feminist politics, 47
feminists, third world, 55
feminists, western, 55–6
feminization of the labour force, 179–80
fieldwork, exclusion of women from in Nigeria, 216–17
flexible employment, 79, 151–4
fodder, 134, 141, 143–4
food consumption patterns, 152
food processing, 217
food production/retailing, 153
food supply chains, 151
foreign direct investment, 174, 180
foreign direct investment, Japanese, 178, 180
formality, 87
fragmentation, 4
fragmentation of production process, 5; *see also* subcontracting; temporary work; work-sharing
fragmentation, women's, 80
free trade/markets, 3
fruit exporters, 150
fruit workers' households, 156
fundamentalism, 7, 9, 44, 55
fundamentalism, religious, 44, 197

gender, 9
gender contracts/arrangements, 164–6
gender division of labour, 5, 132, 154, 179
gender inequalities, 167
gender norms, flexibility of, 146
gender relations, 3, 154–5, 162–8
gender segmentation, 176
gender specificity, 57
global capital, 1
global consumer market, 152
global food chain, chapter 8 passim
global political economy, 6
globalization, 2–3, 49
globalization, gendered, 3–8
globalization, limitations of, 88
governance, global, 2
governance, good, 1, 6–7
growth without employment, 77
growth, export-led, 182
Gujrat, 19

habitus, 43
Hausa women, 216–18
healthcare, 199
health education, 200–11
Hindu nationalist politics, 39
hindutva, 40
hindutva and women, 42–50
hindutva brotherhood, 41, 43
hindutva mobilization, 48
hindutva politics, 40–2
hindutva propaganda, 46
home-based production, 98, 222
household change, 95
household strategies, 133, 154–5
household survival and women's paid employment, 151
housing, 98
human capital, 97
human rights, 26

ideals, bourgeois, 85
illiteracy, 32
IMF, 2, 61, 180
import-substitution industrialization, 3
Indian Constitution, 21
Indian women, chapters 2 and 3 passim
Indonesia, chapter 7 passim

industrialization, 131; India, 38, 48; Indonesia, 131, 135–42
industrialization, export-led, 181
industry, female-intensive, 187
infant/child mortality, 104
infertility, 210
informal employment, 77
informal sector, 4, 78–81, 181–2
information revolution, 2
Iran, chapter 4 passim
Islam, Nigeria, 217
Islamic laws, Iran, 58
Islamification, 54, 59, 65
Islamism, 56, 58, 65–8, 82
isolation, 110–11

Janpath, 19
just-in-time production, 177; see also outsourcing; subcontracting
juvenile crime, 93

Kano River Irrigation Project, 219
Kura, 218–23
Kura women's rice processing group, 219–20

labour, division of, 4
labour flexibility, 160
labour market, 4
labour market feminization, 7, 174, 179
labour migration, 96, 175; see also migrant workers
labour process, fragmentation, 5
labour segmentation, 174, 175–6
legal reform, 86
liberalization, 1; India, 18, 38
lone motherhood, 91; and poverty, 92

Mahila Morcha, 41
male abandonment, 110
marginalization, 2
marginalization of women, 5, 80
market reform, 179
marriage, 9, 61, 96
martyrdom, 61
materialism, 56
Mexico, chapter 6 passim
Middle East, 55

migrant labour, 185–6
migrant workers, 136, 138–9, 175
migration, male, 6
mobilization, 46
modernity, 9, 38, 48
monetization, 217
moral deviance, 110
morality codes, Iran, 58
morality, Islamic, 60
motherhood, 60–2, 83–4, 109
multinationals, Japanese, 177–78

nation-states, 2, 27
nationalism, 39
nationhood, 45
natural resource use and gender, 133–5
natural resources and industrialization, 140–2
natural resources, exploitation of, 131
neo-liberalism, 3, 176
New Delhi Municipal Corporation, 19, 21–2
new economic order, 2
Nigeria, chapter 11 passim

oppression, 166
outsourcing, 5

patriarchal politics, 5
patriarchal structures and labour force, 4
patriarchy, 47, 166–8; differentiated, 166
patriotism, Indian, 40
peak interest groups, 28
peasant production, 156
personal expenditure, 98, 158
police brutality, 30; see also violence
political capacity, 29–31
political participation, Iran, 68–70
political representation, 40, 45
politics, manipulative, 47
pollution, 45
population control, 61–2, 202
population growth, 61, 135
populism, 39, 56
post-colonialism, 18ff

Index

poverty, 8, 92; and children, 102; Chile, 157–8; Tajikistan, 196; Thailand, 183
poverty, perceptions of, 100–2
power, asymmetry, 165–6
power, dispersal of, 26
power, infrastructural, 29–31
power relations, 26
powerlessness, 100
private sphere, 85
production, export-oriented, 4, 78
production, transnational, 4
progress, 83
prostitution, 187
public interest litigation, 28–9
public/private sphere, regulation of, 44
purchasing power of women, 153
purdah, 216–17
purity, 45

Rashtriya Swayamsevika Samiti, 41
religion, 56
religion, politicization of, 42
representation, political, 40
reproductive health, 209
reproduction, 201
resistance, 5
resources, availability of, 14–25
responsibility, gendered, 56
revivalism, 9
rural industrialization, 183

sadre Islam, 70
seasonal employment, 77
seasonal temporary workers, chapter 8 passim
seclusion, 222
secondary poverty, 99
secularism, Egypt, 86; Iran, 63–4
segmentation, vertical/horizontal, 174
sexual availability, 109, 110–11
sexual deviance, 110
sexual favours, 30
sexuality, 42, 201; feminine, 59; masculine, 49
sexually transmitted diseases, 209–10
Sharma, Livleen, 19, 23–4, 31
shift work, 160

Shiv Sena, 41
skill definition, 176
small firms, 181
social capital, 98
social control, 57
social differentiation, 132
social instability, 9
social justice, 27, 32
social stigma, 103
social welfare, Costa Rica, 107–9
Soviet Union, 197–9
special economic zones, 4
stabilization, 3
state autonomy, 29
state capacity, 29; weak, 30
state enforcement agencies, 31
state organizations, 33
state violence, 33
state welfare, 5
state, theorizing, 26
status of women, 6, 82
stereotypes, 91ff, 153
stereotypes, negative, 94–5
stigmatization, 107; and lone motherhood, 109
street-trading, 20–1
stress, marital, 161
structural adjustment programmes, 3, 5; *see also* World Bank
structural adjustment, Egypt, 78; India, 18
subcontracting, 5, 177, 178, 179
subjugation, 46
subsistence production, 8
supermarkets, 153; multiples, 159–62
supraterritoriality, 174
sustainability, 131

Tajikistan, chapter 10 passim
technology development/transfer, 216
temporary employment, Chile, 154–9; Thailand, 188
textiles, 140
Thailand, chapter 9 passim
Thareja Committee, 21, 23, 24, 28
third world, 2
tourism, Thailand, 182–3, 187
trade liberalization, 176

230 Index

trading relations/patterns, 3
trading rights, 21
transmission of disadvantage, 102
transnational corporations, transportation, 2

UK, 159–62
underclass, 93
underemployment, 184
unemployment, seasonal, 184
United Nations, 9

Vedic past, 6
veiling, 44, 59–60, 87
violence, patriarchal, 47
violence, state, 30, 33
visibility, 31–2

water, 133–4, 140–1, 143
welfare state, India, 27

women activists, 7, 47
women and politics, 62–3
women, public role of, 83, 84
women, reification of, 88
women's bodies and political struggle, 44
women's groups, 8
women's movement, 45
women's organizations, 80
women's workload, 142–5
women-headed households, chapter 6 passim
women's labour, 4
wood fuel, 134–5, 141–2
work-sharing, 178
working mothers, 106
working women, Egypt, 78
working poor, 8
World Bank, 2, 61, 180

yarn/textile production, 140